ELIZABETH
Queen of England, France, and Ireland, &c. &c.

HONI SOIT QUI MAL Y PENSE

DIEU ET MON DROIT

KU-426-944

ELIZABETH TUDOR:
THE LONELY QUEEN

SIR ARTHUR MACNALTY ©

By the same author

BIOGRAPHY

HENRY VIII: A DIFFICULT PATIENT
MARY QUEEN OF SCOTS: THE DAUGHTER OF DEBATE
THE PRINCES IN THE TOWER
SIR WALTER SCOTT: THE WOUNDED FALCON
THE GREAT UNKNOWN: A SHORT LIFE OF SIR WALTER SCOTT
THE THREE CHURCHILLS
SIR WILLIAM COLLINS: SURGEON AND STATESMAN
SIR BENJAMIN WARD RICHARDSON

HISTORY

THE DOCTOR IN POLITICS AND DIPLOMACY (*MacAlister Lecture*, 1937)
THE RENAISSANCE AND ITS INFLUENCE ON ENGLISH MEDICINE, SURGERY
    AND PUBLIC HEALTH
THE HISTORY OF STATE MEDICINE IN ENGLAND

First published 1954
Second Impression 1971

SET IN 12PT. IMPRINT AND PRINTED AND MADE
IN GREAT BRITAIN BY THE ANCHOR PRESS LTD.
FOR JOHNSON PUBLICATIONS LTD.
11/14 STANHOPE MEWS WEST, LONDON, S.W.7
ISBN 0 85307 110 1

ELIZABETH TUDOR:

THE LONELY QUEEN

by

SIR ARTHUR SALUSBURY MacNALTY

K.C.B., M.A., M.D. (OXON.), F.R.C.P., F.R.C.S.

Honorary Fellow of the Royal Society of Edinburgh
Fellow of University College, London

JOHNSON

LONDON

TO

B. Ifor Evans,
M.A., D.Litt.
Provost of University College, London

CONTENTS

Acknowledgments

THE sources upon which this biography of Elizabeth Tudor is based are given in the text and in the bibliography. Dr. Routh, President of Magdalen College, Oxford, who died in his hundredth year, advised all writers to verify their references at first hand. In this book it has not been possible to consult the original documents in a number of instances, particularly as regards the Spanish sources, *MS. Simancas*, etc. These are chiefly taken from Froude's *History of England*.

I am grateful to Professor J. E. Neale, M.A., D.Litt., F.B.A., for his kindness in reading part of the book in manuscript and for his criticism and suggestions.

The Editor of *The Times* has given me permission to reproduce an extract from *The Times* of August 24, 1953, in Chapter XV.

I have to thank Sir Charles Dodds, M.V.O., M.D., F.R.S., Harveian Librarian, and Mr. Leonard M. Payne, F.L.A., Assistant Librarian, of the Royal College of Physicians for information relating to the history of the College in Tudor times, and the Registrar for permission to consult the *Annals of the College*.

M. LeFanu, Librarian of the Royal College of Surgeons, has enabled me to consult a number of works relating to surgery in the Tudor period and in particular *The Annals of the Barber-Surgeons*.

My thanks are also due to Mr. Wade, F.L.A., Librarian of the Royal Society of Medicine.

I am indebted to Mr. Frederick Chamberlin, author of *The Private Character of Queen Elizabeth*, and to the publishers, Messrs. John Lane, The Bodley Head Limited, for kind permission to use certain materials relating to the Queen's medical history, collated by Mr. Chamberlin from original sources and published in his book.

Miss Ruth Hubble has given kind assistance in the preparation of the manuscript for the Press.

Lastly, I am obliged to Dr. Donald McI. Johnson for the interest he has shown in the book and his encouragement.

ARTHUR S. MACNALTY.

Introduction

"No scandal about Queen Elizabeth, I hope?"
The Critic.

FOR several years I have been interested in the medical aspects of the reign of Elizabeth Tudor, and I have collected much material upon the subject. The favourable reception given to my book entitled *Henry VIII: A Difficult Patient* has encouraged me to write the life of his younger daughter from a medical view-point.

In regard to Queen Elizabeth the evidence from direct medical sources is scanty. There is the report of Dr. George Owen when he attended her as Princess for acute nephritis in 1554 (see *The Queen's Medical Case-Sheet*, Chapter XV). We have therefore to rely on the despatches of foreign ambassadors at the English Court, accounts in the State Papers and contemporary letters, and to interpret this evidence, which was often based on the pronouncements of the royal physicians, as far as seems reasonable in the light of the medical knowledge of the twentieth century.

The character of the Queen presents a number of interesting medical and psychological problems. For instance, the problem of her marriage which was debated in England and at foreign courts for the greater part of her life: the question of possible congenital defect in this relation; her conduct towards Mary Queen of Scots and her disclaimer of responsibility for her kinswoman's execution; her relations with Seymour, Leicester, Alençon and Essex; her attitude towards her Protestant, Puritan and Roman Catholic subjects; her rule in England; her skilful handling of home and foreign affairs; her self-dedication to the unity and prosperity of her realm; all

9

these and many other phases of her childhood, adolescence and reign are considered here.

The Queen suffered from three serious illnesses in her life. She was subject to moods, caprices, migraine and nerve-storms. For nine years she had a painful varicose ulcer of the leg. But just as Somerset, Northumberland, her sister Mary and Philip of Spain could not intimidate her or break her spirit, so Elizabeth, apparently, never allowed bodily ills to influence her superb judgment and policy, save once after the death of Mary Stuart, when she worked herself up into a state of hysteria. Her physique was excellent, her mode of living regular, and she attained nearly seventy years of age. She told Parliament that she would never be by violence constrained to do anything and added: "I thank God I am endued with such qualities that if I were turned out of the realm in my petticoat, I were able to live in any place in Christendom."

Queen Elizabeth—although surrounded by wooing courtiers, and wise councillors of State, greeted with real affection by her subjects, and occupied with home and foreign affairs, audiences, royal progresses, revels, music, the writing of letters and literary studies—was essentially a lonely queen.

It is a characteristic that impresses one in considering her life as it has impressed modern historians and biographers. Naturally warm-hearted and affectionate she never knew a mother's care, her brother died young, her sister disliked and mistrusted her, and she was surrounded from her youth up by spies and enemies. Hence four chapters of this book are devoted to the perils of her young life which made her hard and cold, sometimes even ruthless and often ungrateful; these characteristics were the armour of her self-preservation. At intervals come glimpses of her true nature. Many times she gave her trust and affection only to have it betrayed. Even in her old age, Essex, on whom she had showered benefits, plotted rebellion. The dangers and isolation of her early years equipped her to rule England at a most critical time, and it is only possible to understand her self-reliant character by knowing something of the vicissitudes of her youth and adolescence. In the duties of high office she never wearied. As Professor Trevelyan observes: "This heroic woman was her own Prime Minister in war and peace for forty-five years, most of them fraught with danger both to the State and to her own much-threatened life."

Historians have already pointed out that the latter part of the sixteenth century was an age of ruling queens, Catherine de Medici in France, Mary Stuart in Scotland and Mary and Elizabeth in England. Of these, Queen Elizabeth was by far the greatest and the most successful. Endowed with the statecraft of a man, which again and again surpassed that of Burghley and Walsingham, which kept Philip of Spain at bay and baffled Catherine de Medici, she used all the wiles and caprices of a woman to reinforce her policy. She gave all she had to the service of her realm and her people. To this end she prayed, she worked, she intrigued, and even sinned. The good she wrought outweighs the evil. She built up the power and prestige of England, preserved it from religious civil war, encouraged arts and industries, and chose her ministers with wisdom.

Several of the anecdotes of the Queen narrated here may be only too familiar to some of my readers. I can only hope that like Diggory with Mr. Hardcastle's story of "Ould Grouse in the gun-room," they will go on laughing at them these twenty years.

I had hoped to include a chapter on Elizabeth's Irish policy. However, considerations of space have rendered this impracticable, and readers will find this information in a recent work, namely, *Elizabeth's Irish Wars*, by C. Falls.

I

King Henry's Daughter

AT Greenwich Palace in the year 1533 there was born
to Anne Boleyn, the second queen of King Henry
VIII, a daughter instead of the expected son which the
astrologers had promised. Hall records the birth in the
following words:

> "On the 7th day of September, being Sunday,
> between three and four o'clock in the afternoon, the
> queen was delivered of a fair ladye, on which day the
> Duke of Norfolk came home to the christening."

As if emblematic of her future destiny, the Virgin Queen
was born in the Chamber of the Virgins, the room being
hung with tapestry representing a history of holy virgins.
The date was also the vigil of the Virgin Mary.

The King glossed over his disappointment. A solemn
Te Deum was sung and the christening of the young
princess was celebrated with great pomp. The Bishop of
London, supported by other bishops and mitred abbots,
officiated. The infant's sponsors were Cranmer, Archbishop of Canterbury, the Duchess of Norfolk and the
Marchioness of Dorset. She was named Elizabeth after
her grandmother, Elizabeth of York.

Princess Mary's governess, Lady Margaret Bryan,
became the child's governess or "lady mistress". Lady
Bryan's husband, Sir Thomas Bryan, was related to the
Queen. Her selection for the post of governess was a wise
one, for she brought up her infant charge judiciously,
tempering a reasonable discipline with much kindness.

Shortly after the arrival of the princess on the stage of life, she became an important person. When she was almost three months old she was removed to Hatfield, "there to remain with such household as the king's highness has established for the same". By the Act of Parliament which settled the succession for the time being, she became heiress-presumptive to the throne in place of her sister, the Princess Mary. She and her establishment were then transferred to the palace of the Bishop of Winchester at Chelsea who was given official charge of the heiress to the throne. It was a responsibility which extended to matters both great and small, for her weaning at the age of thirteen months was the subject of weighty conferences between the officers of her household and the Ministers of State, the whole question at length receiving the royal assent in the following extract from a letter from Sir William Powlet to Cromwell:

"The King's grace well considering the letter directed to you from my Lady Brian and other my lady princess' officers, his grace, with the assent of the Queen's grace, hath fully determined the weaning of my lady princess to be done with all diligence."

Moreover, even at this tender age the shadow of Elizabeth's marriage which was so often the subject of policy and debate almost throughout the course of her life, hovered over her cradle. King Henry at that time was allied with France in opposition to the Emperor Charles V, and sought to cement the alliance by betrothing Elizabeth to the Duke of Angoulème, the third son of Francis I. Henry proposed that the young duke should be educated in England and, if Elizabeth became Queen, that as her consort he should retain his Duchy, independently of the French Crown. These negotiations came to nothing.

In Elizabeth's third year of life her foolish and possibly erring mother was hurried to the block, and her young daughter pronounced illegitimate. It has been alleged that at this time she suffered a certain amount of neglect and indignity. There is some evidence of this in that Lady Bryan had to appeal to Cromwell in order that provision should be made for the child's clothing and other needs. If so, the change must have puzzled and hurt Elizabeth's baby mind. At all events her own personality soon reconciled her to her royal father, for she carried the chrisom of her infant brother, Prince Edward, at his christening, being carried in the arms of the Earl of Hertford, brother of Queen Jane Seymour. In the returning procession she was led by the hand of her sister, Princess Mary, to the bed-chamber of the Queen, who was to die of puerperal fever shortly afterwards. It is said that the child bore herself with royal dignity at this, her first public appearance.

Elizabeth's first diplomatic success was to win back the affection of her father. He grew to like her for those traits in which she so strongly resembled him, her reddish hair, her apt quickness, her occasional outburst of Tudor temper and her love for knowledge. He allowed her to companion Prince Edward to whom she became greatly attached, and later she shared his studies. At six years old she worked a shirt of cambric for him for his second birthday. She also became friends with Princess Mary when they were sisters in adversity. The impression of the subtle Wriothesley, after visiting the two princesses at Hertford Castle, on December 17, 1539 is on record. He reports on Elizabeth most favourably:

"I went then to my lady Elizabeth's grace, and to the same made his majesty's most hearty commendations, declaring that his highness desired to hear of her health and sent his blessing; she gave humble thanks, inquiring after his majesty's welfare, and that with as great a gravity as she had been forty years old. If she be no worse educated than she now appeareth to me, she will prove of no less honour than beseemeth her father's daughter, whom the Lord long preserve."

In 1540 King Henry married Anne of Cleves. Elizabeth,

14

through Lady Bryan, requested the King's permission to visit the new Queen. The King growled out: "That she had had a mother so different from the Queen, that she ought not to wish to see her, but she had his permission to write to Her Majesty." Thereupon Elizabeth penned a tactful letter of congratulation to Anne of Cleves. Later the two met, and after the divorce Anne obtained Henry's permission to see Elizabeth as often as she wished, provided she was only addressed by her as the Lady Anne of Cleves. A firm friendship was formed between the ex-Queen and the princess. Indeed, from an early age Elizabeth had a great craving for love and affection. In Anne of Cleves, in Catherine Howard and in Catherine Parr she strove to find a substitute for that maternal love of which she had been deprived in early infancy. Catherine Howard was of Anne Boleyn's blood, and during the brief period when she was Henry's 'rose without a thorn' took Elizabeth under her special protection, giving her place of honour. The execution of Catherine wounded Elizabeth in this affection. She loved throughout her life and in much of her affection met with cruel disappointment.

When Catherine Howard was beheaded, Elizabeth was still a child though sagacious for her years. She chiefly lived at Havering Bower with her sister, Mary, and it is on record that she was present at the audience given by Mary to the imperial ambassadors in 1543.

As is well known, Henry VIII, "the scholar-king", as Erasmus styled him, insisted on his three children having an intensive education. This was in accord with the influence of the Renaissance and that of the Oxford humanists, who all, Sir Thomas More especially, advocated the higher education of women. More's daughters, Margaret Roper, Elizabeth and Cecelia, were educated in the liberal arts and sciences, Greek and Latin, and Margaret Gigs, his adopted daughter, who married Dr. John Clement, was an accomplished Greek scholar and studied medicine. Sir Anthony Cooke, tutor to Edward VI, gave his four daughters an education equal to that which men received. With other studies it comprised

15

Latin, Greek, Hebrew, Italian and French. These daughters were looked upon as youthful wonders and were warmly extolled by William Bercher in his book, *The Nobylytye off wymen* (1559). One of the daughters, Elizabeth Cooke Hoby Russell, was called by Thomas Lodge the English Sappho. He dedicated *A Margarite of America* to her, and Geoffrey Fenton dedicated his *Monophylo* to her. Lady Jane Grey's education was directed by John Aylmer, afterwards Bishop of London. It was Aylmer who wrote a counterblast to John Knox's book decrying government by women with the pleasing title: *An Harborowe for faithful and trewe Subiectes, agaynst the late blowne Blaste concerninge the gouerment of women*, Strassburg (J. Daye, London, 1559). Lady Jane at seventeen knew Latin, Greek, Hebrew, Arabic, French and Italian and was a student of philosophy.

Other advocates of women's educations were the pundits, Joannes Ludovicus Vives, Princess Mary's tutor, whose teaching on this subject is recorded in his work: *A very frutefull and pleasant boke called the Instruction of a Christen woman*, London, 1529 and Richard Mulcaster who wrote: *Positions wherein those primitive circumstances be examined, which are necessarie for the training up of children, either for skill in their booke, or health in their bodie*, London, 1581.

Women also wrote books. Professor Camden states that over fifty women wrote some eighty-five compositions from 1524 to 1640. Fifty-eight of these books were printed separately, while others appeared in anthologies, liturgies, etc. They were chiefly concerned with religion.

From these examples—and many more might be given —it will be seen that the Tudor standard of female education among the upper and middle classes was extremely high and therefore when Elizabeth was regarded as "a paragon of learning" it meant that she was a woman of outstanding attainments. Julius Caesar Scaliger pronounced her better educated than any of the great men of her time. Miss Strickland said of Elizabeth:

"Those who knew her best were accustomed to say of her 'that God, who had endowed her with such rare gifts, had certainly destined her to some distinguished employment in the world'. At the age of twelve she was considerably advanced in sciences, which rarely, indeed at that era, formed part of the education of princesses. She understood the principles of geography, architecture, the mathematics, and astronomy, and astonished all her instructors by the facility with which she acquired knowledge. Her handwriting was beautiful, and her skill in languages remarkable. Like her elder sister, the Princess Mary, she was an accomplished Latin scholar, and astonished some of the most erudite linguists of that age by the ease and grace with which she conversed in that language. French, Italian, Spanish and Flemish, she both spoke with the same facility as her native tongue. She was fond of poetry, and sometimes made verses that were not devoid of merit*, but she only regarded this as the amusement of her leisure hours, bestowing more of her time and attention on the study of history than anything else."

Elizabeth, though so brilliant intellectually, did not win the palm of scholarship without the dust. The contemporary historian, John Heywood, tells of the hard course of study to which Prince Edward and Princess Elizabeth were kept. As soon as it was light, they were at their books, their first hours being devoted to their religious exercises and the study of the Scriptures. "The rest of the forenoon, breakfast alone excepted, they were instructed in languages and science or moral learning, collected out of such authors as did best conduce to the instruction of princes, and when she was called out to his more active exercises in the open air, she betook herself to her lute or viol, and when wearied with that employed her time in needlework."

* Her epithet for Mary, Queen of Scots: "the daughter of debate, that discord oft doth sow", which occurs in one of her poems is frequently quoted, but most critics do not esteem her poetry.

Thus were laid the foundations of regularity and industry which were of infinite service to Elizabeth when she became Queen. She had a real love of learning and throughout her life set apart three hours a day for study. Grindall, an excellent Greek scholar, and Roger Ascham were successively her tutors. Grindall was appointed in 1544 and taught her Greek and Latin. He died of plague in January 1548. Ascham helped to form her beautiful Italian hand, and both in his book *The Schoolmaster* and in his letters describes the attainments of his royal pupil in glowing terms. As late as 1562 Ascham read Latin and Greek with Queen Elizabeth every day. The first surviving letter of Princess Elizabeth is one in Italian written to Queen Catherine Parr in July, 1544. By the end of the year she had translated Mary of Navarre's poem, "The Mirror of a Sinful Soul", and bound it in a needlework cover made by herself as a New Year's gift to her stepmother.

While the young princess was thus improving her mind, doing her needlework, playing with her young brother and endearing herself to those who had charge of her, King Henry still thought of marriage alliances for her in his changing schemes of international policy. The designated bridegrooms were several and the candidates changed so frequently that Elizabeth may well have satirically inquired each morning: "And who is to be my husband today?" It is hardly to be doubted that she knew of and was interested in what went on, that she noted at an early age that her marriage was an object of high policy, and that she used this knowledge to good effect in after-life.

In 1543, with a view of detaching the Earl of Arran's interest from France and of uniting the crowns of England and Scotland by a marriage between the infant queen of Scots and Prince Edward, King Henry offered the hand of Elizabeth to the son of the Scottish earl. Arran ignored the offer. Henry also had suggested an alliance with a prince of Portugal. In 1544 Henry, much to King Francis's alarm and distress, had become the Emperor Charles V's ally, led his troops to France and captured

Boulogne. In the treaty between Charles and Henry a clause was inserted proposing to wed Elizabeth to the Emperor's son, Philip of Spain, who afterwards married her sister, Mary. This is the first appearance of Philip as one of Elizabeth's suitors; it was not to be the last. Henry had other projects for the bestowal of Elizabeth's hand, but like the rest none came to fruition. Nevertheless, they played their part in the shaping of her character and behaviour.

After repelling the attempted invasion of England by the French fleet in 1545, King Henry's health gradually failed and he died on January 28, 1547. He had been empowered by Parliament to settle the succession. In 1544, at his instigation, Parliament passed an Act which placed Mary and Elizabeth in the order of succession after Edward. Henry's will reiterated the provisions of the Act of 1544, and placed next to Elizabeth the daughters of his younger sister, Mary Tudor, the Duchess of Suffolk, thus tacitly ignoring the claim through his elder sister, Margaret, of Mary, Queen of Scots. Both Mary and Elizabeth received a life annuity of three thousand pounds a year and a marriage portion of ten thousand pounds, provided they married with the consent of the King, their brother, and his council.

In December, 1546, Elizabeth had been removed to Enfield and Prince Edward to Hertford in anticipation of King Henry's death. Camden states that Edward loved his sister dearly, speaking of her as his "dearest sister", or "his sweet sister Temperance". He was distressed at being parted from her and she wrote him a consolatory letter, begging him to write to her.

On January 30, 1547, the Earl of Hertford and Sir Anthony Brown brought Edward from Hertford to Enfield and informed the royal brother and sister that their father was dead. Both children wept bitterly, or as the courtly Heywood phrases it: "Never was sorrow more sweetly set forth, their faces seeming to rather beautify their sorrow than their sorrow to cloud the beauty of their faces."

Princess Elizabeth was now assigned by Edward VI's Council to the care of the dowager Queen, Catherine Parr. The order merely continued the friendly supervision which her stepmother had exercised in Henry's life-time and was welcome to both of them. At the time it seemed to promise the continuance of a happy and sheltered life. Yet in this sheltered environment Elizabeth was to meet the first great peril of her life, a peril which not only threatened her reputation but her very life.

II

Perils of a Princess

HENRY VIII'S will had originally provided for the government of England during his son's minority by a Council in which the Protestant and Anglo-Catholic parties were fairly evenly balanced, the Earl of Hertford being the leader of the former and Gardiner, the Bishop of Winchester, of the latter party. Gardiner's unwise attempt to persuade Henry to sign a warrant committing Catherine Parr to the Tower had caused the King to remove Gardiner from the Council. Hertford and the Protestant party had therefore the preponderance of votes in the Council. Hertford won over the trimmers, Wriothesley and Lisle being the chief ones, took the reins of government in his own hands as Lord Protector and became Duke of Somerset. This rise to supreme power inevitably created for him many unavowed enemies. Among them was his own brother, Sir Thomas Seymour, the Lord Admiral, described by a contemporary as "fierce in courage, courtly in fashion, in personage stately, in voice magnificent, but somewhat empty in matter". In other words he was brave, arrogant, swaggering, reckless in speech and action, but lacking in prudence and discretion; by no means the kind of man to make a successful conspirator. He was thirty-eight years of age, had a fine presence and possessive manners calculated to win a woman's heart. Somerset had given him a post in attendance on the young king who was delighted with his governor. But Sir Thomas, being very ambitious, considered he should be Lord Protector and was by no means content to play second fiddle to his cautious brother. Before Catherine Parr's third marriage he had been a suitor for her hand until Henry VIII took her for his sixth wife, and he knew that she was still fond of him. This marriage with the Queen Dowager would strengthen his position. At the same time his scheming mind surveyed other possibilities. There was young Bess, an intelligent, pretty maid, now of marriageable age in the fashion of the time. If the Council gave him permission to wed the princess he would become the King's brother-in-law. The first step was to gain Elizabeth's consent. An impetuous man, the Admiral. The unreliable writer, Leti, is the authority for the correspondence which passed between Elizabeth and Seymour. With no sense of the fitness of things or shame in intruding upon a daughter's grief, a month after King Henry's death on February 26, 1547, Seymour wrote his proposal of marriage. Elizabeth promptly replied on February 27, to this effect:

"That she has neither the years nor the inclination to think of marriage at present, and that she would not have any one imagine that such a subject had been even mentioned to her, at a time when she ought to be wholly taken up in weeping for the death of the king her father, to whom she owed so many obligations, and that she intended to devote at least two years to wearing black for him, and mourning for his loss; and that even when she shall have arrived at years of discretion, she wishes to retain her liberty, without entering into any matrimonial engagement."

If such was the given reply it constituted a stinging rebuff to a presumptuous proposal. Some similar answer was written with the advice and counsel of Queen Catherine Parr, if not dictated by her. The last words of the letter indicate the key-note of Elizabeth's mind. She ever wished to retain her liberty. The Queen Dowager's advice was sound, for the alliance was highly unsuitable for a princess of the blood royal, yet it was also certainly biased, for Queen Catherine herself loved the Admiral. It may perhaps be surmised that Elizabeth sent the letter with some regret, for she must have been flattered by the Admiral's admiration, even at so inauspicious a time.

The resilient Seymour, by no means abashed at his rejection, turned to his second string, the Queen Dowager. Here he was more successful and married the lady a few weeks after King Henry's death.

Elizabeth was sorely displeased not only for the sake of her father's memory but because of her step-mother's advice in her own case. Princess Mary also felt bitterly on the subject and asked Elizabeth to come and live with her, as a protest. Here again Elizabeth acted wisely. She knew that Seymour might supersede Somerset as Lord Protector and did not wish to come to an open rupture with him and his wife, who had shown her much friendship. In effect she told Mary that what could not be cured must be endured, that they must dissemble the pain they felt at the disrespect paid to their father's memory, and that she could not withdraw from Queen Catherine's protection without appearing ungrateful. Accordingly, for the next year she remained with her stepmother, either at the dower palace at Chelsea or at Hanworth. She had a new governess, Mrs. Catherine Ashley, a relative of Anne Boleyn, and she was much attached to her. Mrs. Ashley was a somewhat foolish woman and a gossip; she had a great admiration for the handsome, swashbuckling Admiral, and constantly spoke of his great qualities to Elizabeth. For his part, Seymour with an eye to the future spared no pains by presents and flattery to win the interest of the governess in his favour. Vives and other educationalists advised young women should be kept away from all men, but despite the standard of strict upbringing many girls of the upper and middle classes enjoyed much freedom; they met young men at weddings, feasts, dances, Christmas revels and other festive occasions. Manners were more free and easy in Tudor times and any household over which Sir Thomas Seymour presided was bound to be an unconventional one. Early morning romps and frolics were instituted by the Admiral. He and

Catherine used to come and tickle the princess when she still lay abed, and on one occasion in the garden, Catherine held Elizabeth while her husband cut her gown into an hundred pieces. Boisterous romping of this kind went on between the Admiral and the young princess of fifteen in the Queen's absence. Seymour began openly to make love to Elizabeth and she seemed not unwilling to receive his attentions. Mrs. Ashley connived at their secret meetings and water-parties by night on the Thames. But even the complaisant governess became alarmed at the length to which matters were carried and remonstrated. Sir Thomas replied with an oath that he would not desist from these frolics, "for he meant no harm".

Queen Catherine, on her return, was shocked at these familiarities for which in the beginning she was partly to blame. She perceived that Elizabeth had developed an infatuation for her husband and that he encouraged it by his behaviour. Elizabeth was taken to task for her unseemly conduct and told by Catherine that she could not remain under her roof. The Queen handled matters skilfully. Elizabeth was touched by the consideration shown to her, and stepmother and daughter parted as friends and afterwards corresponded in affectionate terms. In May 1548 Elizabeth with Mrs. Ashley removed to Cheshunt and afterwards to Hatfield and Ashridge, and everything possible was done by Queen Catherine to hush up Elizabeth's indiscretion. She was, as Elizabeth must have realized in after years, a noble woman and the best of stepmothers. She is said to have told Elizabeth: "God has given you great qualities, cultivate them always and labour to improve them, for I believe that you are destined by heaven to be Queen of England".

Unfortunately, Elizabeth was soon deprived of this wise and understanding friend. On August 30, Catherine gave birth to a daughter and died a week later. She left her unworthy husband all her possessions and to Elizabeth half her jewels and a gold chain.

These episodes between Seymour and Elizabeth which

began as comedy were now merging into tragedy. The Lord Admiral went on with his ambitious schemes. He had obtained from the Duke of Suffolk the charge of Lady Jane Grey, kept her in his house as his ward and intended to marry her to Edward VI while he himself married Elizabeth. To this end he sent his servant, one Edward, to Cheshunt with the news of Catherine's death, with a private communication to his confident, Mrs. Ashley. The governess went to Elizabeth with the news. She added that Edward said, "his lord was a heavy (sorrowful) man for the loss of the queen, his wife", and advised the princess to send the widower a letter of condolence. Elizabeth, who gave little credit to the Admiral's grief, replied: "I will not do it, for he needs it not". She did, however, allow Mrs. Ashley to write such a letter, read it and allowed it to be sent without any comment.

Most authorities state that the Princess refused to see the Lord Admiral, but he secured that Mrs. Ashley, Thomas Parry, the treasurer or cofferer of her household, and others, should continue to press on their mistress the desirable qualities of such a husband. One of her bed-chamber women was so zealous in this mission that Elizabeth threatened to have her thrust out of her presence if she did not desist. Nevertheless, the persistent wooing of so personable a man twenty years older than herself made a deep impression upon her adolescent heart. She blushed when his name was mentioned and liked to hear him praised. She is said to have admitted that she would have married him if the Council's consent had been forthcoming. It should be noted that Elizabeth at this time was suffering from an illness which kept her in bed with Mrs. Ashley in constant attendance on her. (See *The Queen's Medical Case-Sheet*, Chapter XV). Towards the end of the year a report was generally circulated that the Lady Elizabeth was about to wed the Admiral, although Mrs. Ashley, on Elizabeth's instructions replied to the interrogations of Sir Henry Parker, "that he should in no wise credit it, for it was *ne* thought *ne* meant." Seymour, on the contrary, paved a way for his own destruction. Both in his cups and out of them, he spoke scornfully of Somerset and the Council, boasted that he was about to marry Elizabeth, and that he had ten thousand men at his command with whom he would overthrow the regency and obtain supreme authority of the kingdom. All his foolish plots and sayings were reported to the Protector and the Council, who had for months previously kept him under close surveillance. Somerset made an attempt to save his brother by appointing him on a mission to Boulogne, but before the Admiral could leave for France, evidence of his treasonable practices had accumulated, and he was arrested on a charge of high treason on January 16, 1549, and committed to the Tower. Among other things, he was found to have suborned Sharrington, the master of the mint at Bristol, to coin a large sum of false money as supplies for the *coup d'état*, while notorious pirates were to be set at liberty in order to attach them to his cause.

The Lord Admiral's arrest involved Elizabeth in the greatest possible danger. The chief persons of her household, headed by Mrs. Ashley and Thomas Parry, were arrested, imprisoned in the Tower, and closely interrogated by the Privy Council in order to ascertain how far the Princess was implicated in the Admiral's schemes and the nature of the connexion between them. Although Elizabeth earnestly desired to justify herself either before King Edward or the Protector, her request was refused, and she was virtually made a State prisoner in her house at Hatfield, under the charge of Sir Robert Tyrwhit, who had orders from the Privy Council to examine her closely as regards her participation in high treason. She stood alone as so often she was to stand in her life. Her confidants in prison, no counsellor or friend of either sex to advise her, the reckoning for past follies mounting up against her, besides being subject daily to the stern interrogation of a hostile official, whose declared purpose it was to wring a confession of guilt from her unwilling lips and to bring her to shame and possibly to the same fate as her unhappy

mother, the block on Tower Green and the masked headsman. She was, one must repeat, only fifteen years of age;
she was ignorant of what confessions had been wrung in
the Tower from Mrs. Ashley and Parry; she had only herself to rely upon; and had been the not unwilling victim of
an unscrupulous man who had done his best to compromise her for his own selfish ambitions. When
Tyrwhit began his interrogation by informing Elizabeth
that Mrs. Ashley and Parry had confessed everything and
urged her to do the same, she broke down, seemed
abashed and "did weep very tenderly, a long time".
Tyrwhit then imagined his task would be easy and went
on to threaten her with the loss of her honour and peril of
her life unless she confessed. If she complied, as he
advised, the shame would fall on her governess, she would
be forgiven on account of her youth.

Elizabeth saw the snare which Tyrwhit spread before
her and quickly recovered her lofty spirit and self-
command. She avowed nothing, cajolery and threats were
equally ineffective. Tyrwhit reported to Somerset, as
follows: "But in no way will she confess any practice by
Mrs. Ashley or the cofferer concerning my Lord Admiral;
and yet I do see it in her face that she is guilty, and yet
perceive that she will abide more storms ere she will
accuse Mrs. Ashley." Again he wrote to the Protector:
"I do assure your grace she hath a very good wit, and
nothing to be gotten of her but by great policy."

The self-reliant girl would admit nothing, except a few
harmless particulars of the Admiral's reported intentions
to woo her and her reply to Mrs. Ashley: "Though peradventure he himself would have me, yet I think the
Council will not consent, but I think by what you said if
he had his own will he would have had me. I thought
there was no let (hindrance) on his part, but only on that of
the Council". She showed her wisdom by emphasizing
the fact that she would only have married the Admiral
with the Council's consent, which she considered would
not be forthcoming and embodied the admissions in a
letter to the Protector. This document, on February 7,

Tyrwhit forwarded to Somerset with a covering note in which he admits that he has been baffled by the Princess:

> "I do send all the articles I received from your grace, and also the Lady Elizabeth's confession, withal, which is not so full of matter as I would it were, nor yet so much as I did procure her to; but in no way will she confess that either Mrs. Ashley or Parry willed her to any practices with my Lord Admiral, either by message or writing. They all sing one song, and so I think they would not, unless they had set the note before."

Tyrwhit in another vain attempt to wring a confession of guilt from the Princess, had shown her the actual confessions of Mrs. Ashley and Parry, both admitting the familiarities that had occurred between Elizabeth and the Admiral when she was the ward of Catherine Parr. Elizabeth was bitterly incensed. "False wretch", she cried, referring to Parry, "he promised not to confess to death; how could he make such a promise and break it". At the same time she was quick enough to see that these confessions only involved a loss of modesty and discretion on her part, were free from suspicions of treason or from any suggestion of a marriage without the Council's permission. She stoutly maintained her innocence of political intrigue, and eventually felt emboldened to write a letter to the Duke of Somerset in dignified terms defending her honour and vindicating her integrity. "My conscience", she wrote, "beareth me witness, which I would not for all earthly things offend in anything, for I know I have a soul to save, as well as other folks have, wherefore I will above all things have respect unto this same." It is a wonderful letter written in Elizabeth's beautiful calligraphy, remarkable as the unaided composition of one so young.

She wrote with submission to the Protector's authority and that of the Council, yet proudly as became a King's daughter. Her steadfastness, her cleverness, both in what she admitted and in what she denied, saved her head at the cost of some detriment to her reputation. Somerset, too, certainly distressed by the necessity for proceeding against his own brother, may have felt some compassion for the friendless Princess, whom he had carried in his arms at King Edward's christening. The Council acquitted Elizabeth of a share in Thomas Seymour's treason, but dismissed Catherine Ashley as unsuitable for the position she held, and appointed Lady Tyrwhit in her stead, at the same time recommending the Princess to follow that lady's good advice.

Elizabeth had a fit of rage on being deprived of her dear Mrs. Ashley and received Lady Tyrwhit with marked coldness. She also wrote to the Protector another most statesmanlike letter, remonstrating against Mrs. Ashley's removal as likely to reinforce the scandalous rumours that were afoot about her relations with Seymour and asking that they should be contradicted by an official proclamation. This the Council agreed to do. With regard to their request that she would point out the authors of these rumours she wisely replied, "that she should but gain an evil name as if she were glad to punish, and thus incur the ill-will of the people, which she would be loth to have". She never wished to be unpopular "from the cradle to the grave", as Miss Strickland phrased it.

As already indicated, plenty of evidence was forthcoming about Sir Thomas Seymour's treasonable practices without implicating Elizabeth. The only reference to her was in one of the articles of the Bill of Attainder, namely that Thomas Seymour, Baron Sudley, Lord Admiral of England had "attempted and gone about to marry the King's Majesty's sister, the Lady Elizabeth, second inheritor in remainder to the Crown".

On March 4, 1549, Seymour was found guilty of high treason and was executed on March 20. Imprudent to the last, he spent the evening before his execution in writing letters to Elizabeth and Mary, with improvised ink and the point of an aglet, which he plucked from his hose. He concealed them in the sole of a velvet shoe, but they were discovered and read by the Council. The actual text of the contents of these letters are unknown, but Bishop Latimer, who preached a sermon justifying Seymour's death, described them as "of a wicked and dangerous nature, tending to excite the jealousy of the King's sisters against the Protector Somerset, as their enemy".

Elizabeth, with iron will, concealed her grief from the official spies set around her. Her only comment when they told her of Seymour's execution was this: "This day died a man with much wit, and very little judgment".

In after life she showed her attachment to Seymour's memory, the first love of her life, in several ways. As soon as it was possible she reinstated Mrs. Ashley in her favour, and in spite of Thomas Parry having proved to be an unjust steward, guilty of defalcations and of feathering his own nest, on accession to the throne she appointed him the comptroller of the royal household and continued her patronage of him and his daughter as long as they lived. Of significance also is the favour in which she always held Sir John Harrington the elder, Seymour's devoted adherent, and that when she was Queen she accepted from him a portrait of his deceased lord, the Admiral, with a descriptive sonnet.

This tragic story of Elizabeth's first love has been told at some length because it was of great importance in the moulding of her character. Various views have been expressed as to how deeply her affections were involved. Professor Beesly stated that she knew perfectly well that the marriage would not be permitted, and that she only was flirting with a man old enough to be her father, just as she afterwards flirted with men young enough to be her sons. He takes her comment on the news of the Admiral's execution as an example of the utter absence both of delicacy and feeling which characterized her through life. Others would disagree with this opinion and consider that the remark displayed self-control learnt as the result of the danger she had so narrowly escaped. Froude states that the tone in which Elizabeth spoke of Seymour to Mrs. Ashley was one of regard struggling with contempt. He considers that she certainly was never in love with him, "but it might have come to that with time and opportunity". Miss Strickland—and being a woman, her verdict on a woman should be mentioned—had no doubt that Elizabeth had been entangled in the snares of a deep and enduring passion for Seymour. She adds further: "Passion that had rendered her regardless of every consideration of pride, caution and ambition, and forgetful of the obstacle which nature itself had opposed to a union between the daughter of Anne Boleyn and a brother of Jane Seymour".

Bishop Creighton is in agreement with Miss Strickland and considers that Elizabeth dearly loved Seymour with the ardour of a passionate girl, and meditated a secret marriage with him, though she knew his coarse character and had seen the unhappiness of his former wife.

Barnebe Rich, a writer of her reign, said that "the lover is so estranged from that is right and wandereth so wide from the bounds of reason, that he is not able to deem white from black, good from bad, virtue from vice; but only led by the appetite of his own affections and grounding them on the foolishness of his own fancies will so settle his liking on such a one, as either by desert or unworthiness will merit rather to be loathed or loved". (*Of Apolonius and Silla*. A tale on which Shakespeare based *Twelfth Night*.) Perhaps this shrewd analysis represents Elizabeth's frame of mind in regard to the Admiral.

Professor Neale observes that Elizabeth was both cautious and clever in her attitude towards Seymour's wooing, and it is certain that this prudent behaviour, coupled perhaps with the evasions as well as the admissions of Mrs. Ashley and Parry, saved her life. All the same, it is probable that she loved Seymour with the love of a fiery adolescence and that the experience left indelible scars in her mind and heart. As Creighton said, "it was undoubtedly the great crisis of Elizabeth's life, and did more than anything else to form her character". Life and its pitfalls were revealed to her in an abrupt and shocking way. Her friends, Catherine Ashley and Parry, were not wholly to be trusted. Thereafter she trusted only in herself, for love, trust and confidence had their dangers. From the day that Seymour was sent to the Tower, she repressed her feelings, exercised self-restraint and called to her aid all her intelligence to avoid the perils in which her unwise passion for Seymour had involved her. A hard and bitter lesson, but she schooled herself to learn it, to be the loneliest of princesses called to a high destiny. It made her the greater Queen, but something of her better nature, the spontaneous youthful love and affection that is given only once in human relationships departed from Elizabeth as Thomas Seymour's head fell on Tower Green.

III

The Queen's Sister

ELIZABETH dried whatever tears she secretly shed for
the death of the Admiral and fortified herself by
remembrance of the severe lesson she had undergone to
recover her character and to re-establish her reputation.
She well knew she was under a cloud at Court, being
estranged from her brother to whom she was warmly
attached, and under the displeasure of the Duke of
Somerset. As Creighton observed, "she had been detected
as a shameless coquette; she adopted the attitude of a
modest and pious virgin". In this new rôle, she was
helped by Lady Tyrwhit, who knew her well, having been
lady-in-waiting to Queen Catherine Parr. Lady Tyrwhit
seems to have treated her charge, who had so recently
passed through such a fearful ordeal, with sympathy and
kindness.

Elizabeth turned afresh to her studies. At Hatfield she
read with Ascham nearly the whole of Cicero and Livy,
Sophocles, and several orations of Isocrates, as well as
theological studies, the Greek Testament, the writings of
St. Cyprian and the commonplaces of Melanchthon. For
perhaps the only period of her life her dress was un-
adorned and simplicity itself. She gradually earned a
reputation for scholarship and piety which was most
welcome to the reformed party. The King himself was
touched by these tributes and wrote for her portrait. But
Somerset would not allow brother and sister to meet.

The times were troublous. Intrigues and struggles for
political power eddied round the youthful monarch. The
ambitious, reckless, capable John Dudley, Earl of

Warwick, who as Lord de Lisle and Dudley, under Henry VIII, had repulsed the French attempt to invade England in 1545, towards the end of 1550 had overthrown Somerset's power, which he had craftily undermined. Somerset resigned. He was sent for a short time to the Tower, but soon the Council released him, and gave him a place among them. Warwick's administration (1550–53) was precarious and disliked. Somerset began to regain popularity, whereupon Warwick charged him with treason and felony and had him condemned and executed.

The rise of Warwick (who soon afterwards became Duke of Northumberland) for political reasons recalled Elizabeth for a short time to Court. By her prudent conduct she was considered to have atoned for her indiscretions and as the Protestant party regarded her as an adherent to their doctrines and as Northumberland wished to stand well with them, she was bidden to come in state to visit her brother. On March 17, 1551, she rode on horseback through London to St. James's Palace, attended by a great company of lords, knights and gentlemen and some two hundred ladies. Two days later she was affectionately received by Edward at Whitehall. On both occasions she was dressed with much simplicity. "Her maidenly apparel", it was said, "made the noblemen's wives and daughters ashamed to be dressed and painted like peacocks". The Council were sternly examining Princess Mary on account of her adherence to the Romish faith, and Elizabeth's public appearance was devised by Northumberland to divert attention from her sister's recalcitrant attitude. Elizabeth was also present at the festivities held to mark the visit of Mary of Guise, the Queen Dowager of Scotland, to the Court of Edward VI in October, 1551, where again her simple garb contrasted with the brilliant French fashions of Queen Mary's French ladies-in-waiting.

The King was sickly and already a victim of pulmonary tuberculosis. He could not be expected to live long and Northumberland needed a Protestant successor to maintain his authority. Elizabeth, both as daughter of Henry

VIII and favourite of the Reformed Party, offered the best chance to the new Protector's ambitions. It was probably with this in view that he had brought her to Court. If so, he soon perceived that she had a strong will of her own and would be no puppet in his hands. He therefore turned his thoughts to Lady Jane Grey, a sweet and gentle maiden, as likely to serve his purpose better, and from 1552 prohibited Elizabeth's visits to Edward and did his utmost to estrange the dying boy from his two sisters.

Elizabeth, meanwhile, quietly pursued her studies at Hatfield and Ashridge, keeping a watchful eye on events, but avoiding any appearance of being concerned in them. It is of some interest to note, as already indicative of her thrifty disposition, that she was a careful housekeeper, spent little on dress, audited the household accounts; and in one year (October 1551 to October 1552) had a balance in her favour of £1,500.

On several occasions she tried to visit her ailing brother, but permission to do so was interdicted by Northumberland. A letter is extant written by her from Hatfield to King Edward—the exact date is uncertain—in which she states that she had gone half-way to see him, when she was turned back by Northumberland's agents with pretended orders from the boy-king. Elizabeth wrote:

"Two chief occasions moved me much and grieved me greatly—the one, for that I doubted your majesty's health—the other, because for all my long tarrying I went without that I came for. Of the first, I am relieved in a part, both that I understand of your health, and also that your majesty's lodging is not far from my lord marquis' chamber. Of my other grief I am not eased, but the best is, that whatsoever other folks will suspect, I intend not to fear your grace's good will, which as I know that I never deserved to forfeit, so I trust will still stick by me. For if your grace's advice that I should return (whose will is a commandment) had not been, I would not have made the half of my way the end of my journey. And thus, as one desirous to hear of your

35

majesty's health, though unfortunate to see it, I shall pray God for ever to preserve you. From Hatfield this present Saturday.

"Your majesty's humble sister to commandment,

ELIZABETH.

"To the King's most excellent majesty."

In all probability this letter was intercepted and never reached the dying king. Northumberland was busy with his own plans. He had married Lady Jane Grey to his son, Lord Guildford Dudley. Lady Jane was now Northumberland's nominee for the succession, her claim resting on the fact that she was the granddaughter of Mary Tudor, the younger sister of Henry VIII. By playing on Edward's zeal for the Protestant succession, he persuaded him to make a will which set aside the rightful heirs, Mary and Elizabeth, and bequeathed the Crown to Lady Jane Grey. A marriage was also proposed between Elizabeth and the King of Denmark, but the negotiations proved fruitless.

When the King died—and the physicians considered his days were already numbered—Northumberland intended to send Mary and Elizabeth to the Tower, and possibly later to the scaffold, as Creighton surmised, and had all in readiness to proclaim the Lady Jane as Queen.

Pulmonary tuberculosis is an uncertain disease as regards its duration; the patient often shows a transitory improvement and an optimistic outlook immediately before the end. Probably something of the kind occurred in Edward VI's case, for when the boy-king died at Greenwich on the morning of July 6, 1553, Northumberland was taken by surprise and had neither of the royal sisters in custody.

In an attempt to rectify his error, he concealed Edward's death and sent out letters in the King's name to Mary and Elizabeth requesting each of them to visit him in his illness. Princess Mary started to obey the summons, but *en route* was informed of the truth. Thereupon, she fled to Norfolk, and with all her father's courage, proclaimed that she was England's lawful Queen, and summoned her people to support her. The country rallied to her call, and when the perplexed and astonished Northumberland went in pursuit of her, he found her at the head of an army of 40,000 men. His own forces deserted to the rightful Queen, and he was brought back to the Tower as Mary's prisoner.

The careful Elizabeth had also had early news of Edward's death; it is supposed the informant was William Cecil, with whom she was already in communication and on good terms. A real or feigned illness took the Princess to her bed and furnished an excuse for her not obeying the summons to Greenwich. Later, Northumberland sent officers to her, who informed her officially of the King's death, and of the crowning of Queen Jane; and further offered her money and a grant of lands if she would renounce all claim to the throne. Elizabeth boldly replied, "that they must first make their agreement with her elder sister, during whose lifetime she had no claim or title to resign". According to some, she also wrote an indignant letter to Northumberland protesting against the proclamation of the Lady Jane as Queen. Apart from this, she remained in bed at Hatfield and took no share in the conflict that her sister was waging for her rights.

As soon as Elizabeth heard that Mary's success was assured, she went with her train to Wanstead to meet her and paid homage to the new Queen who received her graciously. The royal sisters rode side by side in the state entrance into London, when the youthful charms of the twenty-year-old princess took the popular fancy. She is described as having red-gold hair, an olive complexion, striking eyes, beautiful hands, a fine, moderately tall figure and a dignified mien. "In every look, word, and action, Elizabeth studied effect, and on this occasion it was noticed that she took every opportunity of displaying her hand of which she was not a little vain." (Strickland).

Despite Northumberland's eleventh hour conversion to the old faith, in a last bid for his life, Queen Mary sent him to the block, but for the moment spared Lady Jane Grey and her husband, and kept them prisoners in the Tower.

Not fully realizing the dominating desire of Queen Mary to restore the Roman Catholic religion in England, Elizabeth, trusting in her sister's affection, acted at this juncture with a lack of political discretion which at the same time endeared her to the Reformed party. Queen Mary asked Elizabeth to accompany her to a Requiem Mass for the late King, held in the Chapel of the Tower. She declined this and also other invitations to attend Mass with her sister. Her refusals aroused the displeasure of the Queen and her Council, and when she disobeyed actual orders to conform, some bigots advised that she should be placed under arrest. The Queen sent preachers and members of the Council to admonish her sister; they only obtained a rude reply. This recalcitrant attitude imperilled in Mary's eyes the Catholic succession and was construed by her as disaffection.

Elizabeth in reality was well content to bide her time. She had no wish to overthrow her ailing and prematurely old elder sister, and at once sought to retrieve her mistaken policy. She obtained an audience with the Queen and kneeling before her with tears streaming down her cheeks protested that she had done nothing to offend her majesty "except in the article of religion, in which she was excusable, having been brought up in the creed she at present professed, without having ever heard any doctor who could have instructed her in the other". She asked therefore to study books setting forth the doctrines of Rome and for some learned man to be appointed to instruct her in these doctrines. However doubtful Queen Mary might have been of Elizabeth's true feelings, she accepted this overture and on September 8 Elizabeth reluctantly accompanied her to Mass to celebrate the nativity of the Blessed Virgin. To confirm this impression she wrote to the Emperor Charles V for a cross, chalice and other ornaments for a private chapel which she intended to have. Here, however, she perhaps overplayed the rôle of would-be convert.

It was, however, of the utmost importance to Elizabeth that her sister should recognize her as heiress presumptive to the throne, and that she should have her rightful place at Queen Mary's coronation. If she were passed over, there might still be Protestant claimants in Lady Jane Grey and her sister Catherine, while there was a formidable Catholic aspirant in Mary, Queen of Scots, dauphiness of France, whose claims Noailles, the French ambassador pressed on the Queen. The concessions already mentioned secured Elizabeth's participation as heiress presumptive at Mary's coronation, but now she made another mistake. By the Act which was the initial business of Mary's first Parliament, the marriage of Henry VIII and Catherine of Aragon was confirmed and the legitimacy of the Queen established. No allusion was made to the subsequent marriage of Henry with Anne Boleyn, although the Act tacitly implied that Elizabeth was illegitimate. Inasmuch as nothing was said in the Act on this question, it would have been wiser if Elizabeth had taken no notice. On the contrary, she was much offended and demanded permission to withdraw from the Court. When this request was refused, she held herself aloof and again the Queen was displeased with her. This exhibition of youthful pique was all the more unfortunate in that fresh snares and perils beset her at this time.

The white rose of York had not been entirely merged in the red rose of Lancaster, the aim of Henry VII's policy. It still had a representative in Edward Courtenay, Earl of Devon, whose grandmother was a daughter of Edward IV. Because of this descent his father, the Marquis of Exeter, had been beheaded in 1539, and Courtenay had spent his boyhood a prisoner in the Tower, by order of Henry VIII until Queen Mary released him. Though of weak character, he was handsome, affable and accomplished, and the Queen's wiser statesmen, like Paget, advised her to marry him and thereby affect a second re-union of the Houses of York and Lancaster.

Mary paid no attention to this advice. For many years she had been supported and guided by the counsel of her cousin, the Emperor Charles V, the champion of her mother. He had once been considered by Henry VIII as a possible husband for her, and although this was out of the question now, she desired a closer link with his dynasty, partly through natural affection and partly because a marriage alliance with Spain would help her to re-establish the Catholic religion in England. The Emperor from the same religious motive, and anxious, as he ever was, to have England as an ally in his plans to secure the hegemony of Europe, through his astute ambassador in England, Simon Renard, offered the hand of his son, Philip, now a widower, to the English Queen.

No suitor could have been more welcome to Mary, but in consenting to the match she at once aroused opposition. She would make a foreigner King of England. Even the most devoted of her counsellors shook their heads at this prospect of foreign influence in the affairs of their country. England would be involved in foreign wars and policies in which she had no interest and from which she would gain no advantage. The Queen might forfeit her popularity and the love of her subjects. Mary's proud Tudor spirit would listen to no arguments against the course she was bent on pursuing. She cried out vehemently: "Rather death than marriage with anyone save the Prince of Spain".

The announcement of Mary's betrothal to Philip of Spain was not only repugnant to her people but led to a dangerous plot to depose her. The ringleaders were the Duke of Suffolk, father of Lady Jane Grey, and Sir Thomas Wyatt, a young knight of Kent. Courtenay was the nominal head and it was proposed that he should marry Elizabeth. If Elizabeth knew of the plot, she took no active part in it. At this time she was in equal danger from her friends and her foes. Renard was always sowing seeds of dissension between Mary and herself; the Protestants regarded her as the champion of their religion; and Noailles was tempting her with the promise of French support to entangle herself in the web of politics. The conspirators and other disaffected persons had midnight conferences at the French ambassador's house, but Noailles informed the Court "that though Elizabeth and

Courtenay were proper instruments for the purpose of exciting a popular rising, Courtenay was so timorous that he would suffer himself to be taken before he would act", a shrewd estimate of what was to happen.

As Mary received increasing reports of her sister's popularity, she lent a willing ear to Renard's assertions of Elizabeth's disloyalty, declined to see her privately and allowed the Countess of Lennox and the Duchess of Suffolk to take precedence of her. Elizabeth refused to attend Mass and shut herself up in her rooms. In defiance of the Queen's order, the Princess was visited by the ladies of the Court, which again excited Mary's anger. Renard accused Elizabeth of plotting with Noailles against the Queen, of receiving a French refugee preacher secretly, and advised her arrest. The charges were baseless; and when Paget and Arundel were sent to interrogate Elizabeth, she had no difficulty in disproving them. Queen Mary thereupon felt some sisterly compunction. She sent for Elizabeth, received her kindly, presented her with some valuable pearls and allowed her to go to Ashridge. Even here she was kept under surveillance by Mary's spies and worried with proposals to get rid of her by a State marriage. Charles V suggested the Prince of Piedmont, and the King of Denmark once more appeared as her suitor. Both proposals were inflexibly declined by the young princess, who was content to wait for the Crown of England.

Yet in the early months of 1554, it seemed doubtful if she would be allowed to wait, for her mother's tragic fate once more overshadowed her. The weak Courtenay betrayed the plot to Gardiner under interrogation, and the revolt broke out prematurely. Elsewhere it was easily crushed, but from Kent, Wyatt marched on an unprepared London with ten thousand men.

Mary was always at her best in moments of danger. She appealed to the citizens of London, who rallied to her and succeeded in delaying Wyatt for a day. When Wyatt fought his way from Knightsbridge to Charing Cross, his forces were cut up and defeated and he was made prisoner

41

at Temple Bar. Under torture Wyatt implicated Elizabeth and Courtney in the plot, but exonerated them on the scaffold. As Elizabeth was innocent of conspiracy, he probably considered he might also do his best for Courtenay who had only been a puppet in the proceedings.

When the news first came to Mary of Wyatt's rising, she was highly incensed with Elizabeth and supposed she was deeply involved in the conspiracy. On January 26 Mary sent a command to her sister at Ashridge to repair to London as a safeguard and assured her "she would be heartily welcome". It was a mandate that could not be disobeyed without some urgent cause, but such cause was present, and Elizabeth's state of health interposed delay, a delay that was of advantage to her. She was suffering from inflammation of the kidneys (acute nephritis), possibly as the result of an attack of scarlet fever, her limbs were swollen and dropsical. She was extremely ill and in bed. She sent a message to Mary that she was too ill to travel at present, prayed her majesty's forbearance for a few days, and had her house fortified as a defence against the rebels.

Her enemies and also some historians have regarded her illness as a diplomatic excuse for waiting on the result of the rising, but there is sufficient medical evidence to disprove this assertion.

On February 10 Mary sent Lord William Howard, Elizabeth's great-uncle, Sir Edward Hastings and Sir Thomas Cornwallis to bring Elizabeth to Court. With them she also sent two of her physicians, Dr. George Owen and Dr. Thomas Wendy to see whether the princess was really ill and fit to travel (see Chapter XV.) By this time the rebellion had been quelled, Wyatt had implicated Elizabeth, and acknowledged that he had sent her a message to leave Ashridge and go to Donnington. Also a copy of a letter from her to the King of France was found in an intercepted dispatch of the French ambassador. Finally, the arrested men confessed it had been their intention to set Elizabeth and Courtenay on the throne.

Mary, stirred up by Renard, had repented her former clemency. In the event, Wyatt, Suffolk and his brother,

Sir Thomas Grey, were executed as well as eighty others. There also perished on the scaffold Lady Jane Grey and her husband, Lord Guildford Dudley, on the pretext that they were involved in the conspiracy, but in reality because their existence constituted a possible threat to Mary's tenure of the throne.

Terror and panic were abroad alike for innocent and guilty. Elizabeth, who was usually well aware of the course of events, must have felt highly apprehensive for her future as she summoned strength of will to obey Mary's imperious summons. It was not until Monday morning, February 12, that the doctors pronounced her sufficiently recovered to bear the strain of the journey to London. Weak and ailing, half-fainting, she dragged her swollen limbs to the litter which Mary had sent her. Her condition was so far from well that she could only travel at the rate of six or seven miles a day, and when she arrived at Highgate on the 15th her limbs were so swollen that she could go no further. She had again called up her courage by the 22nd and proceeded through London to the Palace of Whitehall. Simon Renard reported her arrival to the Emperor Charles V in these words:

"The Lady Elizabeth arrived here yesterday, dressed all in white, surrounded with a great company of the Queen's people, besides her own attendants. Her countenance was pale and stern, her mien proud, lofty and disdainful, by which she endeavoured to conceal her trouble." (C.S.P. Span.)

When Elizabeth reached the Palace, she boldly demanded an interview with Queen Mary in order that she might assert her innocence. Mary, instead of the promised welcome, refused to see her and made her virtually a State prisoner, guarded and with few attendants. Elizabeth, as in the Seymour crisis six years previously, had only herself to rely on; her mind must have been greatly agitated; her body ailing and suffering; yet she maintained an intrepid demeanour.

43

The Queen, who had a rough sense of justice, intimated that Elizabeth ought not to be convicted of high treason, unless incontrovertible proofs existed of her guilt. For three weeks the Privy Council, with much wrangling, debated the fate of the princess. The "Spanish Party", headed by the Earl of Arundel and Lord Paget, urged that she should be put to death as a danger to the realm. Renard even intimated to the Queen that Prince Philip would not come to England until both Elizabeth and Courtenay were put out of the way. Bishop Gardiner, who disliked the Spanish match, urged that Elizabeth's severe illness at Ashridge rendered her incapable of actual acts of treason. The Council at first could come to no decision, and when Mary asked the members of it severally if one of them would take charge of Elizabeth, all declined the perilous responsibility.

At length, after an acrimonious debate, it was decided to send her to the Tower. Gardiner, fearing to be out-voted, supported this decision which was conveyed by himself with nine other lords of the Council to Elizabeth. He accused her at the same time of being concerned in the late risings. Elizabeth protested that she was "a true and innocent woman" and begged them to intercede for her with the Queen, which some agreed to do. After this, her attendants were further diminished and she was more rigorously guarded. Next day the Earl of Sussex appeared with another Privy Councillor to say the barge was waiting to take her to the Tower. Elizabeth entreated to be taken to her sister. When this was refused, she asked leave to write a letter. The Earl of Sussex was touched by her appeal and promised to deliver the letter to the Queen. Thereupon, Elizabeth wrote this poignant appeal to her sister. First she protested her innocence; second she implored an interview before she was sent to prison and went on to say:

"You shall never by report know, unless by yourself you hear. I have heard in my time of many cast away for want of coming to the presence of the Prince. And

44

in late days, I heard my lord of Somerset say that if his brother had been suffered to speak with him he had never suffered. But the persuasions were made to him so great that he was brought to believe that he could not live safely if the Admiral lived; and that made him consent to his death. Though these persons are not to be compared to your Majesty; yet I pray God that evil persuasions persuade not one sister against the other; and all for that day they have heard false report and not hearken to the truth knowing. Therefore once again, kneeling with humbleness of heart, because I am not suffered to bend the knees of my body, I humbly crave to speak with your Highness: which I could not be so bold as to desire if I knew not myself most clear as I know myself most true. And, as for that traitor Wyatt, he might peradventure write me a letter; but, on my faith, I never received any from him. And as for the copy of my letter sent to the French King, I pray God confound me eternally, if ever I sent him word, message, token or letter by any means. And to this truth, I will stand to the death."

The two noblemen stood by the door as the young princess penned this epistle in her beautiful calligraphy with slow deliberation, her face puffy and swollen, her eyes brimming over with tears. There was method in her slowness. By the time the letter was finished, the tide had so far ebbed that the rowers could not have shot London Bridge. She had gained another day, and that was everything in this critical time.

As she strove for her life, it is interesting to note how the present peril recalled her previous one and the memory of the Admiral, placed even as she was now, recurred to her. Also, her legs were still swollen and painful, for she could not bend her knees.

IV

Prisoner of State

ELIZABETH'S appealing letter to her sister had its effect afterwards, but for the moment the Queen was adamant. She upbraided Sussex when he delivered it, saying that in her father's time he would have done what he was told.

At nine o'clock the following morning, Sussex and the Lord Treasurer told Elizabeth that they had come to bring her to the Tower forthwith. She replied: "The Lord's will be done; I am contented, seeing it is the Queen's pleasure". As she was led through the palace gardens she glanced up at the Queen's windows in case Mary might show herself and relent. When no face appeared she cried out bitterly: "I marvel what the nobles mean by suffering me, a prince, to be led into captivity, the Lord knoweth wherefore, for myself I do not."

In their haste not to be delayed, Sussex made the rowers shoot London Bridge before the tide had risen sufficiently high for the purpose. The stern of the barge struck against the bridge and was only cleared with much difficulty. If the barge had been wrecked, Elizabeth might have been drowned in the swirling eddies of the waters. The sky was overcast and the rain was falling. As the barge drew near to the Tower, once more the memory of her mother's death within its walls returned to the lonely princess; she also recollected that Lady Jane Grey, in spite of her innocence, had perished there a few weeks previously. She objected to be landed at the Traitor's Gate for she was no traitor, "neither well could she, unless she should step

46

into the water". Sussex, anxious to be quit of his unpleasant duty, told her she had no choice, and offered her
his cloak to protect her from the rain. Indignantly, she
dashed it aside and as she stepped from the barge cried
out: "Here lands as true a subject, being prisoner, as ever
landed at these stairs. Before Thee, O God, I speak it,
having none other friend but Thee alone!" Sussex
answered: "If it were so, it was the better for her".

At the gates several of the warders and servants were
drawn up. As she came near some knelt and "prayed God
to preserve her grace". Elizabeth had hitherto acted as
became her, but she now gave way to an impulse of wilful
petulance, understandable in her condition of ill-health
and agitation of mind. She sat down on a cold, damp
stone and refused to enter the gates. They summoned
Bridges, the Lieutenant of the Tower who came out to her.
"Madam", he said, "you had best come out of the rain,
for you sit unwholesomely." To which she retorted:
"Better sit here than in a worse place, for God knoweth,
not I, whither you will bring me". After some delay, which
she spent in chiding her gentleman usher for weeping,
she was at length persuaded to enter the Tower, but
shuddered with dismay when the doors of her room in the
prison were shut, locked and bolted, and prayed with her
attendants for divine protection.

The Earl of Sussex went back to report to the Council
that he had fulfilled his ungrateful task; and when some
of the nobles urged that Elizabeth should be held with
greater rigour, he uttered a warning:

"Let us take heed, my lords, that we go not beyond
our commission, for she was our king's daughter, and is,
we know, the prince next in blood, wherefore let us so
deal with her now, that we have not, if it so happen, to
answer for our dealings hereafter."

Elizabeth's fate continued to be debated daily in the
Council without any decision being reached. She under-
went a rigorous cross-examination in the Tower conducted

47

by Bishop Gardiner, the Lord Chancellor, with nine other lords of the Council. Gardiner was a most unpleasant man, as Henry VIII had well appreciated. He was a schemer, a trimmer, vindictive and a bigot. He worried Elizabeth with futile questions about her removing to Donnington Castle, as Wyatt had advised, in spite of her explanation that there had been some talk about it, but she had not gone. In the course of this ordeal, she won over one of her judges. The Earl of Arundel, hitherto an advocate for her trial and execution, observed that he was sorry to see her troubled about such vain matters and expressed his conviction of her innocence. This was a powerful ally, for thereafter the elderly earl was a staunch adherent of the princess and strove for her release. Later Elizabeth complained of the close confinement in which she was kept and the Council, probably on Arundel's advocacy, allowed her to walk for part of the day in a high-fenced garden, the other prisoners being strictly warned "not so much as to look in that direction while her grace remained therein".

Among the many Prisoners of State in the Tower at that time was Lord Robert Dudley, son of the Duke of Northumberland, who had been sent there for participation in his father's schemes to place Lady Jane Grey on the throne. Although Elizabeth ostensibly was strictly guarded, it is known that prisoners had subtle means of communicating with one another, and it is possible that Dudley met her secretly and rendered her some service which earned her gratitude and revived her interest in him. He was born on the same day and in the same hour as Elizabeth, had played with her as a child, and, as he afterwards said "had known her intimately from her eighth year". Dudley was soon afterwards liberated and went to the wars in France, but on Elizabeth's accession he was early signalled out for distinction.

These two months of peril in the Tower, when she was alone, weak and ailing, and had only her wits and superb courage to defend herself, helped again to mould her self-eliant character. Once more a stern lesson of life was taught her. Her Queen and sister was estranged from her, her kinsfolk and friends were far apart. She must be all-sufficient to herself. It was the second chapter of the lesson which she had learned six years previously in the Seymour affair. We know from her own lips that she fully realized her danger and even despaired of the issue. In after years when speaking of these dark days she told Castelnau, the French ambassador:

"That she was in great danger of losing her life from the displeasure her sister had conceived against her, in consequence of the accusations that were fabricated, on the subject of her correspondence with the King of France; and having no hope of escaping, she desired to make her sister only one request, which was, that she might have her head cut off with a sword, as in France, and not with an axe, after the present fashion adopted in England, and therefore desired that an executioner might be sent for out of France, if it were so determined."

It was the same tragic request that Anne Boleyn had made, and which was granted to her by summoning the headsman of Calais for her execution.

Bishop Gardiner, as usual, overplayed his hand, as he had done by urging King Henry to send Catherine Parr to the Tower. According to Holinshed, the Queen fell ill and the Chancellor, fearing the accession of Elizabeth if her sister died, sent a warrant to the Lieutenant of the Tower for the immediate execution of the princess. Bridges, observing the warrant was not signed by the Queen, refused to carry it out until he had learned the Queen's pleasure. It is to Queen Mary's credit that, in spite of Renard's ceaseless promptings to do away with her sister, she was highly indignant with Gardiner and sent the trustworthy Sir Henry Bedingfield with a hundred men of her guard to take the command of the Tower and protect Elizabeth. Lord William Howard strongly protested against the treatment meted out to his great-niece. He was one of Mary's staunch adherents and she felt she must placate him. She therefore now decided that neither Elizabeth nor Courtenay should be put on trial, and declined the offer of the Emperor Charles V that Elizabeth should be sent to the Court of his sister, the Queen of Hungary, or to his own Court at Brussels. The Council then suggested imprisonment at Pontefract Castle, but Mary rejected the ill-omened proposal and, on May 19, sent Elizabeth to Woodstock under the charge of Sir Henry Bedingfield. Here she was strictly guarded, but it is likely that the precautions taken were chiefly to protect her from assassination. Miss Strickland gives two instances of such attempts by Gardiner's myrmidons.

Acute nephritis from which Elizabeth had been suffering is a disease of some duration. Recovery may occur in two to four months, or earlier in mild cases, but in many cases after the subacute stage the disease may enter a stationary phase or become slightly progressive. A patient who has nephritis is more susceptible to cold, which may provoke an exacerbation. The cold and damp of Elizabeth's imprisonment in the Tower in addition to the mental distress which she had undergone were unfavourable to uninterrupted convalescence, and it is not surprising that soon after her transfer to Woodstock she had a severe recurrence of her disease. On June 8 she was so ill that Bedingfield sent an express messenger to the Court for two physicians. They were sent and remained in attendance on her for several days. Gradually, her youth and healthy constitution brought about her recovery. It should be noted that the physicians in making their report to the Queen made mention of the patient's loyal sentiments, which are said to have favourably impressed Mary.

In the meantime, Philip of Spain had landed at Southampton with a distinguished train of nobles, which included Alva, Egmont and Ruy Gomez, and was married to Queen Mary in Winchester Cathedral on July 25, 1554. Towards the end of the year Reginald, Cardinal Pole, Mary's kinsman, returned from exile in Italy as Papal Legate bearing with him a bull which confirmed those in possession of Church property provided that the Papal supremacy was restored in England. There followed a solemn reconciliation with Rome in Westminster Abbey attended by Philip and Mary in state. The Romish revival and the Spanish influence at Court caused great discontent among the people and Mary, herself, began to lose much of her popularity in spite of the announcement that she would in due course give birth to an heir or heiress to the throne.

Elizabeth regarding herself as still in danger considered it best to dissemble. She heard Mass, went to confession and professed herself a Roman Catholic. Queen Mary sceptical of these professions sent several divines to interrogate her upon her religious beliefs. Her skill in theology baffled them, as was shown by her famous answer to a question on transubstantiation:

Christ was the word that spake it,
He took the bread and brake it;
And what his words did make it
That I believe and take it.

Her loneliness was accentuated during this period of partial imprisonment at Woodstock. She was restricted in her walks and was allowed few books and writing materials. She heard the song of the milk-maids in the field and often envied their lot. Bedingfield reported that at times she would break out into fits of ungovernable rage, for the ordeal was too galling for perpetual self-restraint. One day she wrote in charcoal on a shutter this poetic expression of her sorrow:

Oh Fortune, how thy restless wavering state
Hath wrought with cares my troubled wit,
Witness this present prison, whither fate
Could bear me, and the joys I quit.
Thou caus'dst the guilty to be loosed
From bands wherein are innocents enclosed,
Causing the guiltless to be strait reserved
And freeing those that death had well deserved

> But by her envy can be nothing wrought:
> So God send to my foes all they have wrought,
>   Quoth Elizabeth, prisoner.

Strange to relate, Elizabeth owed her release from captivity to Philip's influence. Knowing that prince's rigid and glacial cast of mind, it can readily be understood that his reasons for intervention were entirely political. He wished to stand well with the English people, and was aware that she was regarded as a victim of the Spanish match; this impression he desired to remove. He knew that his wife's health was precarious and that in default of an heir to the marriage Elizabeth was likely to succeed her. This he would prefer, because otherwise Mary Queen of Scots and dauphiness of France would succeed, and French influence against Spain would then be paramount in England. His final reason was a project for marrying Elizabeth to the Emperor's adherent, Emmanuel Philibert, Duke of Savoy.

Some historians state that Elizabeth was bidden to the Christmas festivities at Hampton Court, at which she met her suitor, the Duke of Savoy, and declined the offer of his hand, saying, as usual, that she preferred to remain unmarried. Creighton states it was not until the end of April, 1555, that she was summoned, by which time the Duke had been called to the defence of his dominions. On leaving Woodstock, Elizabeth scratched with a diamond on one of the glass casements the following lines:

> Much suspected by me:
> Nothing proved can be,
>   Quoth Elizabeth, prisoner.

It was a tribute from a young woman, elated at her release from prison, to her success in defending herself.

When Elizabeth arrived at Hampton Court, her spirits were somewhat dashed by being restricted to her rooms in the palace. After a fortnight, Bishop Gardiner appeared and asked her to beg the Queen's pardon. This she declined to do, as she had done no wrong. Next day,

Gardiner returned to the charge, saying if she did not own her offence, the Queen would seem to have imprisoned her wrongfully. "Nay", replied Elizabeth, "it may please her to punish me, as she thinketh fit." Gardiner tried some other arguments, but again was worsted by Elizabeth's dialectics. Another week of solitude went by, and then at 10 o'clock at night Mary summoned her. The interview at first was strained, Mary upbraiding her sister for disloyalty, while Elizabeth knelt at her feet imploring the Queen to regard her as ever a loyal subject. In the end Mary was mollified and spoke kindly to her. A shade of distrust lingered as Elizabeth left the royal bedroom. "God knows", she said in Spanish to herself.

Queen Mary's hopes of an heir had proved deceptive. In reality she was suffering from dropsy, the result, according to Sir Spencer Wells, of an ovarian cyst for which no operation could be done in those days. She was depressed and sad at this wreck of her hopes, and Philip's interest in Elizabeth aroused in her a feeling of jealousy. Elizabeth, no doubt, encouraged Philip's admiration from motives of self-interest, although she was careful to be discreet when Mary was present. Prescott in his *History of the Reign of Philip the Second* has a footnote to the following effect in speaking of Philip's suit for Elizabeth's hand when she became Queen:

> "The Spanish minister, Feria, desired his master to allow him to mention Mary's jealousy as an argument to recommend his suit to the favour of Elizabeth. But Philip had the good feeling—or good taste—to refuse. (*Memorias de la Real Academia*, tom. VII, p. 260.)

With security, Elizabeth's vanity again became uppermost. She certainly believed Philip was in love with her and often boasted of this conquest in after-life. She enrolled her brother-in-law in the long list of her admirers and even when he became her deadly enemy, she retained a *tendresse* for him and kept his portrait in her bedroom. If an additional reason is needed for Elizabeth's conciliation of Philip, it is because his good feeling towards her also enabled her to escape the marriage with the Duke of Savoy which Philip and Mary still favoured. Mary would have made the match, but Philip could not press a suitor upon a young woman who had, so he imagined, lost her heart to him. Prince Eric, son of Gustavus Vasa, the King of Sweden, also sought Elizabeth's hand, but she declined his suit on the usual grounds that she was wedded to spinsterhood. There was, nevertheless, mention of a third suitor, the Archduke of Austria.

The Marian persecutions, which have attached a deadly stigma to Mary's name and reign, were beginning, although their chief instigator, Bishop Gardiner, died in 1555. Both Philip and the Pope disapproved of them on political grounds, but Mary's bigotry and desire to root out heresy in her realm could not be checked. War for conscience sake raged, the prisons were crowded and the fires of death blazed forth throughout England.

At this juncture the Emperor Charles V signified his intention of abdicating. Philip was to become King of Spain and the Indies, ruler of the Netherlands, Naples, Sicily and Milan, while Charles's brother, Ferdinand, became Emperor of Germany. Philip had therefore to leave England to meet his father in Flanders, and on September 4, 1555, he embarked at Dover. Mary accompanied him from Hampton Court to Greenwich and Elizabeth came by water to meet them there to bid farewell to her brother-in-law. In October, Queen Mary permitted Elizabeth to reside at Hatfield with the state of a royal princess, and at parting gave her a valuable ring as a token of complete reconciliation.

As the princess passed through London on her way to Hatfield, the warmth of her welcome and the cheers of the people assembled in crowds to greet her astonished her, and she screened herself behind some of her retinue being as if unwilling to court popularity. In her Hertfordshire retreat, to Elizabeth's great joy, Mary had consented to let her have some of her old attendants, in particular her beloved Mrs. Ashley (with her husband), the Parrys and her tutor, Roger Ascham. But though the Queen had greatly relaxed conditions, she did not entirely trust her sister and kept a certain degree of surveillance upon her proceedings.

With or without Elizabeth's consent she was always the focus of Protestant plots. In the spring of 1555, although she had been exonerated, some of the members of her own household had been accused of using spells to destroy the Queen's life. Hardly had she returned to Hatfield when a series of fresh conspiracies began. There was in the spring of 1556 a plot between Henry II, King of France and Sir Henry Dudley to depose Mary and make Elizabeth queen. Two of her officers, Peckham and Werne, were involved and were duly tried and executed, together with John Throckmorton, a member of the same family as Sir Nicholas. Peckham and Werne's confessions implicated Elizabeth, and it is said that she only emerged scatheless through King Philip's interposition. If so, Elizabeth must have once more congratulated herself on the good use she had made of her feminine wiles to secure Philip's friendship. Queen Mary remained outwardly friendly, but she sent Sir Thomas Pope to reside at Hatfield in order to keep a watchful eye on Elizabeth. Sir Thomas fulfilled his duties with tact and discretion, and Elizabeth was wise enough to receive him amicably.

The Marian persecutions continued unabated. Ridley and Latimer by their martyrdom had lit an unextinguishable candle to the Protestant faith in 1555, and in the following year Archbishop Cranmer, Elizabeth's godfather, followed them to the stake at Oxford.

Elizabeth visited London in state towards the end of 1556. Here is the account of her entrance:

"The 28th day of November came riding through Smithfield and Old Bailey, and through Fleet Lane into Somerset Place, my good Lady Elizabeth's grace, the queen's sister, with a great company of velvet coats and chains, her grace's gentlemen, and after a great company of men, all in red coats, guarded with a broad guard of black velvet and cuts (slashes)."

She contemplated staying in London during the winter, and already a little court of her friends and well-wishers had formed around her. She probably learned that this was not looked upon favourably by Mary and also found that the Queen had summoned her in order to press once more—and this time with Philip's insistence conveyed in messages through his ambassador—the suit of the Duke of Savoy. So after a week of protests and refusals "my Lady Elizabeth's grace . . . took her way towards Bishop Hatfield."

After this perturbed visit to London, Elizabeth appears to have faltered for a short time in her stern self-reliance. Anxiety that she might in the end not escape a charge of high treason on account of the incessant plottings in her name against the blood-stained tyranny that now ruled England, the veiled hostility of Mary and the threats used by the Spanish emissaries to force her into an unwelcome marriage, coupled with the strain of playing a part these many weary years, made her contemplate a plan of escape. Through Noailles, Henry II had often urged her to seek refuge at his Court, no doubt with the design of having in his power the one person who stood between his daughter-in-law's succession to the English crown. Noailles had fomented so many plots against Mary that at her instance he had been recalled and replaced by his upright brother, the Bishop of Acqs. When Elizabeth sent secretly the Countess of Essex to the Bishop to ask his assistance in planning the escape to France, the good man wisely pointed out that if Mary had taken refuge with the Emperor Charles V she would not be Queen of England. At a second interview he was even more outspoken, saying that if ever Elizabeth hoped to ascend the throne of England she must never leave the realm. In later years he always held that Elizabeth owed her crown to him, for she took his advice and the momentary fit of indecision and apprehension gave way to her wonted courage to abide the issue of events.

Queen Mary, perplexed with the burden of governing a discontented people, sorely needed the help and support of her husband. Death had deprived her of the counsel of Bishop Gardiner on whom she had chiefly relied. She wrote repeatedly to Philip urging his return and at length sent Lord Paget to reinforce her entreaties.

At last, difficulties with France and the Pope brought Philip back to his wife, when all conjugal persuasions on her part had failed. In this connexion we hear again of Lord Robert Dudley, for in the French wars he had so ingratiated himself with the Spanish King that he sent him to Mary with the welcome tidings of his approach. Elizabeth seems to have been at Court again at this time, for on February 25, 1557, she came from Hatfield to London, "attended by a noble company of lords and gentlemen, to do her duty to the Queen, and rested at Somerset House till the 28th, when she repaired to her majesty at Whitehall with many lords and ladies."

Philip, being short of troops, money and munitions, was anxious to have England as an ally in the French War, and came over to make personal representations to the Privy Council on the subject. It was not a propitious time. The currency was low, distress prevailed among the people, the Flanders debts were heavy and the Queen had relinquished part of her revenue to the Church. A war in any case would be unpopular, particularly one to serve the ends of Spain. Such was the response of Mary's counsellors and Philip would have gone away empty-handed, if events had not played into his hands.

The King of France, imagining that trouble at home would deter Mary from entering the War, helped one of the English exiles, Sir Thomas Stafford, Lord Stafford's second son, and grandson of the Duke of Buckingham, who was executed in Henry VIII's reign, to equip two ships. In these with a small force Stafford sailed from Dieppe, landed at Scarborough and took the castle there. Wotton, the English ambassador in France, had duly warned his Court of the designs of Stafford, and on the fourth day the Earl of Westmorland appeared before the castle at the head of a strong body of troops, and compelled Stafford to surrender. Stafford with several others

57

of his band were sent to London and under torture confessed that the King of France had instigated and supported their enterprise. Stafford was beheaded on Tower Hill and three of his confederates were hanged at Tyburn. Elizabeth's name, fortunately, was not brought into Stafford's conspiracy, although a rumour was set afoot that it was intended to reward the Earl of Westmorland by giving him her hand in marriage. Lord Arundel's suit was also mentioned in another rumour.

The participation of Henry II in Stafford's attempt aroused popular feeling against France and the Council felt justified in declaring open war and acceding to Philip's requests. The King, having obtained his desire, hurried back to Flanders and neither Mary nor England ever saw him again.

The Earl of Pembroke, with Lord Robert Dudley as his master of ordnance, followed Philip in July with 7,000 men. They joined Philip's force of 40,000 men of which Philibert, Duke of Savoy held the supreme command and participated in the great victory of St. Quentin. On hearing of this success, Charles V inquired: "Then my son is at Paris?" But Philip did not follow up the victory; instead he withdrew to the Netherlands. The Duke of Guise, summoned from Italy, at the head of a French army took Calais, the last English stronghold in France, after a gallant resistance on the part of Lord Wentworth the Governor. This success was joyfully hailed by the French and by the English with equal mortification. Queen Mary is said to have averred that after her death the name of Calais would be found graven on her heart.

In the spring of 1558 great preparations were made in England for the invasion of France. The combined fleets of Spain and England were to ravage the French coast, while an Allied army under Philip was to invade France by land. The fleet found Brest too strongly defended, while two great armies, one under Philip and the Duke of Savoy, the other under King Henry and the Duke of Guise, stood arrayed for battle. Philip, ever cautious, preferred negotiation to fighting and the two kings sent their armies into winter quarters, while the diplomatists argued about the restoration of Calais to England and of Navarre to France.

In the meantime, Queen Mary's unhappy and blood-stained reign was drawing to a close. No doubt she had many excellent qualities. Her court was inexpensive and uncorrupt; she lived simply, was a patron of letters and left a legacy for a hospital for old and invalid soldiers which, however, was never appropriated. Apart from religious persecution, justice was said to be fairly administered under her sway, although this is disputed by Protestant contemporaries. She supported trade, being the first sovereign to make a commercial treaty with Russia, and she revoked the privileges of the Hanse Town merchants, because they conflicted with English commerce. In sombre relief and ironically her bigotry, as both the Pope and Philip even realized, was the greatest bar to the re-establishment of Roman Catholicism in England, the great cause which she had at heart. The blood of the martyrs in the Marian persecution was the seed of the Church of England. Her marriage to Philip set the seal on her unpopularity and her reign ended in misery and defeat.

As Mary lay a-dying, according to Philip's wishes, who dreaded the possibility of the Queen of Scots succeeding her, she nominated Elizabeth as her successor and exhorted her to pay her personal debts and continue the Church as she had re-established it. She also sent the Crown Jewels to her sister.

On November 10, the Count de Feria, the Spanish envoy, on Philip's instructions, went to pay his court to Elizabeth, and to offer her the assurances of his master's friendship. Elizabeth received the Count graciously, but when he urged that she owed her recognition as heiress to the throne, neither to Queen Mary nor her Council, but solely to King Philip, she answered proudly that she owed this to the people of England. Referring to Philip's project for marrying her to the Duke of Savoy, she added that she well knew how much favour the Queen had lost by marrying a foreigner. This is de Feria's opinion of Elizabeth after recording this conversation:

"It appears to me that she is a woman of extreme vanity, but acute. She seems greatly to admire her father's system of government. I fear much that in religion she will not go right, as she seems inclined to favour men who are supposed to be heretics, and they tell me the ladies who are about her are all so. She appears highly indignant at the things that have been done against her during her sister's reign. She is much attached to the people, and is very confident that they are all on her side (which is indeed true); in fact, she says 'it is they that have placed her in the position she at present holds', as the declared successor to the Crown".

The astute Spaniard well sums up Elizabeth's meditated policy in these words.

During the last days of Mary's life, Elizabeth remained cautiously at Hatfield awaiting the issue of events. Both time-serving courtiers anxious to salute the rising sun and many of her staunch adherents flocked to Hatfield. Among the latter was Sir Nicholas Throckmorton (Throgmorton in the older spelling) who had been tried for his complicity in Wyatt's rising and acquitted through his legal acumen, much to Queen Mary's indignation. Elizabeth bade Sir Nicholas hasten to Whitehall, and if the Queen were really dead to request a certain lady of the bed-chamber, who was her confidant, to send her as a token, the black enamelled ring which the Queen habitually wore.

It was November 17, 1558. Off sped Sir Nicholas, and while he was on his way to London, Mary died. When he returned with the ring to Hatfield, a deputation from the Privy Council had already arrived there to acquaint Elizabeth of her sister's death and to offer their homage.

Sir Robert Naunton relates that the new Queen sank on her knees and exclaimed: "*O domino factum est illud, et est mirabile in oculis notris!*" "This is the Lord's doing, and it is marvellous in our eyes", which, adds Sir Robert, "we find to this day on the stamp of her gold, with this on her silver, *Posui Deum Adjuratorem meum*, I have chosen God for my helper".

Thus began the glorious reign of Queen Elizabeth the First.

V

The Queen: The Church of England

QUEEN ELIZABETH had been given no easy and simple inheritance. A contemporary memorandum thus describes the unfortunate state of England:

> "The Queen poor; the realm exhausted; the nobles poor and decayed; good captains and soldiers wanting; the people out of order; justice not executed; the justices unmeet for their offices; all things dear; division among ourselves; war with France and Scotland; the French King bestriding the realm, having one foot in Calais and the other in Scotland; steadfast enmity but no steadfast friendship abroad."

Elizabeth, as we have seen, had a stern apprenticeship to Queendom. She had fought for her life alone, she had endured alone. She had no relatives whom she cared for or trusted; no intimate friends, except Catherine Ashley, who had neither wisdom nor judgment to aid her in her problems. But she had one trusted adviser, who remained with her as prime minister for forty years and never left her till death summoned him. This was Sir William Cecil, afterwards Lord Burghley (1520–1598), and his descendants continue to serve their sovereign and their country in high offices of State to the present day.

William Cecil was the son of a country squire. Educated at Cambridge, of which University he afterwards became Chancellor, he married the sister of his scholar friend, Cheke, whose mother kept a small wine shop frequented by undergraduates. This is held to be the only imprudent action of his life. His wife died within three years and he then married Mildred Cooke, a highly educated and intellectual woman; her sister was the mother of Francis Bacon. Cecil was adaptable, as became a budding statesman in those days. He held high office both under the Protector Somerset and Northumberland. At Mary's accession, he lost his place, but conformed to Romanism and was still employed in State affairs. In Mary's reign he was constantly in touch with Elizabeth and became her devoted adherent. On her accession, she appointed him Secretary of State and he became at once her chief adviser. On admitting him to office, she said:

"This judgment I have of you, that you will not be corrupted by any manner of gifts, and that you will be faithful to the State; and that without respect of any private will, you will give me that counsel that you think best."

Loyally and steadfastly did Burghley fulfil his royal mistress's trust in him. The great seal was given to the new Secretary's brother-in-law, Sir Nicholas Bacon, also a man of wisdom and integrity.

Froude pays tribute to the great part Cecil played in Queen Elizabeth's administration in these words:

"Cecil was the presiding spirit; everywhere among the State papers of these years Cecil's pen is ever visible, Cecil's mind predominates. . . . Nothing was too large for his intellect to control, nothing too small for his attention to consider."

He was an excellent civil servant. Elizabeth, who kept supreme decisions in her own capable hands, sometimes rated him, often disputed his advice and sometimes showed her displeasure by keeping him at a distance. All along however, she trusted him implicitly and in the end she usually followed his wise counsel. When he was dying, she visited him and gave food to him with her own royal hand, and she mourned for him as the truest and wisest minister who ever stood by a sovereign's throne.

From the beginning of her reign, Elizabeth followed the example of Henry VIII in courting the popularity of her subjects and in making royal progresses. She was early gratified by being called "Our Good Queen Bess", just as her father had been styled "Bluff King Hal". At the same time she and Cecil were early preoccupied with important problems, which the march of events forced upon them. Of these the most pressing was the state of the national Church.

Bishop Creighton, in a lecture on "The English Church in the Reign of Elizabeth" (*Historical Lectures and Addresses*), observed that a great external change came over England in the sixteenth century, which included three things: (1) a great national revolution in the resolute assertion of England's national independence; (2) a great social revolution; exemplified by the passing of the sway of the nobles, the rise of the wealthy middle classes, the dissolution of the monasteries, importance of manufactures and commerce; (3) a great intellectual revolution consequent on absorption of the New Learning into national life.

These three things played their part in the establishment of the Church of England. Henry VIII for six patient years struggled to preserve the Roman Catholic Church in England as it was, and only the persistent refusal of Pope Clement VII to allow the divorce of Catherine of Aragon led him to break with Rome. The papal authority of Rome had long been resented in England, and Henry in renouncing it was supported by the majority of his subjects. The New Learning also applied criticism to the Romish doctrines and taught men to think for themselves in matters of religion. Under Henry VIII the ecclesiastical system was retained, the services were simplified, and the organisation of the Church continued. There were, however, two parties in the State—the Anglo-Catholics, headed by Gardiner, who desired as little change as possible, and the reformers imbued with the spirit of continental Protestantism. With the latter went some of the politicians, who considered the

Reformed Church could not survive unless it were allied to German Protestantism. Henry, who temporarily yielded to Cromwell's advice on this matter and married Anne of Cleves, had the wisdom to retrace his steps. The Protestant reformers, nevertheless, were still a strong party; they felt the English Church was being reformed too slowly. When Edward VI became king, they seized their opportunity and with the support of Somerset and afterwards with that of Northumberland, they endeavoured to make the English Church a Lutheran one, an innovation which did not accord with the wishes of the people. This explains the reaction under Queen Mary and the ease with which the Mass was reintroduced and the temporary reconciliation with Rome effected. Bishop Gardiner, an unpleasant prelate, was able politician enough to see that, although the old faith might be accepted, the domination of the Pope and Spain would not. Even the Pope and King Philip agreed with him. But the Marian persecutions antagonized the nation, and when Elizabeth became Queen, she was hailed as the champion of the Reformed doctrines. It was never a part which she desired to play, but it was forced upon her throughout her reign by the circumstances of the time.

Elizabeth herself in matters of religion was averse to persecution and was tolerant. Here she was greatly in advance of her age. She greatly disliked the tenets of Geneva and would have been contented to see restored the formulas accepted by her father, Henry VIII, with an English ritual and the Communion Service of the First Prayer Book of her brother, Edward VI. She was constrained to sanction far more sweeping reforms.

At her accession, the Queen desired to proceed cautiously, more especially as she had no wish to antagonize King Philip whose hostility at this juncture, England being still at war with France, might have imperilled the safety of her realm. The Mass for the time being was continued in the Churches. "Mary, late Queen of England, Spain, France, both the Sicilies, Jerusalem, and Ireland, Defender of the Faith, Archduchess of Austria,

5   65

Duchess of Burgundy, Milan and Brabant, Countess of Halspinge, Flanders and Tyrol", was buried in Westminster Abbey with great ceremony and with all the ancient medieval rites, at Elizabeth's command. When Convocation assembled in January, 1559, it was opened formally with high mass. In the royal chapel a crucifix stood on the decorated altar; tapers were lighted and incense was burned. The only innovation was the use of the English litany translated by King Henry VIII, and Elizabeth's objection to the elevation of the consecrated Host, "because she liked not the ceremony". When the Queen was crowned in Westminster Abbey on January 15, 1559, it was according to the ceremonies of the Roman pontifical. Dr. Heath, Archbishop of York, refused to officiate and Dr. Oglethorpe, Bishop of Carlisle, crowned the Queen.

Elizabeth, although anxious to exercise a temporising policy, soon realized that her people were in favour of the reformed religion, and that she must conciliate the reforming party, now augmented by the return of Marian exiles from the Continent. Cecil also saw this was necessary; and with the Queen's sanction a commission was set up to consider how the reformed religion could be most safely re-established. It included such eminent divines as Parker, Cox, Grindal and May. To minimize controversy preaching was forbidden, but the Gospels, Epistles, the Ten Commandments, the Lord's Prayer and the Creed were to be read in English. A conference was ordered between the Marian bishops and the leading reforming divines, but after two days of incompatibility the bishops withdrew. Elizabeth's first Parliament met on January 30. It restored the first fruits of ecclesiastical benefices to the crown and passed the "Act of restoring to the Crown the ancient jurisdiction over the State, ecclesiastical and spiritual". The Queen refused the title of "Supreme head of the Church", but accepted that of "supreme governor, as well in spiritual and ecclesiastical causes as in temporal". In case this assumption offended Philip II, she explained to the Spanish ambassador that

66

this title meant very little. She did not intend to be "head of the Church", but she could not let her subjects' money be given to the Pope any more. The Act of Uniformity, passed at the end of April, with certain alterations in the Communion Service, ordered the Second Prayer Book of Edward VI to come into use. The religious settlement generally was welcomed by the English people. Bishop Creighton observes that "the number of staunch Romanists or strong Protestants was very small".

The clergy raised no substantial opposition to the change. Out of 9,400 clergy only 192 refused to take the oath of supremacy; the recusants included all the bishops, except Kitchin of Llandaff. They were ejected from their sees. Some went into exile, others like Heath, Archbishop of York and Tunstal, Bishop of Durham, into friendly custody. Even the persecuting Bonner was given a house in the Marshalsea prison.

Queen Elizabeth in her wisdom never interfered with the spiritual authority of the Church and often prevented Parliament from interfering in ecclesiastical matters. Archbishop Pole, who died the day after Queen Mary, had left a number of vacant sees and after the ejection of most of the Marian bishops, it was difficult to find bishops to consecrate Matthew Parker, the new Archbishop of Canterbury, who had been Anne Boleyn's chaplain. She had entreated him before her death to watch over her little daughter, and he was always Elizabeth's friend.

The above-mentioned difficulty was overcome by summoning three previously consecrated bishops of the reformed opinions, Coverdale who had been Bishop of Exeter; Scory, Bishop of Rochester, then of Chichester; and Barlow, Bishop of St. David's, then of Bath. Coverdale's Genevan doctrines prevented his being re-appointed to a see under Elizabeth. Parker was reluctant to be Archbishop, but at length yielded to pressure. A man of learning, moderation and piety, he skilfully piloted the Church of England at this difficult time. He had a most able coadjutor in John Jewel, Bishop of Salisbury, who in 1562 published his well known "Apology of the Church of

England" in Latin, and had a large share in the writing of the "Homilies", which were a collection of sermons for parish priests to read in Churches.

Much as Elizabeth esteemed Archbishop Parker there was one matter in which they differed—Elizabeth preferred a celibate clergy. Parker, a married man, was firm and insisted on the right of the clergy to marry. Elizabeth had to agree, but perhaps one may tell once more the well-known story of how she scored off Mrs. Parker after the Archbishop and his wife had entertained her at Lambeth Palace: turning to her hostess, the Queen said: "And you, madam I may not call you, mistress I am ashamed to call you, and so I know not what to call you; but, howsoever, I thank you."

Leading features of Parker's episcopacy, during which he combated the extreme views of the rising sect of Puritans, are the adoption of the Thirty-nine Articles in 1562, in the amendment of which Elizabeth, herself, participated, and the magnificent folio of the Bishops Bible which appeared in 1568 and 1572. Its size and price prevented its general circulation. Elizabeth was equally fortunate in her choice of Parker's successors in the see of Canterbury, Archbishop Grindal and Archbishop Whitgift. All three Archbishops kept the Church of England in a *via media* between the doctrines of Rome and those of Geneva. This suited the moderates, although it was repugnant to the extremists. Above all things, Elizabeth was anxious to avoid bitter religious wars in her realm such as were distracting France and the Netherlands. She is not always given the credit for her success in this policy, but it was a notable achievement and entirely due to herself, for Burghley and Walsingham, both staunch Protestants, were always pressing her to emerge as the champion of the Huguenots and the revolting Netherlanders. She knew well that these civil wars on the Continent kept France and Spain from being a menace to England. She disliked rebellious subjects, and equally was aware that the revolts must be maintained in England's interest. She knew that her people sympathized with the

Huguenots and the Netherland Protestants, so she affected not to notice the numbers of English volunteers who went across the Channel to aid the insurgents. She sent help both secretly and openly to the Huguenots when the League seemed likely to prevail, and she allowed Huguenot and Dutch refugees to take shelter in her land and to augment English manufactures and crafts. She refused to go to war with Philip of Spain or Charles of France and kept their ambassadors at her Court.

The Queen's tolerant policy in matters of religion was partially successful.

"Silently, almost unconsciously," wrote J. R. Green, "England became Protestant, as the traditional Catholicism which formed the religion of three-fourths of the people at the Queen's accession died quietly away. At the close of her reign the only parts of England where the old faith retained anything of its former vigour were the north and the extreme west, at that time the poorest and least populated parts of the kingdom."

The older parish priests, who although they had conformed were Catholic at heart, gradually died and were replaced by Protestant clergy. Their instruction and preaching inculcated the Reformed doctrines in the new generation. The beliefs of the Universities changed. Oxford, which in 1558 was "a nest of Papists" became later ultra-Protestant, and bred Puritans. There was a new literature, a much wider general education among the middle classes, the fruits of the teaching of the Grammar Schools, and towards the end of the reign scholars like Archbishop Whitgift, Lancelot Andrewes, Bishop of Winchester, the greatest theologian of his age, and Richard Hooker, who defended and expounded the position of the Church of England in his treatise on "The Laws of Ecclesiastical Polity", were found among the clergy. Hooker was one of the luminaries of Elizabethan literature. His treatise bore the stamp of profound learning and was written in language of rare dignity and massive eloquence.

Another incentive to Protestantism was John Foxe's *History of the Acts and Monuments of the Church* popularly known as *Foxe's Book of Martyrs*. The first part was published in Latin at Strasburg in 1554 (reprinted at Basel in 1559). The first English edition appeared in 1563, in folio. It was sanctioned by the bishops and went through four editions by 1587.

Elizabeth's reliance on time to establish the Church of England was thus justified, and she reigned sufficiently long to see the effects of her wisdom. Her system of compromise in matters of faith and worship, of being tolerant with Roman Catholics so long as they outwardly conformed to the State religion, and of fining recusants to make them attend Church, proceeded tranquilly for the first twelve years of her reign.

Romish priests were still to be found, especially in the northern counties and Mass was said in Catholic private houses. It was only when the Queen perceived that the fanaticism and hostility manifested by certain papists, at the behest of Rome, endangered her personal safety and Government that she devised stern measures of repression.

In 1561 there was even the brief prospect of a reconciliation between the Church of England and the Church of Rome. Lord Robert Dudley, with or without the Queen's sanction, had alleged to Philip II that if the Spanish King favoured his marriage with her, she might incline to Roman Catholicism and make an alliance with him. De Quadra, the Spanish ambassador, was in charge of the negotiations and saw both the Queen and Dudley. Cecil was in despair. The new Pope, Pius IV, was calling a continuation of the Council at Trent for the discussion of religious controversies. A temperate policy was to be the order of the day. Representatives were invited from the Church of England and a papal nuncio was about to leave Rome to invite the Queen of England to unite with the Pope in the common interests of Christianity. Philip through de Quadra sent a personal message to Elizabeth begging her to receive the nuncio. In the end, the Queen changed her mind. She referred the proposal to her

Council and asked them to answer it. They did so. The visit of the nuncio was firmly declined; neither directly or indirectly could England recognise the authority of the Pope; for the same reason no English bishops or ambassadors could attend the Council at Trent—"where no manner of person might have voice or decision but such as were already sworn to the maintenance of the Pope's authority." Finally, it was stated: "her majesty could hope no good from it, as tending only to confirm those errors and those claims which had occasioned the disorder of Christendom."

Thus when the Council of Trent was summoned for its third and last session in 1562, Anglicans were unrepresented as well as Lutherans and Calvinists. The decrees promulgated on its dissolution in 1563 were, in the main, the authoritative exposition of the dogmas of the Romish faith, and of the papal claims to authority. The Roman Church emerged with the aims of rooting out heresy by sword and the stake and asserted that England must be brought back by force of arms to its allegiance. This confusion of spiritual with temporal power was a disastrous policy.

As long as the prudent Pius IV (1559–1566) was Pope, a cautious attitude towards England was maintained, but on his death this course was altered. The first step, often previously urged by English Catholic refugees who longed to see the fires of Smithfield rekindled, was the excommunication of Queen Elizabeth by Pope Pius V (1556–1572). The papal bull *Regnans in Excelsis* deposed her and absolved her subjects from her allegiance. At first kept secret, it was issued in February, 1570, after the failure of the northern rebellion. Philip II and Charles IX refused to allow its publication in their kingdoms, regarding it as a blow to sovereign authority. A copy was found nailed to the door of the Bishop of London's palace on May 15. One John Felton was hanged, drawn and quartered for giving the bull to a poor student.

Queen Elizabeth, mindful of her father's attitude towards his excommunication, troubled herself little about her own, but the Parliament of 1571 was alarmed. It passed bills, making the introduction of papal bulls into the realm, as also the conversion of members of the Church of England to Romanism, high treason. It was also made high treason for anyone to claim a right to the succession of the Crown during the lifetime of the Queen, or to say that it belonged to any other person than the Queen. This Parliament imposed the Thirty-nine Articles on the clergy; previously these had only been sanctioned by Convocation. Puritan in temper, it went too far for the Queen's tolerant disposition, and introduced several bills for the Protestant reform of religious worship, which were either dropped by the House of Lords, or failed to receive the royal assent.

The majority of English Roman Catholics refused to look upon Elizabeth as illegitimate and a usurper and to accept Mary, Queen of Scots as the true queen. But there was a fanatical minority who meditated the deposition and even the murder of Elizabeth.

It was on account of this minority that Elizabeth was driven to change her tolerant policy towards Roman Catholics, not so much for their religious beliefs but because they were enemies to the State. She could always feel the pulse of her people, and she knew that the spirit of the time was now Protestant, more Protestant than she herself wished. Her people were shocked by the atrocities enjoined by Philip in the Netherlands, by the massacre of St. Bartholomew and by the ceaseless plots secretly abetted by Rome in favour of the captive Queen of Scots.

Certain of the English Catholics in the latter part of the sixteenth century were earnest and active in endeavouring to remove Elizabeth. Among these was William Allen, a former Fellow of Oriel, who had resigned the headship of St. Mary Hall early in Elizabeth's reign. In order to train English Catholics for the priesthood he founded a Seminary at Douai in 1568, which in the first five years of its existence sent nearly a hundred priests to England. They were sent to maintain the old faith and, if necessary, were to embrace martyrdom. Pope Gregory XIII furnished funds for the seminary, and Allen eventually received a Cardinal's hat and was named Archbishop-Designate of Canterbury. In 1579 Allen through Mercurian, General of the Jesuits, secured the services of two English Jesuits, Robert Parsons, ex-fellow of Balliol and Edmund Campion, ex-fellow of St. John's, both men of learning and eloquence. In 1580 they came to England in disguise. Their mission was a failure. The majority of their co-religionists had no wish to dethrone the tolerant Queen, far less to assassinate her, or to invite invasion from Spain or France. Parsons fled back to Rome. Campion was arrested, tortured and tried. When he was imprisoned in the Tower, the Queen, who knew his scholarly abilities, sent for him and examined him as to his beliefs in the presence of Leicester and Burghley. Although several times offered a pardon, probably at the instance of Elizabeth, if he would deny the Pope's right to depose his lawful sovereign or hear a Protestant sermon, he refused, although he acknowledged Elizabeth as Queen, as the new interpretation of the Papal bull permitted him to do, and wished her a quiet and prosperous reign. So he was duly executed.

J. R. Green states: "The death of Campion was the prelude to a steady pitiless effort at the extermination of his class. As far as facts can now be ascertained, during Elizabeth's reign two hundred and fifty Catholics suffered for religion, while others perished in the filthy and fever-stricken gaols into which they were plunged. The work of reconciliation to Rome was arrested by this ruthless energy; but on the other hand, the work which the priests had effected could not be undone. The system of quiet compulsion and conciliation to which Elizabeth had trusted for the religious reunion of her subjects was foiled; and the English Catholics, fined, imprisoned at every crisis of national danger, and deprived of their teachers by the prison and the gibbet, were severed more hopelessly than ever from the national Church."

73

Protestants and Parliament exaggerated the danger of the Jesuit missionaries. Recusants were imprisoned, leading Catholics closely watched or put in ward. Statutes were passed which prohibited the saying of Mass in private houses, the fines for recusancy or non-attendance at public worship were increased to twenty pounds a month, and it was enacted that "all persons pretending to any power of absolving subjects from their allegiance, or practising to withdraw them to the Romish religion, with all persons willingly so absolved or reconciled to the See of Rome, shall be guilty of high treason." Few Roman Catholic laymen were executed or brought to trial, their oppression being limited to financial exactions, restriction of their movements and search of their houses for priests or treasonable correspondence. Thus through the ill-starred attack of the Pope in a vain attempt to subjugate England once more to Rome, the tolerant policy of Elizabeth partially failed. The antagonism to Rome was further increased through the issue by Cardinal Allen, as a prelude to the Spanish Armada, of a pastoral letter. This released the terrible anathemas levelled by Rome at Queen Elizabeth and, at the same time, urged the faithful English Roman Catholics to rise in arms and welcome His Catholic Majesty, King Philip II, the Spanish Champion of their religion. The letter went on to attack Elizabeth in the most reprehensible terms. She was described as filthy and illegitimate; her subjects were absolved by the Pope from their oath of allegiance to this wicked monster—"the scourge of God and shame of womankind." It was also considered by the Pope, by Cardinal Allen and King Philip a meritorious act to assassinate her. King Philip by a similar instigation had already disposed of his most formidable adversary in the Netherlands, William of Orange, in 1584.

This vituperation again defeated its own objects. Most English Catholics were disgusted by it and remained true and loyal subjects to their Queen.

Towards the latter part of Elizabeth's reign, the attitude of the Puritans, who were discontented with the ritual and

74

organisation of the Church of England, troubled Elizabeth. The Puritans, strongly Calvinistic as the result of association with Geneva and with the Huguenots and the Dutch, opposed the hierarchy in the Church, bishops and canons, vestments and surplices, kneeling at Holy Communion, the use of the ring in marriage and the sign of the Cross in baptism. The Queen, herself, was proud of being the head and defender of the national Church, of its services and ritual and of her bishops. She perceived that the ultra-Protestant clergy constituted a menace to the Crown, and would overthrow the peaceable middle line in religion which was so popular with her people. In fact she regarded them as much traitors as the emissaries of Rome. Puritans were not punished if they conformed, but if they obtruded their opinions they were harshly treated while Anabaptists and adherents to other strange sects were hanged or burned at the stake. The Puritans' religious meetings were suppressed for "prophesying", which was their name for extempore preaching; their pamphlets were regarded as provocative of sedition; and John Parry who wrote tracts in scurrilous terms against the bishops and the Church services under the name of "Martin Mar-prelate" was hanged for treasonable libel.

The Queen's fears carried her too far. The Puritans were not traitors. One man who had one hand struck off for intemperate zeal, took off his hat with his other hand and shouted, "God save the Queen". Archbishop Grindal was considered by the Queen to be too gentle with these schismatics, and this gave great offence to her. She insisted that the "prophesyings", which Grindal had allowed to be revived, should be absolutely forbidden. Grindal declined to comply with the royal command, and as a result the Archbishop was "sequestered" for five years, and though he continued to exercise some of his archiepiscopal functions was formally debarred from holding a convocation. Archbishop Whitgift, Elizabeth's "White-gift" as she called him, was a great English divine of the new learning, unprejudiced by exile at Geneva. He pleased the Queen by introducing a much sterner discipline in the Church. All the clergy had to subscribe to three articles affirming the royal supremacy, the lawfulness of the Book of Common Prayer and their assent to the Thirty-nine Articles. Many Puritans subscribed, some went into exile, others were contumacious and even suffered death for their religious convictions. The persecution of the Puritans is a blot upon the memories of Elizabeth and Whitgift. Yet there was in truth a grave risk that these zealots, as intemperate as their Roman Catholic persecutors, might destroy the Church which Queen Elizabeth had been at such pains to establish; and continued toleration was impossible at that time.

Neal, the historian of the Puritans, although bitterly blaming the cruelty wreaked upon them, testified to the service Queen Elizabeth rendered to religion in these words:

> "However, notwithstanding all these blemishes, Queen Elizabeth stands upon record as a wise and politic princess, for delivering her kingdom from the difficulties in which it was involved at her accession, for preserving the Protestant Reformation against the attempts of the Pope, the Emperor and the King of Spain abroad, and the Queen of Scots and her Papish subjects at home. . . . She was the glory of the age in which she lived, and will be the admiration of posterity."

It was Elizabeth who consolidated and established the Church of England with the help of a group of great men, the makers of the Church of England as it exists today. These men were Parker, Jewel, Sandys, Cox, Horne and others, Grindal the Puritan and Whitgift the Anglican.

It is often alleged that Queen Elizabeth as the result of her learning was imbued with something of the atheistical attitude present in some of those who were steeped in the lore of the Renaissance, and of which Sir Walter Raleigh and Christopher Marlowe were accused. It has been said that she cared nothing for religion except as an instrument of policy, that she was utterly worldly and if the occasion had served would as soon been a Roman Catholic as a Protestant Queen. The Queen's own history confutes this view. Her intellect and education made her highly tolerant of opposing views, until Romish aggression, plots and threatened assassination drove her into religious persecution. She was a Christian Queen believing in the essentials of Christianity rather than in dogma. The princess whose first thought when imprisoned in the Tower was to kneel and ask for divine succour; the Queen whose first thought on hearing that the Crown of England had fallen to her lot was to ascribe to God the glory; the Queen who upbraided Henry IV for deeming that Paris was worth a Mass; the dying woman who begged Archbishop Whitgift to continue praying for her at her bedside —all these things and the sacrifices she made for Christian beliefs and the welfare of her country, in spite of many sins and imperfections, go far to show that religion was the strength and mainstay of her lonely life.

VI

The Marriage Problem

FROM the cradle up to forty years of age, and—perhaps even later—the question of Elizabeth's marriage exercised the minds of English Ministers of State and those of the chief sovereigns of Europe. In Appendix I will be found a list of the different husbands proposed for Elizabeth, beginning with the Duke of Angoulême, when she was one year old, and ending with the Duke of Alençon when she was 36. They amount to twenty in all, ranging in degree from knights to crowned monarchs, and even this list is probably not exhaustive. All these twenty suitors were considered either by Elizabeth herself, or by other responsible persons as serious aspirants to her hand.

Certain princes who wished to marry the Princess have been mentioned in earlier chapters. Some of these, like Prince Eric of Sweden and the Prince of Denmark, renewed their suits when she became Queen. It is remarkable in those days of early marriages that Elizabeth was not married off as a child by her father, that in adolescence, even when infatuated with Seymour, she refused to make a clandestine marriage, that Philip and Mary failed to unite her to the Duke of Savoy or to Philip's son, Don Carlos. On these latter occasions much pressure was brought to bear on the Princess, but she withstood it and even the inclination of her own heart, in the case of Seymour.

When Elizabeth became Queen, it was confidently expected that she would marry and that her children would ensure the Tudor dynasty. Professor Beesly said that if the nobles of England could have foreseen that Elizabeth would have eluded this obligation, she would probably never have been allowed to mount the throne. Even before she was crowned, her brother-in-law, King Philip II, after much searching of heart and weighing the *pros* and *cons*, as a sacrifice to duty offered his hand to the young Queen. With his insatiable passion for writing memoranda, he set forth his reasons in a letter to his Ambassador in London, which de Feria unwisely showed to certain ladies of the court who conveyed its substance to the Queen. This knowledge did not enhance the value of the offer.

England was still at war with France and the ally of Spain. The country was in no state to resist a French invasion. If Elizabeth married Philip, it would be Philip's interest to protect England. The statesmen in the new Queen's cabinet were in favour of the proposed alliance. Elizabeth, however, knew the position of continental affairs better than her advisers. She was aware that Philip would never dare stand aside to allow King Henry II of France to place his daughter-in-law, the dauphiness, on the throne of England. Whether she married Philip or not, for the time being he must protect England in his own interests. She gave de Feria no positive refusal; spoke of the honour which had been done her; the value to the realm of the alliance, but added his friendship was as sufficient for her protection as his love. She did not desire to marry and doubted whether the Pope would grant a dispensation to marry her sister's husband. De Feria was so displeased with this reply that he absented himself from the Coronation. A month later, the Queen gave de Feria a more definite refusal. Meanwhile, she was in secret correspondence with the French king, who wished to make treaty with her, if she would marry a nominee of his own. In March peace was made between Spain and England and France at Cambray—Calais was left in French hands, subject to a forfeit of 500,000 crowns if not restored to England within eight years. Elizabeth through her own wits emerged unmarried from this marriage imbroglio. What is more she had gained breathing space for England to restore its finances, build up its fleet and strengthen its defences, without committing herself or the kingdom to a foreign alliance. She had the courage to tell de Feria that "her realm was not too poor, nor her people too faint-hearted, to defend their liabilities at home and to protect their rights abroad." Thus, early in her reign she struck the Elizabethan note.

This success taught Queen Elizabeth the inestimable value of her marriage as a trump card in the game of diplomacy. It was a card which repeatedly took tricks and never went out of her possession. She played it for fifteen years or more. She enjoyed the coquetry, the courtships, the revels and the excitement of the game. To change the metaphor, with consummate art, she used the possibility of her marriage as a weapon of defence, and with singular selfless devotion dedicated it to the protection and welfare of England. Being a woman, at times she wavered and thought seriously of matrimony, but ever her head ruled her heart and she drew back in time— sometimes only just in time—and the deluded suitor ruefully departed. Only a Queen endowed with superb statecraft could have maintained this attitude so long and so successfully.

Never was woman so badgered to marry. The subject was raised, much to her displeasure, in the first Parliament of her reign and thereafter many times. Again and again she replied to their pressing petitions in ambiguous terms. This is what she told her first Parliament and it indicates the attitude she consistently maintained:

> "She intended to spend her own life for the good of her people, and if she married she would choose a husband who would be as careful for them as herself. If, on the contrary, she continued in her present mind, she could not doubt but that with the help of Parliament the succession might be secured, and some 'fit governor be provided, peradventure more beneficial to the realm than such offspring as might come of her.' Children

were uncertain blessings and might grow up ungracious. For her it would be enough 'that a marble stone should declare that a Queen having reigned such a time lived and died a virgin.' (Speech of the Queen: *Commons' Journal*, Dewes, I Elizabeth.)"

When Philip II announced his betrothal to Henry II's daughter, Elizabeth of France, Queen Elizabeth professed to be piqued that he had so soon consoled himself for the failure of his suit to her. She affected one or two little sighs and told de Feria that King Philip could not have been so very much in love with her, or he would have waited three or four months. When the ambassador referred to her refusal, she replied that she might well have changed her mind. (De Feria to Philip, April, 1559: *MS. Simancas*.)

King Philip was out of the running, but there were other suitors. "The Council," wrote de Quadra, the new Spanish ambassador, "are in an agony to have her married to someone," and the Queen was under constant pressure in this first year of her reign to select a consort.

King Philip sent her the choice of his cousins, Ferdinand and Charles the Austrian archdukes, sons of the Emperor of Germany. Elizabeth received the proposal favourably and even discussed it with the Imperial ambassador. Ferdinand withdrew but the Archduke Charles, at intervals, was regarded as her suitor for some nine years. The house of Burgundy was traditionally popular with the Queen's subjects, and they would have accepted the Emperor's younger son as embodying no danger to English liberty. In the end, Elizabeth without making any promises, stipulated that the Archduke must come over and woo her in person. This was not feasible, and so at length the Archduke was eliminated.

Even those who came to woo in person had no better success. The King of Denmark, having failed with his son, sent his nephew, Adolphus, Duke of Holstein, to try his fortune. He was young, handsome and accomplished. Elizabeth made much of him, creating him a Knight of

6   81

the Garter and granting him a life pension. Rejecting his suit, she sent him away with rich gifts. Earlier in the year, John, Duke of Finland, the second son of the King of Sweden, also handsome and talented, had arrived to plead the revived suit of his brother, Prince Eric. He was received by the Queen with great cordiality, as well as by the London crowds to whom he threw handfuls of silver money. Doubting his brother's success, he fell in love with Elizabeth and became a suitor himself. The jealous Eric, having succeeded to the throne of Sweden on the death of his father, promptly recalled his brother and sent a plenipotentiary Nicholas Guildenstiern, to continue the negotiations, promising the Queen "that he would quickly follow to lay his heart at her feet."

"The Swede and Charles, the son of the Emperor", wrote Bishop Jewel, "are courting at a most marvellous rate. But the Swede is most in earnest, for he promises mountains of silver in case of success. The lady, however, is probably thinking of an alliance nearer home."

King Eric's suit was finally rejected in 1560 after he had attempted to reach England, and had been driven back to Helsingborg by stormy weather.

Another aspirant was the Earl of Arran. He was also a revived candidate, for his father, then the Earl, now the Duke of Chatelherault, had been approached on the subject by Henry VIII in 1543. The Duke was the powerful head of the House of Hamilton, and the next heir to the Scottish crown. Arran was two years younger than Elizabeth, an earnest Protestant, and brought up on the Chatelherault estates in France from whence he had escaped to Scotland. The Lords of the Congregation were ready to renounce their Queen if she sent a French army into Scotland and to make Arran King Consort if he married Elizabeth and thus united the two kingdoms of England and Scotland under one monarch. A proposal for the marriage was formally made to the Queen of England by an embassy from the Scottish parliament, and the Protestant members of her Council strongly supported it. Sir Nicholas Throckmorton, her ambassador in France, was also in favour of the Arran alliance. The embassy consisted of Lethington and the Earls of Morton and Glencairn. In the meantime, Henry II of France had died, and the danger of French intervention in Scotland diminished. Elizabeth returned her usual indefinite reply to the proposal concerning the terms of which the Lords of the Congregation had informed Francis II. The Earl of Arran came to England, was concealed in Cecil's home in London, and was inspected by Elizabeth, who found him almost a mental defective and no fit husband for her. The Earl was sent back to Scotland, figured as an unsuccessful suitor for the hand of Mary Queen of Scots and eventually became completely insane.

It was Elizabeth's practice in playing the diplomatic game of matrimony, as one suitor receded or was discarded to bring forward another. Thus, when Arran the Protestant suitor departed, she turned again to the Catholic Archduke, wrote to Philip that it would give her pleasure if his cousin would come to England, and annoyed her Protestant subjects by restoring the crucifix in the chapel royal and having service celebrated with the priest in full vestments. When the Spanish ambassador became too pressing on the subject of the alliance, she told him that at present she did not wish to marry but might change her mind when she saw the Archduke. Then she began to favour the King of Sweden's proposal, so that it was impossible to discover her intentions from her language. For this ambiguous and vacillating behaviour Queen Elizabeth has been blamed alike by her contemporaries and by posterity. But this behaviour, although often deceitful and sometimes undignified, was her defence against internal and external diplomatic insistence on marriage; it was a feminine weapon and she used it in the interests of peace and for the protection of her kingdom. Like Queen Penelope, when similarly beset by importunate suitors, at night she undid the web of alliances which she had woven in the daytime.

Besides the foreign suitors, there were at least three Englishmen who desired to marry her. One of the three was Sir William Pickering, a courtier who had been concerned in Wyatt's conspiracy and had been pardoned. According to Paulo Tiepolo (*Venetian Papers*, Vol. 1, pp. 36–37) he was about 36 years old, "of tall stature, handsome and very successful with women." He returned from the Continent in the Spring of 1559 and for a time was regarded as one of the Queen's suitors. This turned his head; he was rude to several nobles of the court; and by the end of the year, though he retained his place at court, he was no longer favoured by Elizabeth. Another aspirant, already mentioned, was Fitzalan, Earl of Arundel, the father-in-law of the Duke of Norfolk. Elizabeth liked him for his former championship of her when she was a prisoner in the Tower. From time to time his pretensions were mentioned, but he was an elderly widower, who had served under three sovereigns and three creeds. As Froude wrote: "But he moved in a cloud, suspected of aims which he could not avow, without a conviction, without a purpose, feared by all men and trusted by none."

The third English aspirant was Lord Robert Dudley, next to Sir Thomas Seymour the best beloved by Elizabeth of all her suitors. As we have seen, Elizabeth and Lord Robert had known each other as children, and had been fellow prisoners in the Tower, under the shadow of Queen Mary's dire displeasure. Later, Dudley had served in France and had ingratiated himself with King Philip of Spain.

On the accession of Elizabeth, Dudley, handsome, self-seeking and ambitious rose rapidly in her favour. He was made her Master of the Horse with the fee of 100 marks per annum and was given the lucrative post of land commissioner for compounding the fines of those desirous of declining the order of Knighthood. Next, the Queen made him a Knight of the Garter and appointed him Constable of Windsor Castle and Forest, and Keeper of the Great Park.

Historians differ as to the merits and demerits of Robert Dudley, Earl of Leicester. Many have regarded him as the one case in which Elizabeth's shrewd judgment of men went sadly astray in promoting "a valiant warrior, who never drew a sword; . . . a noble courtier, who never kept his word," as the satirical epitaph in *Drummond's Collection* hath it. Much of the obloquy which assailed him in his life-time and subsequently was due to the description given of him in *Leycester's Commonwealth*, which was ascribed to the Jesuit, Robert Parsons, and popularly known as *Father Parson's Green Coat*, though it is doubtful whether Parsons wrote it. It was published at Antwerp in 1584 and first entitled *The Copye of a letter wryten by a Master of Arts at Cambridge.* This libellous book had an instantaneous success. It was translated into French, Spanish and Italian and was widely circulated in spite of Elizabeth's Order in Council banning it. She added the assurance that the contents were completely false. Sir Philip Sidney wrote an eloquent *Defence* of his uncle. It was long unprinted and generally ignored. Modern historians are inclined to take a much more favourable view of Leicester's abilities and character. As Sir Walter Scott remarked, at an earlier date: "It is possible that slander, which very seldom favours the memories of persons in exalted stations, may have blackened the character of Leicester with darker shades than really belonged to it." He was by turns, Roman Catholic, Protestant and Puritan as the variable winds of policy inclined him. That was Renaissance politics. The Emperor Charles V and his son, King Philip, those devoted Catholics, both took up arms against the Holy See for their own advantage, albeit with hypocritical excuses, and Henry of Navarre, the champion of the French Huguenots, became a Catholic King of France.

There was something in Leicester besides his good looks that appealed to Elizabeth. He was one of the few people of her world to whom she could talk more or less freely, and she believed in his affection for her. This period, soon after her accession, was the summer of her

85

life, and she sunned herself in the admiration and flattery of her suitors. There is a description of Elizabeth sitting under an awning in the royal barge, manned by the Queen's watermen, richly clad in the royal liveries, with the banner of England fluttering in the breeze. In the background are her ladies and the nobles and gentlemen of the Court. Standing before her are the Imperial ambassador, the Duke of Finland and Lord Robert Dudley all vying with one another to win her sole attention. Stately as any swan the royal barge moves over the silver waters of the Thames which runs more softly to a tune of love as the pretensions of the Archduke of Austria and the King of Sweden are advanced. Lord Robert is the only one of the three who speaks for himself, and he obtains the longest audience, the tenderest smile and the most encouragement from the young Queen.

William Cecil, anxious to put everything in order, could not understand the original statecraft of his sovereign: "Here is a great resort of wooers and controversy among lovers," he wrote, "would to God the Queen had one, and the rest honourably satisfied."

Elizabeth indeed was on the verge of selecting one, but it was one whose selection as a Consort, Cecil and the Queen's subjects considered most unsuitable. Lord Robert Dudley was a married man. At the age of eighteen he had married Amy, daughter and heiress of Sir John Robsart, a Norfolk squire of good estate. The marriage was celebrated in 1550, with the King's approval, for Edward VI records in his diary: "Sir Robert Dudley, Third son to the Earl of Warwick, married to-day Sir John Robsart's daughter, after which marriage there were certain gentlemen that did strive who could first take away a goose's head which was hung alive between two great posts." This cruel feature of the wedding festivities evidently impressed the young King.

Dudley neglected his wife, did not bring her to Court and immured her in the country, latterly at Cumnor Hall, the property of the son of Dr. George Owen, who had inherited it from his father. Here Lady Robert Dudley was under the care of Anthony Forster, Dudley's Steward and Mrs. Owen; and she was visited from time to time by Sir Richard Verney who was one of Dudley's agents, the Varney of *Kenilworth*. Court gossip, marking the increasing intimacy between the Queen and her Master of the Horse, doubted if the lady could or would be allowed to live much longer. As early as April, 1559, de Feria reported:

"They tell me that she is enamoured of my Lord Robert Dudley, and will never let him leave her side. He offers me his services on behalf of the Archduke; but I doubt whether it will be well to use them. He is in such favour that people say she visits him in his chamber day and night. Nay, it is even reported that his wife has a cancer on the breast, and that the Queen waits only till she die to marry him." (de Feria to Philip. *MS. Simancas.*)

By 1560 the picture looks black indeed. It may be that Dudley himself did not plot the murder of his unfortunate wife, but that the sycophantic scoundrels in his service thought her elimination would pave the way to their master's marriage with the Queen and incidentally benefit themselves. This is the charitable view of Dudley taken by Sir Walter Scott in *Kenilworth* and by Froude in his *History*. At all events, the omens were threatening for Amy Robsart. There is the circumstantial account of Ashmole (*Antiquities of Berkshire*) that Dr. Walter Bayly, Regius Professor of Physic in the University of Oxford, was approached by Lord Robert Dudley's henchmen, Anthony Forster and Verney, for a potion for Dudley's Lady.

"The doctor upon just cause and consideration did suspect (their design), seeing their great importunity, and the small need the lady had of physic, and therefore he peremptorily denied their request; misdoubting (as he afterwards reported) lest, if they had poisoned her under the name of his potion, he might after have been hanged for a colour of their sin."

In January 1560, de Quadra, the new Spanish ambassador, relates that Dudley was spoken of as "the King that is to be", but with universal indignation at the prospect. De Quadra had no liking for the favourite. He regarded him as the worst young fellow he had encountered. "He is heartless, spiritless, treacherous and false." (De Quadra to the Count de Feria. *MS. Simancas.*) Lord Robert was intriguing against William Cecil, who was then endeavouring to arrange the marriage with Arran and Elizabeth. Cecil, on his return from Scotland, was so perturbed by the favourite's success that he contemplated resigning his office and according to de Quadra was even driven to confide in him—see the latter's long letter to the Duchess of Parma of date September 11 (*MS. Simancas.*) The alleged conversation between Cecil and the ambassador took place on September 3. De Quadra wrote that Cecil said he perceived the most manifest ruin impending over the Queen through her intimacy with Lord Robert, who had made himself master of the state and of her person with the intention of marrying her. The realm would not tolerate the marriage. He would retire into the country, but he expected he would be sent to the Tower before they would let him go.

> "Last of all he said that they were thinking of destroying Lord Robert's wife. They had given out that she was ill, but she was not ill at all; she was very well and was taking care not to be poisoned; God, he trusted, would never permit such a crime to be accomplished or allow so wicked a conspiracy to prosper."

On the following day, de Quadra alleged also that Elizabeth, on her return from hunting told de Quadra that Lord Robert's wife was dead or nearly so, and begged him to say nothing about it. De Quadra shrewdly observed in his letter: ". . . I do not feel sure that she will immediately marry him, or indeed that she will marry at all." Amy Robsart was then alive and in view of this statement, it has even been asserted that it shows Elizabeth's complicity in a plot to murder her. If there is any truth in this account it is much more likely that Dudley, perhaps misinformed by Verney and Forster, told the Queen that he had heard his wife was not likely to live much longer.*

On Sunday, September 8, Amy is supposed to have sent off all her servants to Abingdon Fair. She and Mrs. Owen dined together. When the servants returned from the Fair they found their mistress lying dead on the floor of the hall at the foot of the great staircase.

Lord Robert Dudley was in attendance on Queen Elizabeth at Windsor. Bowes, a messenger, arrived from Cumnor to tell him of his wife's death. Dudley had received some previous tidings from Cumnor which had disquieted him, for his cousin, Sir Thomas Blount, had left to make inquiries about Amy's health before the news arrived. Dudley was now seriously alarmed "for the talk which the wicked world would use". In this he was right, for within three days, it is said, there was not a village in England where the tragic news was not known, and Dudley named as the instigator of his wife's murder. Ashmole bluntly related that Forster and Verney were responsible for sending the servants to the Fair, that they removed Lady Robert to another bedroom, stifled or strangled her with the help of a serving man, bruised her head very much, broke her neck and at length flung her down stairs "believing the world would have thought it a mischance, and so have blinded their villainy".

Dudley in his apprehension did not go to Cumnor Hall himself, but sent a letter after Blount desiring that the strictest inquiry should be made into the circumstances; that an inquest should be held immediately and "the

* Professor J. E. Neale informs me that the whole account in de Quadra's letter will not stand up to historical criticism; and Froude himself, who is chiefly responsible for its promulgation, said that it was more likely either that de Quadra invented the story for the Duchess of Parma's amusement, or that Cecil played upon the bishop's credulity.

A.S.M.

discreetest and most substantial men should be chosen for the jury". Blount was to use all devices and means for learning of the truth without respect to living person; he was not to dissemble but to tell him faithfully and truly whether the death happened by evil chance or villainy. He added that he had sent for his wife's half-brother John Appleyard, with others of her friends, to be present at the inquest.

The first inquest, so far as can be judged from Blount's letters to Dudley, was brief and the verdict was "it was a very misfortune". The public outcry, however, was so great that Dudley insisted that a more searching and stricter inquiry should be made. After this, the jury returned a verdict of accidental death.

Though Lord Robert had been thus formally acquitted, a cloud rested on his name. As Cecil wrote in after years, "he was infamed by his wife's death". Seven years later John Appleyard, who had received money and other favours from Dudley, said that Lord Robert had prevented him making further inquiries into his sister's murder. He was examined by the Privy Council and personally by Cecil. He withdrew his charges, and no further proceedings were taken. Amy Robsart was first quietly buried in Cumnor Churchyard, but later her remains were buried in the chancel of St. Mary's Church at Oxford with much pomp and ceremony. Her husband did not attend either funeral.

The mysterious death of Amy Robsart, whether accident or murder, proved in the end an insuperable bar to the marriage of Elizabeth and Dudley, though neither realized this at first. Yet Dudley was stunned and frightened by the uproar and was driven to seek the advice and help of Cecil, whose power was completely restored by his rival's humiliation. Cecil responded to the appeal and Elizabeth told Cecil in October "that she had made up her mind and did not intend to marry Lord Robert". General belief took a contrary view. The Queen of Scots and France said: "The Queen of England is about to marry her horsekeeper, who has killed his wife to make room for her." Sir Nicholas Throckmorton, the English ambassador, reported this to Elizabeth, and was so concerned that he sent his Secretary, Jones, to tell her how her reputation was suffering abroad. The Queen heard him patiently, explained that the matter of Amy Robsart's death had been contrary to what was reported and that Dudley was then in the Court and the affair touched neither his honesty nor her honour. Elizabeth seemed ill and harassed. Dudley was still in favour, but the creation of the earldom which she had promised him was delayed in spite of his reproaches. Sir Henry Neville wrote to Throckmorton that the Queen when urged to marry Dudley, "would pup with her lips; she would not marry a subject . . . men would come to ask for my lord's grace"; and when it was pointed out that she might make him a king, "that she would in no wise agree to".

Elizabeth, thwarted by the dangerous situation into which her affection for Dudley had brought her, was a creature of moods. At one moment she sent for the foreign ambassadors and told them she had no intention of marrying Lord Robert and inclined towards the Archduke or King Eric. At another time she showed de Quadra how far removed Dudley's apartments were from her own and then soon afterwards installed him in rooms on the same floor as her own for the sake of his health.

In January, 1561, Sir Henry Sidney, Dudley's brother-in-law, came to de Quadra with an extraordinary proposal. If King Philip would support the Queen's marriage with Lord Robert, they would restore the old religion by way of the General Council. "He then went on to press me to write to your majesty to forward the affair in such a form that Lord Robert should receive the prize at which he aims from your majesty's hands". (*MS. Simancas.*)

The Bishop of Aquila learnt later that Elizabeth, though indignant at the reproaches of the Protestant preachers about her encouragement of Dudley, had consented to this approach with much reluctance, and only at the passionate entreaties of Lord Robert. For once she let her heart rule her head. Cecil restored to high favour, managed to get control of the affair. He persuaded Elizabeth to support Henry of Navarre and the Huguenots in opposition to Spain; he asked Lord Paget, who favoured the alliance with Spain, to speak to the Queen; to her surprise, he advised against the marriage with Lord Robert and endorsed Cecil's policy. Lord Robert had an interview with de Quadra, which did not carry matters further. When Philip's reply arrived, his support of the match was saddled with such conditions that the Queen at once realized their impossibility. Nevertheless, she continued to encourage Lord Robert's hopes. One day in June, 1561, Elizabeth embarked on her barge to watch the games on the river. She stood on the poop alone with Lord Robert and de Quadra, who relates the incident. The Queen and Lord Robert began to talk nonsense. Lord Robert said, as the Bishop-Ambassador was on the spot, there was no reason why they should not be married if the Queen pleased. She doubted if de Quadra knew sufficient English. After further trifling de Quadra spoke to them seriously. First let them restore religion and good order; and then they could marry when they pleased—and gladly would he be the priest to unite them. After which no doubt Elizabeth changed the conversation. The passionate love which the Queen had entertained for Lord Robert settled down into a steady affection which endured throughout her life. A proof of this is that in 1564 she proposed him as a husband to Mary Queen of Scots; and in that event was prepared to nominate Mary as her successor. Mary said the match was unequal, but she would consult her advisers. She well knew that no true friend would advise her to accept a husband whom Elizabeth dared not marry, although even in 1564 Philip considered such a marriage might be a means of restoring "the true ancient and Catholic faith, and will bring back the realm under the obedience of the Pope and the Holy See". (Philip II to de Silva.)

Elizabeth told Sir James Melville, the Scottish ambassador, that she intended to make Dudley a great earl.

"I take him as my brother and best friend." She would have married Lord Robert herself had she been able. As she might not she desired her sister of Scotland to marry him. On Michaelmas Day, Dudley was created Earl of Leicester at Westminster in Melville's presence. At the ceremony the Queen could not refrain from putting her hand on Lord Robert's neck and smilingly tickling him. She asked Melville how he liked him and when the Scot made a tactful answer, "Yet," says she, "you like better of yonder long lad," pointing towards Lord Darnley, who, as nearest prince of the blood, bore the sword of honour that day before her.

Her intuition did not deceive her. Mary married Darnley, much to Elizabeth's displeasure. Leicester continued to serve his Queen, deluded with the hope of eventually marrying her, serving her at home and in the Netherlands, squandering a fortune in entertaining her at his Castle of Kenilworth, helping her to rule England, encouraging crafts and manufactures, promoting sound learning and discipline in the University of Oxford as its Chancellor and writing letters of loyalty and affection to his Queen up to the end.

In the early years of the reign, Elizabeth's affection for Leicester made her highly indiscreet, and she was the more so out of bravado and because he was so unpopular and, as she considered, unjustly blamed for his wife's death. No historian of standing considers that Elizabeth's relations with Leicester or any other man were anything more than imprudent. When she thought she was dying of smallpox in the autumn of 1562, de Quadra reported to Philip II:

"The Queen protested at the time that although she loved and had always loved Lord Robert dearly, as God was her witness, nothing improper had ever passed between them." (*MS. Simancas*).

For the pacification of her country, she abandoned her intention of marrying Leicester in 1560, although she kept him on tenterhooks for years afterwards. He was then in her mind added to her list of suitors whom she might bring forward when others became too pressing. In 1569 the Earl of Arundel instigated his son-in-law, the Duke of Norfolk, to inquire of Leicester if the Queen really wished to marry him, and then they would use their influence to sanction their honourable union. Leicester humbly thanked them. Arundel and Norfolk then asked Elizabeth the same question, and she resolutely answered that she pretended not to marriage with him. (Fénélon.)

Elizabeth not only used the possibility of her marriage as an admirable instrument of policy, but she was also exceedingly vain and greedy of admiration and flattery for so intellectual a woman. She imagined herself not only as the Queen of two Kingdoms, but also as the Queen of Hearts, surrounded by young and handsome princes, nobles and knights dying for love of her, while she remained, "in maiden meditation, fancy free." That was the fashion of the times, and of the old romances. It is depicted in *Love's Labour's Lost*, where the characters mouth the extravagant language of Eupheus, and in *As You Like It*, where Orlando hangs his verses to Rosalind on trunks of trees, and the lover sighs like a furnace. The ambitious "young courtiers" like Walter Raleigh and Christopher Hatton played up to her, and Leicester when he grew middle-aged, portly and red-faced had to continue playing the juvenile lead to his elderly leading lady.

Elizabeth might have been Queen of France, but that would have linked England with France, involved her in war with Spain, and alienated her Protestant subjects. Catherine de Medici, the scheming Queen-Mother of France, proposed successively Charles IX and the Duke of Anjou (afterwards Henry III) to Elizabeth as husbands. In her usual way she first encouraged and then discouraged King Charles, until in 1570 he married the beautiful Elizabeth of Austria, daughter of the Emperor Maximilian II. "At all events", said Elizabeth with a smile to the French ambassador, "he remained true to the name". She pursued the same tactics with the Duke of

Anjou, until he offended her by saying in 1570 "that he would not marry her, for she was not only an old creature but had a sore leg". In 1571, when further pressed by his mother, he repeated charges against Elizabeth's honour. Catherine having previously reassured herself there was no truth in the allegations, dealt faithfully with her son, for she wrote to Sir Francis Walsingham and Sir Thomas Smith, as follows:

"I bare him in hand (for it grieved me not a little, and the King, my son, as you know) that of all evil rumours and tales of naughty persons, such as would break the matter, and were spread abroad of the Queen, that those he did believe and that made him so backward." (Sir Thomas Smith to Burghley, Paris, March 22, 1572.)

Although Elizabeth had jocularly remarked to the French ambassador at the wedding of Burghley's daughter with the Earl of Oxford, on the same day on which the Earl of Worcester and Lord Dudley also were married "that so many marriages at one time seemed a presage that her own would soon take place", she saw it was time to decline Anjou's suit of her own accord before he broke off the negotiations. This she did in January, 1572.

Anjou having proved so laggard a wooer, Queen Catherine substituted her youngest son, the Duke of Alençon in his brother's stead. This was at first a manoeuvre to cover Anjou's withdrawal, but Alençon, an ambitious and imaginative prince of twenty years, set to work in earnest. Though short in height, pitted with smallpox, with a frog face and a bulbous nose, he cast himself for the rôle of a hero of romance with the painted, bewigged Elizabeth, now in her fortieth year, as the youthful heroine. In the letters Alençon wrote, Elizabeth was Madame de Lisle, and he was Don Lusidor. Ambition also led him to favour the Huguenots; and at the end of 1572 he sent M. Maisonfleur, a Huguenot, to speed his wooing and to suggest that he should flee to England and seek his royal bride. Elizabeth would give no definite

95

answer, and in the meantime Alençon went to prison for being concerned in a Huguenot plot and was not released until Charles IX died in 1574. The whole prolonged and undignified affair is bound up with Elizabeth's defensive policy against Spain and her consequent attitude towards the Netherlands (see Chapter XII).

As Bishop Creighton has pointed out, Alençon was a political adventurer; he hoped either to marry Elizabeth or to secure the Crown of the Netherlands, and if possible to succeed in both enterprises. Elizabeth was determined he should do none of these things, and by keeping Alençon, Leicester and her ministers on tenterhooks for years, she gained valuable time and avoided decisive action.

In 1578 Alençon went to help the Netherlands. He knew he could not maintain himself there without the Queen of England's help. So did Elizabeth, and to get him away she sent the long wished-for invitation to England. Alençon then sent a gentlemen of his household named Simier to make inquiries. He arrived in January 1579, and ingratiated himself with the Queen who petted him, called him "her *petit singe*", and spoke much of her marriage. When one of her ladies compared Leicester favourably to Alençon, Elizabeth cried: "Do you think me so unmindful of my royal dignity as to prefer my servant, whom I myself have raised, to the greatest Prince of Christendom."

The proposed marriage was unpopular and a preacher in the Chapel Royal had the temerity to say that England could not tolerate a second foreign marriage after that of Queen Mary, whereupon the Queen left in high displeasure. But the Council told Simier his terms for the alliance were unacceptable. The Queen told him she was resolved to marry Alençon and adjured him to be patient. Alençon, after being kept in suspense for seven years, now pressed to come to England. This Leicester and others opposed. While Elizabeth was hesitating, the astute Simier told her that the Earl of Leicester was secretly married to Lettice, the widowed Countess of Essex. She was a daughter of Sir Francis Knollys and had been Leicester's mistress for some time previously. Elizabeth was much incensed at the marriage and even thought of sending Leicester to the Tower. Within a short time she forgave him, but she retained her animosity against the Countess. Leicester had one legitimate son, Robert, who died in 1584, aged four years, "the noble impe", as he is described in an inscription on his tomb in the Beauchamp Chapel at Warwick. Leicester was accused of having poisoned the Earl of Essex by "an Italian recipe." The latter appears to have died of a flux while Deputy in Ireland. Leicester also had an illegitimate son, Robert, by Lady Sheffield, the "little western flower" of the *Midsummer Night's Dream*. Robert was born in 1574. Leicester had him educated at Christ Church with the status of an earl's son. In 1604 he said his mother was secretly married to Leicester, and, although she gave evidence to this effect, the claim was disallowed by the Star Chamber. Robert voyaged to the New World, joined an expedition to Cadiz, sent lengthy letters on many subjects to James I and Henry, Prince of Wales, and died in Italy aged 75 leaving thirteen children by his last and surviving wife.

To return to the Alençon affair. To punish Leicester for his presumption in re-marrying, Elizabeth allowed the Duke to pay a short visit, made much of him and called him her "*grenouille*". It was then that the Puritan lawyer, John Stubbs, and his printer had their right hands struck off for writing and publishing a protest against the French marriage. Sir Philip Sidney also protested in a letter to the Queen. She had to reconcile Sidney with the Earl of Oxford, who had picked a quarrel with him. The Lords of the Council came in a body to voice their objections. When they left the presence, Elizabeth turned to Walsingham and burst into tears. She said she was only desirous of doing what was best for the kingdom, "to marry and have a child and continue the line of her father"; she had hoped "all would approve of this laudable purpose". The Councillors returned and submitted, saying they would die at her feet rather than offend her. Elizabeth now carried her dissimulation so far that a definite marriage

7   97

treaty between herself and Alençon was drawn up. It was signed by Simier and was only delayed until Parliament should be in a more placable mood to sanction it. In the meantime, the Queen had obtained what she wanted. Alençon had left the Netherlands and, deluded by Elizabeth's promises, had broken off negotiations for a marriage between him and Philip II's daughter. Burghley asked the Queen to make up her mind. She preferred to continue to keep Alençon in suspense. The Duke had accepted the sovereignty of the Netherlands which gave Elizabeth another excuse for postponing her decision. In 1581 the marriage project was revived and Commissioners from France came to arrange a fresh treaty. Henry III was prepared to assist his brother in the Netherlands and would make a treaty with England. Elizabeth raised diplomatic objections but the King proved amenable to all her suggestions. In the end she said she loved the Duke but could not marry him at present for fear of exposing her country to a war. She had, however, much against her will, to give two hundred thousand crowns for the renewal of the league with France.

In November, Alençon once more returned to press his suit and in the presence of the French envoy, Elizabeth at Greenwich Palace kissed her suitor, drew a ring from her finger and placed it upon his, at the same time saying to the envoy: "Write to your master that the Duke will be my husband." She then summoned her household and presented the Duke to them as her betrothed. As the Frenchmen went out in triumph, Sir Christopher Hatton, one of her constant admirers, came to her in tears. She told him to be of good heart for she intended to ask more than the French King would give. "But if he does," demurred Hatton, "how will you escape?" "With words," she replied, "the current coin in France. Moreover, when the field is large and the soldiers cowardly, there are always ways for creeping out." Accordingly, she demanded the suppression of the Seminary of Rheims, the denunciation of the Scottish Treaty and the restoration of Calais. This last demand was an impossibility, but

Alençon refused to go at first. He vowed he must marry the Queen or be derided by the world, and offered to become a Protestant. Elizabeth had to lend him her handkerchief to wipe his eyes, so moving was the scene! At length the little Prince was persuaded to leave, and Elizabeth went as far as Canterbury to bid him farewell. She sentimentally declared that she would give a million crowns that her "dear Frog should again be swimming in the Thames, and not in the marshes of the Low Countries."

This farce lowered the Queen's dignity and for the time being disgusted her ministers. Elizabeth did not care, because she had succeeded in keeping France in opposition to Spain without committing England to war. Here again she was wiser than Burghley and Walsingham. The drama held the boards until 1585 when Alençon, after being expelled from Antwerp, died in May of that year. Elizabeth played it out to the end, assuring the French ambassador with tears and regrets that she was now a widow who had lost a dearly loved husband.

This was in fact the final occasion on which Elizabeth pretended to contemplate marriage and she deceived Alençon, the French King, Simier, her Council, Parliament and her people in order to maintain the balance of power between France and Spain and to keep England out of war. She was 51 when Alençon died and settled into spinsterhood in the eyes of her contemporaries. In her own eyes and up to the last year of her life, she was still the Queen to be wooed by devoted courtiers, a Queen whose smiles exalted and whose frown rendered them miserable. Old and young, Leicester, Raleigh, Hatton— even the youthful Essex—had to adore the woman to retain the Queen's favour. She never wearied of adulation and compliments and refused to look into a glass in old age for fear it should convince her of the ravages of time. Ben Jonson told Drummond of Hawthornden that, knowing this, some of her flighty ladies in making her up would impertinently rouge the royal nose. Let us hope the story is not true.

The reasons for Elizabeth declining to marry and perpetuate the Tudor dynasty have been several— congenital defect, coldness of temperament, masculine nature, and high policy. The question of congenital defect is examined in Chapter XV, where it is shown that all the evidence is against this supposition. The other reasons may be considered together. Professor Beesly wrote: "She was a masculine woman simulating, when it suited her purpose, a feminine character. The men against whom she was matched were never sure whether they were dealing with a crafty and determined politician, or a vain, flighty, amorous woman." Bishop Creighton wrote: "Personally she was attracted by physical endowments and let herself go in accordance with her feelings up to a certain point. But she was both intellectually and emotionally cold."

With great respect the views of these eminent historians in this connexion must be differed from. Heredity, for example, is opposed to them. Can one imagine the daughter of Henry VIII and Anne Boleyn an emotionally cold woman? As a child all accounts show that Elizabeth was warm-hearted, impulsive and affectionate. She fell in love with Sir Thomas Seymour like any normal adolescent might have done, and it was only the wise counsel of Queen Catherine Parr and her intellectual abilities that saved her from disaster. Twice as a young woman she saved her head by her circumspection and intellect. Before she came to the throne, she had learned to control herself and to repress her natural affections. She had the normal woman's desire to marry and have children, but she would not enter into a loveless marriage. For a time she was in love with Leicester and it is held would have married him, if it had not been for his unpopularity. As with Seymour, she only drew back from the contract just in time. She herself acknowledged that she loved him dearly, but she sacrificed her hopes of marriage for the welfare of her country. Sometimes her natural feelings came to the surface, as when on hearing of the birth of James I, she left the dance and cried out bitterly, that the Queen of Scots was mother of a fair son while she remained but a barren stock.

Leicester, himself, on August 6, 1566, gave La Forêt, the French ambassador, his account of the marriage problem:

"I believe not in truth that the Queen will ever marry. I have known her from her eighth year, better than any man upon earth. From that date she has invariably declared that she would remain unmarried. Should she, however, alter that determination, I am all but convinced she would choose no other than myself. At least, the Queen has done me the honour to say as much to me, and I am as much in her favour as ever."

Elizabeth, though her voice was deep, and she was endowed with her father's vigorous physique and bluff speech, was not a masculine woman. Surrounded by her wooing courtiers she was in truth very feminine, a romantic of the Renaissance. She gave them nicknames: Leicester was her "two eyes", just as Christopher Hatton was "her lydds (eyelids)", and her mutton, and Alençon her "*grenouille*". As for high policy that was, as already explained, the chief reason for her refusal to marry when she realized that a union with Leicester was impossible.

Elizabeth's ultimate real reason for remaining unmarried was shrewdly divined by Sir James Melville, the Scots ambassador:

"You think, Madam," he said, "that if you were married you would be but Queen of England, and now you are both King and Queen. I know your spirit cannot endure a commander."

That was the fact. Elizabeth was a great Queen and kept her dignity inviolate. Whatever condescensions she would allow her favourites, a line was drawn beyond which not even the cherished Leicester dared presume. On one occasion when he rebuked one of her ushers in her presence she rated the Earl roundly for his temerity: "I will have here but one mistress and no master," she said.

VII

Elizabeth and Scotland

THE Scots are a proud and patriotic nation. Henry VIII, guided by Wolsey, after the Battle of Flodden pursued a conciliatory policy towards them and continued this for the chief years of his reign. James V's refusal to meet him at York in 1541 and the alteration in temper due to his chronic ulcer and the effects of head injury at a tournament, led Henry to send an invading force into Scotland under the Duke of Norfolk and finally resulted in the disaster of Solway Moss in 1542. Soon afterwards, James V died after hearing with grief of the birth of his daughter, the ill-fated Mary, Queen of Scots.

Another factor in Henry's unfortunate change of policy was the fact that at that time Scotland was a Roman Catholic country, owning spiritual allegiance to the Pope. This circumstance, especially in the eyes of the King's Protestant advisers, was a threat to the maintenance of the Reformed doctrines in England.

The Earl of Arran, Henry's brother-in-law by his marriage with the widowed Queen Margaret, became regent and was anxious to keep on good terms with England. Certain banished nobles, who had lived in England under Henry's protection, returned to Scotland, while there were others, converts to the Protestant faith, who were attached, on that account to England and hostile to French alliance. These influential men were in favour of a marriage treaty between the infant Queen of Scots and the young Prince Edward which would ultimately unite the two kingdoms. If Henry had exercised the patience and discretion which earlier he had displayed, he would have secured all he wanted. His demands, including the desire that the infant Queen should be handed over to him to be brought up at the English court, were so insistent and peremptory that they wounded Scottish national pride. Cardinal Beaton succeeded in uniting a large and powerful body of the nobles in opposition to the English alliance. It was joined by the Earl of Arran who declared himself for the French interest. The enraged Henry raided Scotland by sea and land with indifferent success and further increased his unpopularity with the Scottish people. Even the assassination of Cardinal Beaton, his inveterate political foe, failed to benefit his cause. At this juncture Henry VIII died, but the Protector Somerset pursued an equally blundering policy. Thanks chiefly to Dudley, Earl of Warwick, the battle of Pinkie Cleugh was won, but Somerset failed to follow up his success and withdrew into England.

As might have been expected, this defeat led the Scots to seek the aid of France. An assembly of nobles at Stirling offered the hand of their young Queen to the French dauphin and agreed that she should be brought up in France. In return Henry II was to give immediate assistance to Scotland. The Queen-Mother, Mary of Guise, used her art and address in favour of this project, which was at once accepted and ratified by Henry II, who sent over six thousand troops under M. d'Esse. The Earl of Arran was bribed by the bestowal of the dukedom of Chatelherault and a substantial pension from King Henry to resign the regency in favour of the Queen-Mother; and the infant Queen was sent over to France with suitable attendants—"And thus," wrote Sir Walter Scott, "ere Mary knew what the word meant, she was bestowed in marriage upon a sickly and silly boy, a lot which might be said to begin her calamities."

Mary of Guise, with the aid of the French troops, retook Haddington from the English and expelled the other garrisons which they had established after the Battle of Pinkie. Afterwards, a peace was made by the Duke of Northumberland, between France and England in which Scotland was included. Time went on. The Queen-Regent had her difficulties, for the Scots resented the presence of the French troops and the favour shown to them. She prevailed upon the Scots to support France in the war between England and Spain, but they took up a defensive attitude and refused to invade England.

In 1558 two important events occurred—Elizabeth became Queen of England and the marriage of Queen Mary and the dauphin was celebrated. This ceremony further linked France with Scotland. It was a menace to Elizabeth, for Mary was not only heir of England in right of her grandmother, Margaret, the sister of Henry VIII, but many Roman Catholics regarded her as having an immediate instead of a contingent claim to the English throne, Elizabeth in their eyes being illegitimate. Thus early was Elizabeth brought into conflict with her cousin through the pretensions of Mary, who was persuaded by Henry II to style herself Queen of England and to use the arms of England. Grave apprehensions were entertained of a French invasion of England based on Scotland, in order to remove Elizabeth and to place the Queen of Scots on the English throne. The ambitious Henry II had such an expedition in mind. The treaty of Cateau Cambresis (March, 1559) which concluded peace between France, Spain and England was attended with a secret compact between Philip II and Henry II that each monarch should suppress heresy in his own dominions and where necessary in other countries. A double marriage was to cement the peace; Philip II engaged to marry Elizabeth, daughter of the French king and Emanuel Philibert, Duke of Savoy, was to marry the king's sister. Marguerite. England, if involved, might therefore have had no help from Spain.

In this menacing crisis two pieces of good fortune favoured Elizabeth. The first was the death of Henry II, who was accidentally and mortally wounded by the lance of the captain of his guard, Count Montgomery, in a tournament held to celebrate the marriage festivities. The second was the outbreak of the Reformation in Scotland.

The Scottish Reformation, unlike the English one, came from the people and besides renouncing the supremacy of the Pope was mainly concerned with changes of doctrine and worship. Its moving spirit was John Knox (c. 1505 or 1515–1572). He was educated at the University of St. Andrews, became a Lutheran Minister and falling a prisoner to the French troops, toiled for eighteen months as a slave in the French galleys. In 1549, at the intercession of King Edward VI, he was released and spent four years in England as a royal chaplain, preaching at Amersham, Bucks, and elsewhere. He declined the bishopric of Rochester in 1552. On Queen Mary I's accession, he fled to the Continent, residing chiefly at Geneva, where he was much influenced by Calvin. At the same time he kept in touch with the advocates of reform in Scotland, who in 1557 bound themselves to religious revolution by the First Covenant and recalled Knox to Scotland in 1559. Knox was a man of undaunted courage and endowed with a fluent eloquence. He was often violent and coarse which promoted his influence in a violent and coarse age. His intellectual and theological learning enabled him to reason with the educated nobility; his spirit and zeal convinced the mass of the people. By his preaching at Perth and St. Andrews and by his labours in Edinburgh, he built up a strong Protestant party in Scotland, which received the support of a number of Scottish nobles, who cast covetous eyes on the wealth of the monasteries and ecclesiastics. These nobles put themselves at the head of the Protestant movement and were known as "The Lords of the Congregation".

At first the Queen-Regent adopted a policy of toleration towards the Protestants, and, although they were encouraged by the accession of Queen Elizabeth to take possession of the churches in Perth and burn down a monastery, they maintained a moderately quiet attitude for a time. Urged, however, by her two brothers of the house of Guise, and previously by Henry II after the peace of Cateau Cambresis, to stamp out Protestantism in Scotland, the Queen-Regent against her better judgment took proceedings against the Reformers. Although on two occasions she withdrew discomfited, her actions incensed the Protestants who were stirred up by John Knox to open rebellion in June, 1559. Perth, Stirling and Edinburgh were occupied, abbeys and monasteries were destroyed and the monks ill-treated and dispersed. In the churches images were destroyed, tombs defaced and the Mass made to give way to King Edward's service. This popular rising swept away the Roman Catholic religion in Scotland. The French general, d'Oysel, had fortified Leith with his troops and thither the Regent retreated in expectation of an army arriving from France to maintain her authority.

These revolutionary changes propounded a difficult problem for Queen Elizabeth. The Lords of the Congregation could not make headway against a regular French army and they looked to the Protestant Queen of England for support. This Elizabeth was reluctant to give for several reasons. One was that she never willingly assumed the role of a Protestant champion; she was only sometimes driven to assume this part by the pressure of political events; another was that she did not like to encourage subjects to rebel against their lawful sovereign; the third was that she rightly summed up most of the Scottish Protestant leaders as treacherous, greedy and self-seeking, who thought more of getting hold of church lands and treasure than of the Reformed faith. They were unlikely to give proper support to an English army, for all Scots hated foreigners. On the other hand, if the Reformation were crushed in Scotland, French influence would be predominant there and she was likely to lose her throne. It was at this juncture that her marriage to the witless Earl of Arran was proposed (see Chapter VI).

The Queen adopted her usual temporising policy. A supply of money was sent to the Lords of the Congregation, and they were assured that she was opposed to French domination in Scotland. When a further force of 2,000 French troops had arrived to aid the Queen-Regent and the Lords asked for an English army, they were told they must fight their own battles—were there not enough fighting men in Scotland to overcome the small French forces? The Scots Lords became more active, proclaimed the deposition of the Regent, caused her to flee from Edinburgh, and besieged her and the French garrison in Leith. But their activity was soon expended, their forces disintegrated, and later the Queen-Regent, who was now in bad health and broken in spirit, sought refuge in Edinburgh Castle.

The outlook again seemed threatening for England. It was reported that large forces of troops were on their way from France to Leith. Once landed, the Scottish Protestant party would be crushed and a combined Scottish and French invasion of England would follow. As a counterpoise to this threat Elizabeth contemplated seeking King Philip of Spain's aid, opened negotiations with the Spanish Ministers in the Netherlands, and, having seen and discarded Arran, once more considered the Archduke Charles as a possible husband, although she said she had been told he was not over-wise, and that he had an over-large head, "bigger than the Earl of Bedford's".

Philip replied that if Elizabeth went to war with France in Scotland, he would oppose the Queen of France and Scotland's invasion of England, but on his own terms. He would send a Spanish army into England to repel the invasion. Cecil, Bacon and the rest of the Council were in favour of the Queen's acceptance of this offer, and Elizabeth, herself predisposed to caution, inclined at one time to their view. Then the courage of the Tudors awoke in her. She looked round to see what a year of prudent and intensive administration had effected. Through the excellent financial measures of Sir Thomas Gresham, confidence in England had been restored in Antwerp, then the *bourse* of Europe, and considerable sums could be borrowed for the prosecution of a war; the English fleet, ever dear to her father, had been re-established, equipped and manned; munitions and arms had been imported; defence troops once more lined the coasts of England; and the garrisons on the Border had been strengthened and augmented.

The risk was great. Elizabeth must win or probably lose all. She, a young Queen, was pitting her own knowledge of statecraft against the considered advice of her wisest Councillors who bade her trust in Philip of Spain. But she knew Philip through and through. If Spaniards once gained a footing in England they would never leave it. She also knew the courage and valour of the English people and was prepared to trust them. The lonely Queen made her independent decision to expel the French forces from Scotland and her loyal Council proceeded to carry out a policy which they had initially opposed. The Duke of Norfolk and Lord Grey headed a English army assembled on the Border. With the aid of the Scottish statesman, William Maitland of Lethington, and Cecil, a treaty was drawn up between Elizabeth and the Lords of the Congregation, which made it clear that Mary's authority was not in any way challenged. The English troops were only sent to assist the Duke of Chatelherault, the heir-presumptive to the throne, to expel the French invaders. Cecil had inserted in the draft a clause about maintaining "Christ's true religion", which Elizabeth promptly struck out. She had no intention of favouring John Knox's propaganda.

While all this was planning, Elizabeth covered her designs with a cloak of feminine irresolution embroidered with diplomatic deception. She sent Sir Nicholas Throckmorton as her ambassador to France, instructing him as follows: "If they shall ask whether she means to aid the Scots or no, he may assure them that at his departure hence no such thing was meant." She assured the Queen-Regent of Scotland that "all the foundation of her doings was laid upon honour and truth which she esteems above all things". Hardly had these words been penned when her fleet sailed for Berwick with orders to the admiral that "he might provoke a quarrel, if he did not find one".

The readers of this century, who have seen more glaring acts of perfidy committed by hostile nations, like the betrayal of Austria and Czechoslovakia by Hitler and the attack on Pearl Harbour, may possibly regard

Elizabeth's deceptions with a more tolerant eye than their Victorian forebears or even than that of her contemporaries The Bishop of Aquila (de Quadra) writing to the Count de Feria admitted she always outwitted him:

> "Your lordship will see what a pretty business it is to have to treat with this woman, who, I think must have a hundred thousand devils in her body, notwithstanding that she is for ever telling me she yearns to be a nun, and to pass her time in a cell, praying." (*Spanish Calendar*: Elizabeth. Vol. I.)

Nevertheless, when with her the Spanish ambassador succumbed to her cleverness, for in a letter written on October 2, 1559 to the Emperor Ferdinand on the subject of the Archduke's marriage, he wrote:

> "We chatted on this subject very pleasantly for some time, and in a vastly different mood from her other conversations about her not wishing to marry." (*Ibid.*)

In the matter of giving or not giving aid to the Scottish Reformers, Elizabeth, one must repeat, had been thrown upon her own resources by her Council. Accordingly, she used the arts of deception and reticence which she had been driven to adopt in the perils of her adolescent life.

On March 28, 1560, the Duke of Norfolk, who had only reluctantly accepted the Chief Command, and Lord Grey marched into Scotland and besieged Leith. At the same time the stronghold was blockaded from the sea by the English fleet. A gale in the Channel dispersed the threatened reinforcements from France, but the campaign was somewhat inglorious, and the Scots hindered rather than assisted, the citizens of Edinburgh refusing to give shelter to the English wounded after an attack on Leith had been repulsed. The blockade prevented food and supplies reaching the garrison and this together with the death of the Queen-Regent brought about the surrender of Leith. On hearing of the death of her mother

Queen Mary sent a French envoy to arrange terms of peace with England. Elizabeth sent William Cecil as her plenipotentiary and he ably conducted the negotiations. On July 6, 1560 the Treaty of Edinburgh was signed. It secured substantial advantages for England: Elizabeth's title as Queen of England and Ireland was recognised; the King of France and Queen Mary were to cease from using the title and insignia of these realms for all future time; the French troops were to withdraw from Scotland; Offices of State were only to be held by Scots; the government during Mary's absence was to be vested in a Council of twelve nobles, seven nominated by the Queen and five from the Estates. Further the treaty removed the threat of invasion from Scotland.

The Queen of Scots very unwisely, and no doubt by the advice of the Guises, refused to ratify the treaty. Its provisions were carried out in Scotland and the Queen's refusal only proved a future source of trouble to herself. Cecil returned, a successful diplomatist, to England, to be congratulated by his friends and colleagues. Elizabeth, then much swayed by Dudley, accorded him no thanks. She grumbled at the financial cost of the campaign, desired an indemnity, and left Cecil to pay his own expenses. Cecil was treated with such coldness that he contemplated resigning, but the tragedy of Amy Robsart brought Dudley to seek his aid and Elizabeth soon took her faithful Prime Minister back into favour. (See Chapter VI.).

Queen Elizabeth must have realized that her courageous action had secured for England further advantages. Independently of King Philip's proferred aid and contrary to his injunctions, she had protected the kingdom by her own forces and in her own way. She had defied the powers of France, and France had not challenged her authority. She had placed the Catholic Duke of Norfolk in command of her army, the noble hostile to her Protestant reforms, and he had proved loyal and dutiful. "England once more stood before Europe as an independent power, able to take care of itself, aid its friends, and annoy its enemies." (Beesly.)

This achievement made the young Queen a little too self-confident and her support of the French Huguenots did not result in a similar success. The Guises were the leaders of the French Catholics who were the dominant section of the nation. Dreading the encroachments of the House of Lorraine, Catherine de Medici, the Queen-Regent, allowed the Chancellor l'Hôpital to issue the Edict of January, 1562 by which some measure of toleration was for the first time shown to the Calvinists. They injured their cause by forthwith demanding greater privileges. The Catholics would have none of such mercy towards heretics and plunged into a civil war which, seven times interrupted by precarious truces, was always renewed and devastated France for thirty-two years. The Duke of Guise seized Charles IX and his mother and transferred them to Paris. The Huguenots proclaimed the Prince of Condé defender of the King and protector of the kingdom; in a few weeks they captured more than two-hundred towns including Rouen, Lyons, Tours, Montpellier, Poitiers, Grenoble, Orleans, and Blois. The Guises appealed to Philip of Spain to support the Catholic cause. He sent them an army of 3,000 Spanish veterans. Condé on his side appealed to Elizabeth.

Elizabeth reflected. The triumph of the Catholics in France would strengthen Queen Mary's position with English Catholics and might cause civil war in England. She knew her people still resented the loss of Calais and that intervention in France would be popular with her Protestant subjects. Her main reasons for action were political; and she consented to send help to the Huguenots with the stipulation that Dieppe and Havre should be placed in English hands as guarantees for the ultimate restoration of Calais. The English forces occupied Havre and did little. Rouen fell to the Catholics, the Huguenots were defeated and a temporary peace was made between the contending parties after which the evacuation of Havre was demanded. Elizabeth complaining of the desertion of the Huguenots refused to do this and the Earl of Warwick stoutly affirmed that he would defend the town with his garrison "to the last drop of their blood". The Queen-Mother's army, Condé being in it with other Huguenots, besieged Havre. Typhus appeared in the town and the English, sadly reduced in numbers, abandoned it on July 28, 1563. Peace was concluded between England and France in April, 1564. It was a peace between the two countries which Elizabeth never broke. She had learned her lesson. Henceforth, she chiefly relied on encouraging the deep-rooted antagonism between France and Spain to protect her realm.

VIII

Elizabeth and Mary Stuart

MARY STUART is one of the most tragic figures in history; James V, on his death-bed wept at the news of her birth. "It came with ane lass and it will pass with ane lass", he said prophetically. She was born in December, 1542 into an ill-starred dynasty. James I and James III were murdered; James II and James IV were killed in battle. Mary herself and her grandson, Charles I, died on the scaffold, while James VII (James II of England) the last Stuart King who reigned in Great Britain, ended his days as an exile in a foreign land.

Mary became Queen of Scots when six days old. The Battle of Pinkie Cleugh (1547) was fought between England and Scotland, because the Scots refused to place her under the charge of the Protector Somerset as the child-bride to Edward VI. Ten thousand men died for her sake when she was four years old, and others were to die for her by steel, axe or rope in the years to come.

The fates gave her tall stature, beauty, infinite charm, a sensitive and romantic heart and high moral endowments. All these gifts were powerless to shield her from the malign influences that surrounded her, the clash of politics, the intrigues and plots of wicked men that in their turn drove her to plots and conspiracies. She is the endless theme of novels, plays and poetry. Many adore her at the present time and cherish a glove that once covered her hand, a piece of embroidery that she worked, a tress of her hair or a wine-glass with twisted stem which once touched her lips. She is still and ever must be "the daughter of debate".

A child of tender years, with her four Maries of her own

8

age, Mary Fleming, Mary Beaton, Mary Livingstone and Mary Seton, she crossed the seas to France to be out of danger from the agents of Somerset and to be educated and brought up at the Court of Henry II in order that she might wed the dauphin.

The Thirty Years' War which Charles VIII, Louis XII and Francis I had waged with ephemeral success in Italy had associated France closely with the beauty, wisdom and art of the Italian Renaissance. Francis I was thus led to emulate the great lords of Italy, the Popes, the Medici, the Visconti in their patronage of Italian genius. He welcomed at Fontainebleau that wonder of the world, Leonardo da Vinci, painter, sculptor, anatomist, engineer, physicist, writer and musician; he adapted one of his palaces into an Italian counterpart, decorated by the perfect painter, Andrea del Sarto, Benvenuto Cellini and Primaticcio; he founded the College of France and filled it with scholars from Florence and other parts of Italy; and he wedded his son and successor to the niece of Pope Clement VII, Catherine de Medici. Thus the French Renaissance drew its life-blood from Italy. Writers translated Ariosto, Petrarch, Tasso, Boccaccio and Macchiavelli into French and the nobles and ladies of the Court read them as well as students and men of letters. Rabelais, Ronsard, Montaigne, du Bellay and others gave of their native genius to France.

The magnificence, the beauty and the arts and science of Italy bestowed its priceless heritage upon the awakened intellect of France. Yet, the association with the famous cities of the Italian Republic in which at one time they were welcomed as liberators, at another regarded as enemies, bestowed evil as well as inestimable gifts. For the great nobles of Italy, who loved the sonnets of Petrarch, the pictures of Leonardo, Titian and Raphael were too often steeped in vice and intrigue, poisoners, hirers of assassins and of brutal *condottieri*. These evils permeated the Court of the Valois, along with the appreciation of letters and the beautiful things of life, while the strife of warring creeds began to menace peace and prosperity. One cannot begin even to understand something of Mary Stuart's character unless it is realized at the outset that she was a child of the Renaissance.

Like her English cousins, Mary, Edward VI, Elizabeth and Lady Jane Grey, she was bred up in the learning and accomplishments of the Renaissance. She knew something of Greek and Latin, at thirteen years of age she recited in the great gallery of the Louvre before a courtly audience a Latin oration composed by herself; she spoke French, Italian, English and Spanish. She became a poet and when Ronsard and du Bellay wrote odes in her honour, she was able to answer them in metrical French. This gift of poesy was often a solace to her in after life. She sang, and played the lute; she danced gracefully; dressed well in flowing robes, for she disdained hooped skirts; moreover, she was a good rider, loved outdoor exercise and the pleasures of the chase. Her physique was excellent and when young she was never tired. In those happy days in France, her young slender hands grasped the cup filled with the zest and joy of life and she drank eagerly from it. In a highly critical *milieu* she won golden opinions. Her uncle, the Cardinal of Lorraine informed Mary of Guise that her daughter was improving, and increasing day by day in stature, goodness, beauty, wisdom and worth. He added:

"She is so perfect and accomplished in all things, honorable and virtuous, that the like of her is not to be seen in this realm, whether among noble damsels, maidens of low degree, or in middle station."

Mary became a favourite of King Henry II who often talked with her. On April 24, 1558, at fifteen years of age, she was married at Notre Dame to the dauphin, Francis, a year younger than herself. The two children were fond of each other, but the boy bridegroom suffered from bouts of fever and was too often in the hands of his physicians. By the marriage treaty drawn up by the representatives of France and Scotland, the Dauphin received the title of

"King of Scotland". The French—the Guises took the leading part—prevailed on Queen Mary to sign some secret documents in which in the event of her death without issue Scotland was bequeathed to France as well as her rights of succession to the Crown of England and Ireland. This secret treaty was not divulged to the Scottish representatives.

Mary Stuart was now the future Queen of France. King Henry and her ambitious uncles put before her the prospect of another crown, that of England. This will-of-the-wisp was again and again to lead her into misfortune and finally to death.

As mentioned in the preceding chapter, as soon as Elizabeth on her accession assumed the customary title of Queen of France, an empty assumption to be that country's ruling sovereign, which was continued by the wearers of the English Crown up to the Treaty of Amiens in 1802, Henry II by way of retaliation caused his daughter in-law, Mary, to be styled Queen of Scotland and England and had the Arms of England quartered with those of Scotland. Elizabeth never forgave Mary this, for she was extremely sensitive to any claims upon her crown—she regarded the act as a declaration of her own illegitimacy and of Mary's superior right to the English throne and resented it deeply. It was one of the reasons—if not the main one—which led her to support the Lords of the Congregation, to encourage for a moment the wooing of the Earl of Arran, and to do her utmost to prevent Mary returning to Scotland. The reported beauty, charm and accomplishments of her Scottish cousin excited the jealousy of the woman as well as the apprehensions of the Queen.

As Cecil observed to her: "The longer the Scottish Queen's affairs remain in disorder, the better for Your Majesty's cause". Mary became Queen of France in July, 1559, on her husband's accession to the throne as Francis II. The boy and the girl Queen were still under the tutelage of the Queen-Mother and it was Catherine de Medici who dragged the reluctant girl of seventeen to the

window to witness the gruesome executions of the conspirators of Amboise (1560).

Mary's queen-consortship of France was brief. She
was a devoted wife to her invalid husband and in a gallant
and amorous Court no word affecting her reputation
assailed her. King Francis, in spite of the care of that
prince of surgeons, Ambroise Paré, died of a cerebral
abscess, supervening on middle-ear disease, on December
6, 1560, and his brother, Charles IX, reigned in his stead.

His widow mourned sincerely for Francis and expressed
her sorrow in verse—"*Sans cesse mon coeur sent le regret
d'un absent.*" She woke from her grief to find that she was
less considered and less welcome at the Court of the
Valois than before. This was due to the attitude of the all-
powerful Queen-Mother, who cherished some resentment
for an unfortunate speech of Mary's reflecting on the
mercantile origin of the Medici. Mary could never learn
to restrain her tongue or to keep from making a witty jest
when silence had been better. She had already made fun
of Elizabeth and Leicester, as Sir Nicholas Throckmorton
reported. And now the evil star of Mary Stuart led her
into another action which exacerbated the antagonism of
Queen Elizabeth towards her. As we have seen, she
had refused to ratify the Treaty of Edinburgh, which was
interpreted that she still claimed the Crown of England.

It was time for her to leave France, the land she knew
and loved, if she intended to keep the Crown of Scotland.
Her half-brother, James Stuart, came over to France, and,
although he was already in Elizabeth's pay, probably
advised her both in his own interests as well as hers, that
with all these intrigues with England afoot, she should
without delay return to her kingdom. Yet in spite of this
advice and pressing messages from Scotland, she postponed her departure on one excuse or another. She
visited her Guise relations at their country chateaux, she
waited for Charles IX to be crowned at Rheims. Then at
length, heedless of the offence she had given, she sought a
safe-conduct from Elizabeth to pass through England to
Scotland, should sickness or rough weather make this

necessary. It would have been gracious and politic in Elizabeth to grant this application. It might have served as an opportunity for the royal cousins to meet, and for the elder Queen to influence the younger. Unfortunately, Elizabeth used the request as a counter for bargaining. She would grant no safe-conduct until Mary ratified the Treaty of Edinburgh. Mary's reply was one of affronted dignity. In two interviews with Sir Nicholas Throckmorton—who had given her much good advice—she said she was sorry his Queen had refused her so unkindly. She was quite able to return to Scotland without Elizabeth's passport. She had only denied her cousin's friendship. When Throckmorton spoke of Mary's assumption of the Arms of England, she said this had been done under the command of King Henry II and of her husband. Since their deaths she had neither borne the Arms nor the title of England. As for ratification of the Treaty of Edinburgh she would consult her estates when she returned to Scotland. In conclusion she hoped that the wind would be so favourable that she would not need to land in England. On learning of her cousin's attitude, Elizabeth at once sent the passport. It arrived two days after Queen Mary had sailed from Calais; she watched the coast of France as long as it was in sight.

On August 19, 1561, under grey skies and in thick mist, she set foot again on her native land at Leith. She was received by Lord James Stuart, escorted to Holyrood and welcomed with rough music by her subjects. It was a harsh contrast from a polished Renaissance court to the rough and almost barbaric conditions of the Scottish capital. Her chief friends were her ambitious half-brother and Maitland of Lethington, her Secretary, both Protestants. She made the former, Earl of Mar and her chief adviser. Her beauty, youth and kindness at first won the affection of many of her subjects. But the chief party in the state were the Calvinistic Lords of the Congregation, rich with Church lands and antagonistic to a Catholic Queen. They wished to make her a convert to the Reformed Religion. She listened to insults and invective sermons from John Knox, always hostile, untouched by her youth or kindly character. Little wonder that after hours of State business and sermons, she sought recreation in hunting, hawking, and other sports, while music and dancing occupied the evening, and recalled something of the festivities which had surrounded her in France. These recreations scandalized the protestant preachers who regarded them as vanities and sin. The nobles, many of them in the pay of Cecil, were as was their wont, turbulent, self-seeking and disloyal to their Stuart Sovereign. Mary's father, James V, writing to Mary of Guise when he asked her to marry him, said of them: "There is not a nobleman in any realm who has not been seduced from his allegiance by promises and bribes. Even my person is not safe; there is no guarantee that my wishes will be performed or that existing laws will be obeyed". This state of affairs persisted, as Mary found to her cost.

In the first few years after her return to Scotland, she ruled wisely and well by the counsel of her half-brother, Lethington, and that prudent adviser, Sir James Melville. She exchanged cordial letters of friendship and gifts with Elizabeth, but the Treaty of Edinburgh remained unratified, and Elizabeth refused to acknowlege Mary as her heir-presumptive.

"She was not so foolish," she said, "as to hang a winding-sheet before her eyes or make a funeral feast while she was still alive."

The unwise insistence of Queen Mary on this subject was another source of offence which rankled with Elizabeth. Clearly, if Elizabeth had made such a pronouncement, it might have encouraged the Catholic party in the realm to remove her by rebellion or even assassination, in order to secure a Queen professing the old faith.

With her brother's aid, he was now the Earl of Murray, Queen Mary crushed the rebellion of the Earl of Huntly in 1562. In so doing she injured one of the most powerful

Catholic families in Scotland. Soon afterwards she took the first step which led to the loss of her crown.

Naturally enough, like Elizabeth, she was pressed to marry by her subjects. The Earl of Arran was forthwith rejected. The Archduke Charles, refused by Elizabeth in the end for being too Catholic, was rejected by Mary for being too nearly a Lutheran. Philip II had no wish for her to marry the infant Don Carlos, already under his displeasure. Mary refused the proffer by Catherine de Medici of Charles IX's hand if she would wait two years for him. More from policy than friendship, she desired English approval of her marriage; she sent Sir James Melville to England to obtain Elizabeth's advice.

Elizabeth was a doubtful adviser. She had been thwarted in her project for marrying Leicester and, as she was not allowed to marry the man of her choice, thereafter never approved of anybody marrying, especially the beautiful Queen-widow of Scotland. As the Queen of England's probable successor it was politic on Mary's part to consult her. Indeed, with all her personal prejudices against Mary, Queen Elizabeth seems to have addressed herself seriously to the problem; only as usual, putting the interests of England first and those of Mary and Scotland second. In the first place she informed her cousin that she must not marry into the Royal House of Spain, France or Austria for that would upset the balance of power in Europe and lead to war between England and Scotland. As we have seen, Mary accepted this advice. Later with a self-sacrificing air Elizabeth offered Leicester as a consort and promised to make him a duke, if Mary accepted. Randolph, the English ambassador, conveyed this offer to the Queen of Scots with the promise that as Leicester's wife the Queen of England would nominate her as successor. Mary had hoped that Elizabeth would have suggested Darnley. She was surprised and secretly affronted by the proposal, but commanded herself sufficiently to promise favourable consideration of it. Historians have doubted whether Elizabeth made the offer in all sincerity, Froude and Beesley consider that she did.

This was also the opinion of Cecil and others of her Council. Elizabeth said herself she held Leicester in such esteem that if he were wedded to the Queen of Scots, he would never permit any hostile action to be taken against her.

Elizabeth was curious about Queen Mary and asked Sir James Melville many questions about her looks and accomplishments in comparison with herself. On hearing that Mary played "reasonably for a Queen", she allowed Melville to discover her playing on the virginals, "exceedingly well". She expressed her longing to meet Mary and from time to time suggestions were made for a meeting at York which did not come to pass any more than James V's promised meetings with Henry VIII.

Henry Stuart, Lord Darnley, "the long lad", as Elizabeth called him, was son of the Earl of Lennox and Lady Margaret Douglas, daughter of Margaret, formerly Queen of Scotland and sister of Henry VIII. Through his mother he was therefore Queen Mary's first cousin and the grandson of Elizabeth's aunt, and thus a possible claimant to both the crowns of England and Scotland, in default of issue by the present Queens. He was a Roman Catholic. Queen Mary deemed that a marriage with Darnley would strengthen her claims to the English throne. She had already recalled the Earl of Lennox to Scotland and reversed his attainder. He did not recover the patrimony of Angus, his father, for that was in possession of the Earl of Morton, Chancellor of the Kingdom, but Mary promised him other estates. Lennox sent for his son and Sir James Melville was asked to support this appeal. Elizabeth for a time suspended permission. Mary then pretended that she was ready to marry the Earl of Leicester and deluded both Maitland and Randolph that she was going to do so. Cecil noted: "Mr. Randolph writeth at length of the Queen of Scots' allowance of my Lord of Leicester, and giveth great appearance of success in the Marriage." Elizabeth was also deceived, all the more readily as she knew that the Earl of Murray and other Scottish nobles were strongly opposed to their Queen wedding a Catholic. In an unguarded moment she allowed Darnley leave of absence for three months to assist Lennox in the recovery of his property. It had been better for her and for Darnley to have sent him to the Tower.

It seems probable that Queen Elizabeth relied too much upon the influence of the Earl of Murray to prevent the Darnley marriage. But of late Queen Mary had secretly set at nought the counsel of the one supremely able Minister that she possessed. Two years, previously, M. de Moret, the ambassador from Savoy, had brought in his suite to Queen Mary's Court, an Italian of thirty years of age, named David Rizzio. He became the Scottish Queen's secretary and her favourite. Like the unfortunate Chastelar, he was an accomplished musician and played and sang to the Queen and her ladies. He hated the Reformers and had a genius for intrigue. Gradually, he supplanted Murray as adviser on the Queen's policy and ironically enough, he strongly urged her marriage with Darnley. Darnley came to Edinburgh. His youth and good looks attracted Mary. She also imagined he would be a docile husband, and after first rejecting him promised to marry him. There were strong protests from Murray, Chatelherault, Argyle and Randolph on behalf of Elizabeth and cautious advice from the Duke of Alva. The English Queen also sent Sir Nicholas Throckmorton with instructions to prevent the match. It was too late. The marriage took place in the Chapel of Holyrood on July 29, 1565, and all writs were ordered to run in the joint names of Henry and Mary, King and Queen of Scotland.

Elizabeth during this year was reported by de Silva, the Spanish ambassador and de Foix, the French ambassador, to be suffering from bouts of fever off and on, which may have been malaria. It is possible that this illness prevented her from handling the Scottish crisis with the firm touch that she had displayed when she supported the Lords of the Congregation in 1560. The Protestant lords, headed by Murray, assembled at Stirling, took up arms and sought aid from Elizabeth, which Sir

Nicholas Throckmorton believed would be forthcoming. She sent them money, appointed Bedford and Shrewsbury her lieutenants in the north, and reinforced the garrison of Berwick by 2,000 men. She also sent Tamworth, a creature of Leicester's, to Scotland to protest. The incensed Mary requested Elizabeth to content herself with the government of her own kingdom. The Scottish Queen acted with vigour; she gathered a strong force around her, rode with them on horseback, steel cap on head with pistols at her saddle-bow, and chased her discomfited brother into England, for his confederacy had broken up, and some of the ardent Protestants, Morton, Ruthven and Lindsay, had now joined her, being Darnley's kinsmen and pleased with his elevation.

Lord Bedford offered to lead his troops across the Border to attack Queen Mary's army. He even proposed doing it on his own responsibility, and letting Elizabeth disown him, if she wished. Elizabeth would have no war. She abandoned the cause of the Protestant Lords immediately to their grief and chagrin. She secretly gave Murray a pension; openly she upbraided him before the French and Spanish ambassadors for instigating rebellion against his lawful sovereign; she wrote an account of this interview to Queen Mary; she instructed Randolph to tell the Queen of Scots that although the Darnley marriage had interrupted the friendship which had subsisted between them, yet that she desired only to act honorably and kindly towards her.

The defeat of the lords and the conciliatory attitude of the English Queen placed Mary Stuart on the pinnacle of success. No power in Scotland or England seemed capable of resisting her authority. Murray expressed the belief that he and his friends were wrecked for ever. Towards the end of the year Queen Mary's popularity with her people was increased by the news that she was pregnant.

At this moment of her triumph, conciliation would have been the path of wisdom. Sir James Melville urged such politic generosity upon his mistress. Mary was intending to call a Parliament to pass bills of attainder against Murray and Argyle and their chief confederates, and to confiscate their estates. Melville advised her to withdraw this measure, to pardon the rebels and then "she might command their devotion for ever". His counsel was reinforced, unexpectedly, by that of Throckmorton, who was indignant that his activities on Elizabeth's behalf with Murray and the rest had been repudiated by her. For this disinterested action Elizabeth and Leicester cherished animosity against him. It was even alleged that Leicester much later poisoned Sir Nicholas.

The hapless Mary, flushed with success, despised wise counsel and listened only to Rizzio, who urged that now was the time to throw off the yoke of the Lords of the Congregation and re-establish the Catholic religion in Scotland. Then, with the help of Philip of Spain and the Catholic party in England, she would be able to wrest the crown from Elizabeth and rule over the three kingdoms. Froude considers that with this project in view Elizabeth was in great danger. It seems more probable that the threat of invasion from Scotland would have united the English nation, Protestant and Catholic, against the aggressor. Rizzio did not know the English.

The news that the rebel lords were to be stripped of their estates and that the Catholic religion might be restored caused great consternation among the Protestant nobles of Scotland enriched by Church lands. They took steps to prevent this catastrophe and found a ready instrument to their hand in Darnley. Within six months of her marriage, Queen Mary realized that she had lavished her affection upon a weak, headstrong, dissipated young man, who was unworthy of sharing in the royal authority. Darnley was ambitious of the chief power and when this was denied him, treated the Queen with scandalous disrespect. Seeing this, the alarmed nobles, Morton and others, made him their tool. They persuaded him that Rizzio was the enemy of the Scottish nation, the spy and paid agent of foreign princes, the Queen's lover and the barrier to his rights as King of Scotland. The murder of the detested foreigner was planned; intimation of the date was sent to the banished noblemen in England so that they might return to Edinburgh; Randolph and Bedford were also informed and sent the tidings to Cecil on March 6, 1566. They also wrote to Elizabeth as follows:

"A great business is in hand in Scotland, which will bring about the recall of the Earl of Murray, so that we have forborne to forward your Majesty's letters in his behalf". (*Scottish MSS.*).

The story of Rizzio's barbaric murder at Holyrood on March 4, begun in the presence of the Queen of Scots and completed by sixty dagger-thrusts out of the presence-chamber, is only too well known. The sullen aspect of the irresolute Darnley, the grim, spectre-like visage of Lord Ruthven, risen from a sick-bed and clad in complete armour, the Queen of Scots indignantly confronting the murderers, her ladies weeping, her officers of the household alarmed and helpless, the table spread for supper, the lute whose strings the Italian had plucked to accompany a love-song only a few minutes before, lying on the floor, the cries of the dying man, "*Madonna, io sono morto guistizia, guistizia!*" These were the terrible things that lingered for ever in the outraged Queen's memory. When she heard that Rizzio was dead, she said: "Then farewell tears, we must now study revenge." In that tragic hour all love died for the husband who could expose his wife and his Queen to such an ordeal, and imperil the life of their unborn child.

The murder, as planned, was to bring back the exiled lords, to unite the Protestant Party again and to maintain the Reformed Religion in Scotland. At first the murderers were triumphant and Darnley held Mary a prisoner in her room. By simulating affection and showing him the danger he was in as a Catholic in the hands of the Pro-testants, the Queen effected a reconciliation. He betrayed the whole conspiracy and the names of the plotters, and in the night of March 11, they both fled from Edinburgh to the castle of Dunbar. Here Mary was joined by Huntly, Athole, Bothwell and others, her most faithful nobles, and an army of eight thousand men stood ready to march. Within a few days Queen Mary was in Edinburgh Castle and the chief conspirators had fled. Morton, Ruthven, Brunston and Car of Faudonside escaped to England; Maitland of Lethington sought refuge in the hills of Athole. The Earl of Murray and his companions benefited by the misfortunes of their friends. The Queen pardoned them for their share in the late rebellion on condition they broke off entirely with Morton and his associates. On meeting her half-brother while still a prisoner in Holyrood, Mary had wept in his arms and embraced him. They seemed completely reconciled yet, probably, each mistrusted the other's sincerity.

On June 19, 1566, Mary's son, afterwards James VI, was born. Elizabeth received the news with chagrin (see Chapter VI), but soon dissembled, promised to be godmother, regretted she could not attend the christening and sent a present of a massive gold or silver-gilt font worth £1,000. She had previously replied to Mary's protest against rebels like Morton and Ruthven being harboured by sending Melville to Scotland with assurances of sympathy and help; she wrote to Darnley advising him "to please the Queen of Scots in all things"; she warned Murray to be faithful to the Queen his sovereign, under pain of her own displeasure. Ruthven was dead, but she ordered Morton to leave the country, accompanied by a private hint that no great search would be made for him if he remained in England. However, Mary, probably by Murray's advice and wishful to allay the apprehension of her Protestant nobles, received Morton into favour soon afterwards as well as Maitland and Argyle. These measures, together with the birth of her son, once more placed the Queen of Scots in a strong position. Du Croc, the French ambassador, said he never saw Her Majesty so well beloved, esteemed and honoured, nor had so great harmony ever prevailed at court. Secure in Murray's wise counsel she might well have continued to rule in Scotland.

126

Tired of dissembling, she now threw off the pretence of affection for Darnley and treated him with contempt. So too did the Protestant lords, indignant at his betrayal of their conspiracy. Maitland and Morton were ready to engineer a divorce for the Queen, although, as a devout Catholic, she could hardly entertain this. Irresolute and depressed, Darnley wandered from place to place and thought of seeking refuge in England. Unfortunately, he was persuaded by du Croc to abandon the idea.

Yet even as Mary Stuart seemed most secure, her heart led her to disaster. She was neither licentious nor wanton as her enemies have alleged—none today believes the scandal about Rizzio—but she was a daughter of the Renaissance, a true Romantic, and fell passionately in love with the most unsuitable of men. This was James Hepburn, Earl of Bothwell, Lord High Admiral of Scotland. Though brutal and profligate, he had lived much in France, had fought for Mary of Guise, and had a French veneer of courtesy which attracted Mary. Murray at one time had accused him of plotting his murder and Bothwell was exiled to France. When Murray was out of favour Mary recalled Bothwell, and he helped her greatly after Rizzio's murder. One of her conditions of Murray's replacement in her counsels was that he should be reconciled with Bothwell.

It was at this juncture that Queen Elizabeth called a Parliament in order to obtain supplies. This Parliament with much persistence refused to grant them unless the Queen named her successor. She trounced them forcibly for their presumption, but in the end only succeeded in evading compliance with the request by reducing her financial demands by half and promising to give consideration alike to marriage and the succession question. It was clear to the English Queen that both her Catholic and Protestant subjects wished her to settle the succession. The Catholics favoured the Queen of Scots, the Protestants Lady Catherine Grey who had wedded the Earl of Hertford to Elizabeth's great displeasure. Queen Mary was near the goal of her desire, for Elizabeth might very well have had to meet the wishes of many of her subjects by nominating the Scottish Queen, if events in Scotland had not altered the situation.

Bothwell had now become the Queen's chief adviser, and was to all intents and purposes the ruler of Scotland. Although he was married to Lady Jane Gordon, sister of Mary's faithful counsellor, the Earl of Huntly, he arranged for a divorce from her as the first step towards marrying the Queen. The only obstacle after this was Darnley, whose life was not to be allowed to interfere with the plans of a ruthless, brutal and ambitious man. Mary, as many other women had done, became infatuated with this forcible personality. It was a devouring flame, expressed in passionate French love sonnets and frantic and deplorable deeds.

In October the Queen of Scots was residing in Jedburgh to superintend the proceedings of the circuit courts. While there she heard that Bothwell had sustained a wound in the hand in an affray with an outlawed borderer. As soons as the courts were over she went from Jedburgh to the Castle of Hermitage in Liddisdale, twenty miles distant, to visit Bothwell and returned the same day. After this fatiguing journey she became seriously ill with a fever and was laid up for a month. The tapestry which she and her Maries worked during their stay is still to be seen at Jedburgh.

Darnley was not present at the splendid christening of his son at Stirling on December 17. He was residing in the Castle, shut up in his own room, and received without notice or distinction. It was Bothwell who greeted the guests. Darnley lingered for a week among festivities in which he had no share and then joined his father in Glasgow where he took the smallpox. The Queen sent her physician to attend him, but did not visit until January 24, 1567. Their meeting was a friendly one and the poor dupe was persuaded by Mary—almost certainly at Bothwell's instigation—to return with her to convalesce at Edinburgh in a solitary house, called the Kirk o' Field. in the suburbs of the City; the site now covered by the

University buildings. Mary regularly visited him and sometimes slept in the house. In spite of this reconciliation there were persistent rumours that the King of Scotland was to be done away with, for the chief conspirators, Bothwell, Argyll, Huntly, Maitland and Sir James Balfour made little secret of their intentions. The prudent Earl of Murray left Edinburgh the morning before the deed and afterwards disclaimed all previous knowledge of it. Mary passed the evening of Sunday, February 9, with her husband and then returned at eleven o'clock to Holyrood, for the wedding festivities of Sebastian, a musician married to Margaret Cawood, her favourite waiting woman. At two o'clock in the Monday morning the Kirk o' Field was blown up with gunpowder under Bothwell's direction and Darnley and his page were found dead in the garden, possibly strangled when fleeing by Bothwell's myrmidons. Mary received the news calmly and professed that she had only escaped being involved in the tragedy by changing her mind about spending the night at the Kirk o' Field, a statement which was received with incredulity. She showed no grief and took no active steps to investigate the crime; she neither summoned Lennox nor recalled Murray. Accusations were levelled in Edinburgh against herself and Bothwell and she found it expedient to go with Bothwell and her chief adherents to Lord Seton's house near Prestonpans, where in the intervals of state business the royal party amused themselves with hunting and shooting.

The news of the murder shocked Europe. The Pope and Philip of Spain expressed their displeasure; Catherine de Medici and Charles IX wrote to Mary that if she did not discover and punish the assassin, she would cover herself with infamy, and that she could expect for the future no friendship or support from France. (Drury to Cecil, March 29, 1567—*Border MSS.*) Elizabeth sent Killigrew as her ambassador to Mary. He conveyed a letter of friendly advice written by Elizabeth in her own hand in which she urged her cousin to lay her hands upon the man who had been guilty of the crime—"to let no interest, no persuasion, keep you from proving to every one that you are a noble princess and a loyal wife". Well would it have been if Mary had taken this wise and disinterested advice. Instead, she rushed to her own destruction, and Murray, knowing his life was threatened by Bothwell, departed for England on his way to visit France and Italy. Bothwell's fellow conspirators were disgusted at the pretensions of the ruffianly border earl and plotted to make away with him. They had not murdered Darnley to exalt Bothwell in his stead. Without any withdrawal of the Queen's favour, Bothwell, indicted by Lennox for the murder of his son, had a mock trial, which he attended surrounded by a powerful body-guard and was found not guilty, the prosecutor having not put in an appearance. Elizabeth again attempted to warn Mary of her folly in screening Bothwell, but she was too late. Queen Mary had paid a visit to her infant son at Stirling and on her way back was abducted by Bothwell at Linlithgow and taken a willing prisoner to the Castle of Dunbar. As de Silva wrote to Philip on May 3: "All had been arranged beforehand, that the Queen, when the marriage was completed, might pretend that she had been forced into consent." Mary's marriage to Bothwell took place on May 15, immediately after his own divorce. Nemesis quickly followed. In spite of Bothwell's advocacy of Protestantism, in spite of his supper at the Ainslie Tavern where he extorted the consent of the Protestant leaders to his espousal of the Queen, the lords rose in arms. A month later, Mary surrendered to the insurgents at Carberry Hill on condition that Bothwell's life was spared, and became a prisoner in Loch Leven Castle, where on July 29, she was forced to abdicate in favour of her son and to nominate the Earl of Murray, Regent. Bothwell fled to his dukedom of Orkney, became a pirate, and ended his days insane, in 1578, ten years later, in a Danish prison.

The downfall of the Queen of Scots released Elizabeth from the dilemma of recognising Mary as her heir or of taking a husband. But in her own interests she could not approve of subjects in revolt against their sovereign, and her remonstrances probably prevented Mary being executed for Darnley's murder by her indignant subjects.

Elizabeth sent Throckmorton with instructions to get the infant James entrusted to her care. But she refused to say that she would acknowledge him as her heir, and her peremptory messages to the Scottish lords that she would not permit them to imprison and coerce their lawful Queen only annoyed them. In fact, some of them would have been willing to keep Mary as Queen if she had consented to renounce Bothwell. Elizabeth became unfriendly to the Scottish Government and this attitude made Mary regard her as a true friend.

Mary escaped from Loch Leven on May 2, 1568; the Hamiltons joined her with an army which was defeated at Langside by Murray's forces on May 13. The Queen fled from the battle-field, and had ample time to take ship for France or Spain, as her faithful friends advised her. But both Catherine de Medici and Philip had been severe with her. In England she believed she had a party. She took the fatal resolution of crossing the Solway and throwing herself into the hands of Elizabeth.

IX

The Captive Queen

MARY STUART was never a realist like her cousin Elizabeth. If she had been, she would have abandoned all idea of marrying Bothwell, as Elizabeth had done in the case of Leicester. Now safe at Carlisle under Lowther's protection, the romantic queen saw no danger. If Elizabeth did not receive her, she would give her a free passage to France. Froude notes the fantasy in which she indulged in these words:

> "She saw herself in imagination kneeling at Elizabeth's feet before the assembled barons of England, an injured and beautiful supplicant flying for protection against her rebellious subjects; a few passionate words would dispel the calumnies which clouded her fame; a thousand swords would leap from their scabbards to avenge her, and she would return in triumph to Scotland escorted by the English chivalry."

The tidings that the Queen of Scots had taken Elizabeth's repeated promises of help and friendship at their face value and had sought refuge in England came as unwelcome news. Both the Queen of England and her Council were "perplexed in the extreme". At first Elizabeth's natural impulse, as the French and Spanish ambassadors, M. de la Fôret and de Silva, record, was to support Mary's cause, to receive her and to entertain her as her rank and greatness deserved. The royal intellect, however, soon rose superior to the heart. She read the masterly memorandum which Cecil presented to her, entitled "Things to be considered on the Queen of Scots' coming to England" in his own hand. The wise Minister saw it was necessary in the first place to learn whether the Queen of Scots was guilty or innocent. If she were innocent, she must be restored to her throne and enabled to punish those who had slandered her to cover this rebellion. He hinted this was not a likely possibility, and went on to consider what was to be done if she were guilty. She could not then be replaced as Queen upon an unwilling people, a proven murderess. She could not be allowed to pass to France, because she would certainly bring foreign armies into Scotland and crush the Scottish Protestants of whom England was the natural guardian. Again she was heir-presumptive to the crown of England; and not heir-presumptive only but "she had openly made challenge to that crown, not as second person after the Queen's majesty, but before her". She had not ratified the Treaty of Edinburgh. She thought she had a great party in England who would stir up trouble. On the other hand, to detain the Queen of Scots in England was equally dangerous. She would practise and make a party to seize the crown at the first opportunity and would stir up all evil English subjects in the cause of religion. Finally, Cecil came to the conclusion that it would be best, supposing her guilt proved, to devise means whereby it could be covered up and the Queen of Scots restored to nominal sovereignty, the Earl of Murray having the real power. The Protestant religion to be established in Scotland, the Treaty of Edinburgh ratified, and Mary bound not to remarry without Elizabeth's permission. No clearer exposition of the situation could have been drawn up. Cecil's appraisement of the risks of detaining Mary in England was amply justified by after-events. Elizabeth must have appreciated the advice, but she seemed reluctant to take it and still reverted to her original idea of receiving the fugitive at her court.

She was not well at the time, according to de Silva's dispatches to Madrid, having suffered from fever (? malaria) and "a great excess of bile". These ailments may have made her more than usually irresolute.

The interview between the two queens might have been arranged had it not been for Mary's unwise conduct. Instead of remaining in seclusion until the Queen of England's pleasure was known, she held a court at Carlisle where she received a number of the English Catholic nobility, including Thomas Percy, Earl of Northumberland, who would have escorted her to his seat at Alnwick, if Lowther had not prevented it.

On hearing this news, the compassion of the woman was quenched in the indignation of the Queen. She now saw the danger of a rival Queen, the heir-presumptive, at large in her Kingdom, a younger woman, beautiful and charming, who might so easily win over the Catholic nobles to her cause. Forthwith she agreed with Cecil that Mary's share in the murder of Darnley must be investigated, and that she could not receive her until her innocence was proved. Lord Scrope was sent to Carlisle, to replace Lowther; a troop of two hundred men was sent to guard Mary and to prevent her escape; and Sir Francis Knollys, Elizabeth's cousin, was sent to communicate her wishes to the Queen of Scots and to report on her behaviour. Elizabeth wrote to Mary that she would "have care both of her life and honour". "Does it seem strange," she added, "that you are not allowed to see me? I entreat you to put yourself in my place. When you are acquitted of this crime I will receive you with all honour; till that is done, I may not."

Mary Stuart, at first indignant, at length consented to submit her cause to the arbitration of Elizabeth. Mary and the Regent were asked to submit their evidence to a Commission at York, consisting of the Duke of Norfolk, the Earl of Sussex and Sir Ralph Sadler. Private assurances were given by Elizabeth to both parties concerned. Mary was told that her restoration to the Scottish throne would be effected without detriment to her honour. Murray was told that if Queen Mary were found guilty of crime she should not be restored. The Commissioners opened their court in October, 1568. Murray came armed with the famous "Casket Letters", a bundle of love-letters and sonnets, which had passed between Mary and

Bothwell and which, if genuine, revealed Mary's guilt and infatuation. The authenticity of these letters must nowadays remain unverified, for only copies, some of which seem to have been forged, are available. It is presumed that James VI destroyed the originals to preserve his mother's reputation. They had passed through several hands before they came into the Earl of Morton's possession who gave them to Murray. Mary protested they were forgeries. Murray, an upright man, must have believed they proved his sister's guilt.

While the Commission was sitting, Elizabeth learned the unwelcome news that an intrigue was on foot to marry the Queen of Scots (she had been divorced from Bothwell) to the Duke of Norfolk. Murray had agreed to this scheme, but later divulged it to Elizabeth. The offended Queen revoked the Commission and set up another inquiry in England comprising her chief nobles and statesmen. The casket letters were produced and read by them. The Bishop of Ross, Mary's advocate, made the best defence possible. If the Queen of Scots had an interview with the Queen of England she would explain why Murray should not be permitted to advance charges against her honour.

Queen Elizabeth then had her terms privately communicated to her captive. It appeared impossible to restore Mary to Scotland for that would mean her execution by her subjects. Of her own free will she was to confer the crown of Scotland on her son and the regency on Murray. James was to be brought up in England and his mother was to live in England as long as Elizabeth wished. The proud Mary, by whom voluntary retirement and sacrifice of her rights was never to be entertained, refused to make this declaration. She derided Elizabeth's veiled threat that if she did not the trial must go on to "the great extremities". She was encouraged in her inflexibility by the strained relations that now prevailed between Spain and England. Elizabeth therefore was constrained to keep Mary Stuart her prisoner and the inquiry into her conduct was abruptly terminated without any decision. Murray went back to Scotland. He had been tricked by Elizabeth into bringing forward accusations against Mary on the understanding that her deposition would be confirmed. Instead, Elizabeth left everything inconclusive, first for the interests of England and secondly from a generous impulse towards a sister queen. Her letter to Mary on January 20, 1569, though tempered with admonitions, reveals her womanly sympathy with her captive. She wrote:

The Queen of England to the Queen of Scots

"It may be Madam, that in receiving a letter from me, you may look to hear something which shall be for your honour. I would it were so—but I will not deceive you. Your cause is not so clear but that much remains to be explained. As I understand it, my heart which directs my hand forbids me to write, because the fruit of a sorrowing spirit is bitter, and I had rather something else than pen of mine should shed such drops on you. Your commissioners will tell you what has passed. If they do not tell you also what sincere goodwill I have myself shown towards you, they deceive you and they do me too much wrong. Only let me advise you this: Let not the fine promises, the pleasant voices, which will do you honour through the world, wrap you in clouds and hide the daylight from your eyes. Those do not all love you who would persuade your servants that they love you. Be not over confident in what you do. Be not blind nor think me blind. If you are wise, I have said enough."

(Extract. MSS. Queen of Scots. Quoted by Froude.)

Mary Stuart was never wise. Even when pretending to be guided by Elizabeth she had been urging her uncle, the Cardinal of Lorraine, to arrange for a French army to be sent to Scotland to restore her. She preferred to be a crowned prisoner rather than a queen without a crown.

While the Commissions were sitting, Queen Mary had

been removed from Carlisle to Bolton Castle, and in June 1569 Sir Francis Knollys thankfully gave up his wardenship of the captive Queen to the Earl of Shrewsbury. Mary's presence in England had already brought discord with her. The people, as a whole, were for the most part Protestants and loyal subjects of Queen Elizabeth. The noblemen and chief gentlemen of England seem to have been grouped into four political parties. One, which included Cecil and Bacon, who were also Protestants, and wanted the Queen to support the Huguenots and the Dutch in the Netherlands, and to execute the Queen of Scots or at least to place her in rigid custody in the Tower. Elizabeth, being more far-sighted than her advisers, wished to reign impartially and to avoid war. The second party, which included the Earl of Sussex, were also loyal subjects. They were in favour of good relations with France and Spain, advised their Queen to marry the Archduke of Austria, to recognize Mary as her heir-presumptive and to wed her to an English nobleman. The third party was composed of pro-Catholics like Norfolk and Arundel. They were only half disloyal, had secret correspondence with Spain through the Spanish ambassador, desired to remove Cecil from office, to wed Mary to Norfolk, to force Elizabeth to recognize the Queen of Scots as her successor and to restore the Roman Catholic religion. Finally, a fourth party in the North, headed by Northumberland and Westmorland, wished to put Queen Mary on the throne and to marry her to Don John of Austria, the natural brother of King Philip II. The aims of the three last parties bore a certain resemblance in that they favoured the claims of Mary to the English crown, but in their main differences lay Elizabeth's strength. Leicester, the trimmer, had secret relations with most of these parties.

About this time a quarrel had broken out between England and Spain which had a bearing on home affairs. Elizabeth, like her father, desired a strong navy to protect her realm from invasion and to build up commerce. To this end the adventurous youth of England must be trained in seamanship. The most economical method of doing this was to encourage the merchant adventurers; in other words, she turned a blind eye to piracy, when Spanish ships were seized as prizes and their goods sold in England. Her treasury derived an income from these exploits, which interrupted Spanish communications with the Netherlands and intercepted Philip's treasure ships from the New World. The Queen and Leicester took shares in these ventures, which paid a substantial dividend; they included Hawkins's traffic in the negro slave trade, which had been begun by the Spaniards. Moreover, trained seamen and the ships themselves could be assembled for the defence of England, if so required. It was an efficient and economical method.

Philip retaliated in 1564, when England was preoccupied with the war with France, by seizing all the English ships in Spanish harbours and closing his Flemish ports to English traders. Elizabeth then promised to put down piracy but little was done to stop annoying the Spaniards, and a Commission which met at Bruges to settle differences between England and Spain was ineffective.

Tension further increased in December, 1568, when some ships conveying a large sum of money, which Philip had borrowed from the Genoese for his war in the Netherlands, put into English ports and were seized by Elizabeth. Philip protested and in retaliation took possession of English ships and their crews in Spanish harbours. Elizabeth then imprisoned all the Spaniards and Flemings in London and seized their possessions. Philip threatened war and this threat encouraged the English Catholics, who supported Mary Stuart.

In April, 1569, the Huguenots were defeated at Jarnac, and Elizabeth, under a threat of war with France, closed her ports to Huguenot refugees and prohibited attacks on French merchant vessels. She desired at all costs to avoid further hostilities with France.

Both the Norfolk party and that of the Northern lords asked Philip to send them troops from Alva's army in the

Netherlands in order to free the Queen of Scots. Philip preferred them to take action first before he intervened.

As regards the Southern scheme for marrying Mary to Norfolk, the Duke was too irresolute to ask Queen Elizabeth's consent, although she was perfectly aware of the plot, twitted him about it and warned him to renounce it. Elizabeth also took steps to prevent a rising. Arundel and Pembroke were kept under strict observation; Norfolk was sent to the Tower and the whole scheme collapsed. The Queen took sterner measures with the Catholic northern party. She summoned Northumberland and Westmorland to appear before her. Instead the earls mustered their forces and after having Mass said in Durham Cathedral marched south to free Mary. Elizabeth had previously ordered Mary to Tutbury Castle from Wingfield in Derbyshire, but when the rebels were nearing Tutbury they heard that Elizabeth had transferred her to Coventry. Their followers forsook them under pursuit from Elizabeth's forces. Northumberland fled to Scotland, was imprisoned by the Regent, and two years afterwards was sent back to Elizabeth who had him executed for high treason. Westmorland escaped to the Netherlands and died there. By Elizabeth's orders, stern vengeance was executed by the Earl of Sussex on the rank and file, some seven hundred being hanged. She had been greatly alarmed and for once was less magnanimous than was her wont. Thus ended the rebellion of the Northern earls. It revealed to England and the Continent that Elizabeth by her wise rule possessed the trust and confidence of the greater part of the nation.

In the meantime, a party for the Queen of Scots had come together in Scotland. The Regent Murray was taking steps to crush it with some secret aid from Elizabeth, although she refrained from assisting him openly. Unfortunately, this wise ruler was assassinated at Linlithgow on January 23, 1570. Elizabeth mourned his death as that of her best friend.

Murray's death was the signal for civil war to break out

in Scotland between the King's party and the Queen's party. The King's party chose the Earl of Lennox, Darnley's father, as Regent. His position was not very firm and Elizabeth sent an army into Scotland, which routed the Hamiltons and the Borderers, ravaged their lands and burned their houses. But the civil war raged throughout Scotland and in an attack by the Queen's party on Stirling, the Earl of Lennox was shot dead. John, Earl of Mar, succeeded as Regent.

Meanwhile, Mary Stuart was condemned by Elizabeth to spend for nearly twenty years the weary life of a captive Queen, moved about from one castle or manor to another without her leave being asked and in the care of gaolers who covered their real duties by pretending to be her hosts and guards. She was during her long imprisonment at different times at Bolton, Chatsworth, Sheffield, Wakefield, Buxton, Wingfield, Tutbury and Fotheringay. If she had resigned herself to imprisonment or acquiesced in it; if she had declined to encourage rebellion in England, and had ceased communication with the Pope, Philip of Spain and her kinsfolk in France beseeching them to stir up revolt and to declare war on England; if she had shown herself docile and inoffensive, it is quite possible that she might have regained the Scottish crown or even have become Queen of England by outliving Elizabeth, though this last contingency is more doubtful considering her state of health. But it was not in Mary Stuart's nature to be any of these things. She made herself the centre and rallying-point of countless Catholic plots and schemes. She caused many men to die for her in vain; and she was a constant source of peril and anxiety to Elizabeth and of care to her advisers.

Although she owed much to Elizabeth, as Elizabeth told her in one of her letters, she never would acknowledge it. Yet while the English Queen is blamed for holding her a prisoner, she might have done much worse by her. Elizabeth might have solved her problem by transferring Mary to the Scottish Lords, who would have executed her. Again Elizabeth might have prevented much of her captive's plotting by keeping her in strict custody in the Tower, a measure which Burghley and others repeatedly advised Elizabeth to take and to which she would never consent.

Instead, the Queen of Scots was treated with considerable kindness for those days, restriction being only placed on her exercise and recreation, when conspiracies were afoot. She had a royal canopy over her chair and Turkey carpets on her floors. She was permitted a small court and was treated with the respect and ceremony due to a Queen. All this was done at Elizabeth's personal expense and Mary was allowed to receive the rents from her estates in France, which she expended for the most part in subsidizing plots against England. Her days were spent in prayer, in reading, in needlework and embroidery, in writing letters and French verse, and in scheming for release from captivity. The romantic Queen always imagined herself as a heroine immured by an enchantress in a castle who would one day be released by a band of devoted knights who would place the crown of England on her head. For her woes and wiles many went to their deaths, yet she still plotted and hoped. For some time Elizabeth and Mary exchanged letters; at length the former ceased to answer her captive's recriminations and protests. Mary continued to write and from time to time she sent presents to Elizabeth. In all her schemes, she was under the close surveillance of Cecil and Walsingham's highly efficient secret service, which guarded the life of Elizabeth and the security of England.

Lord Shrewsbury had a masterful wife, Elizabeth, the famous "Bess of Hardwick". In her long life she was four times married and with each marriage she grew richer and more powerful. By her second husband, Sir William Cavendish, she had three sons and three daughters —the only children she ever had; and through her influence every one either became a peer or married a peer or became the founder of a peerage. Lord Shrewsbury was her fourth husband and as his wife she became the custodian of Mary Stuart. Accordingly, as the Scottish

Queen's prospects brightened or clouded, Bess was Mary's partisan or treated her with severity. Lord Shrewsbury had a most difficult task in trying to keep the peace between his royal charge and his wife.

In retaliation Queen Mary took a vindictive delight in writing to Elizabeth all the scandals which Bess repeated to her about the Queen of England and her favourites. The original is among The Hatfield Papers. Bess, having quarrelled with both Shrewsbury and Mary, informed Elizabeth that her husband was too friendly with the Queen of Scots, a libel which Elizabeth was much too shrewd to credit.

In 1574 Elizabeth had been somewhat concerned because Lord Charles Stuart, Darnley's younger brother, had secretly married Elizabeth Cavendish, Lady Shrewsbury's daughter, but both the husband and wife died within a year or two, leaving a daughter, the ill-fated Arabella Stuart. Elizabeth nevertheless maintained her trust in Shrewsbury and it was not misplaced. On several occasions he asked to be relieved of his onerous charge. In 1584 when at length Queen Elizabeth transferred Mary to the charge of that veteran diplomatist, Sir Ralph Sadler, and allowed a separation between Shrewsbury and his shrewish wife, the Earl in kissing his sovereign's hand on a new appointment thanked her for ridding him of two she-devils!

Queen Elizabeth had greatly added to her difficulties in ruling a united England by receiving and keeping the Queen of Scots. Burghley and her Protestant subjects could not understand it. A rigorous prison, transfer to Scotland or the block was their answer to the problem. Elizabeth could never forget that both she and Mary were directly descended from Henry VII, and for nineteen years she resisted pressure from her Council and Parliament to put Mary to death. As she has recorded in the doggerel verses, of which Sir Walter Scott was surprised that Elizabeth's taste could permit her to be guilty, Mary's presence in England harassed her constantly. "That doubt of future foes exiles my present joy." It preyed constantly on her mind. For some time she clung to her original scheme of restoring Mary in Scotland, if she could make her subservient.

In 1570 the Peace of St. Germain was made between Charles IX and the Huguenots, and the Guises were out of favour. Catherine de Medici, for she was the moving spirit in the affair, then suggested a triple alliance between France, England, and Scotland, which was aimed at destroying the encroaching power of Spain. This alliance was to include the restoration of Mary, a condition which Elizabeth was prepared to accept. But the English Queen learned at the same time that behind this alliance Catherine had a plan for marrying Mary to the Duke of Anjou. Such a marriage would have made Mary too powerful and she therefore, with Cecil's full approval, played her usual trump card of matrimony. She proposed to marry Anjou herself (see Chapter VI), but she was still willing to enter into the triple alliance and to restore Mary, who had instructed her representative, the Bishop of Ross, to accept all the English Queen's conditions, though once again ruler of Scotland she had no intention of keeping them. Negotiations began, but the Regent's party refused to permit Mary's return; and Mary herself, on hearing of Elizabeth's simulated intention to wed Anjou, preferred to remain a captive than go to Scotland as the puppet of Elizabeth. Elizabeth then discarded Anjou without impairing her good relations with France. Her policy had been thoroughly successful in alienating Catherine's support of Mary, and to please Catherine she was prepared to coquette with Alençon (see Chapter VI).

As the prospect of Elizabeth or France restoring her receded, the Queen of Scots turned to Philip of Spain. The outcome of this was the so-called Ridolfi plot, which was practically a revival of the Southern scheme for marrying her to the Duke of Norfolk. Ridolfi, an Italian banker, was the intermediary of the conspirators—Norfolk, Arundel, Southampton, Cobham, the Spanish ambassador, the Bishop of Ross and Queen Mary—with the King of Spain. Two years before, the Duke of Norfolk had been pardoned by Elizabeth for his previous conspiracy and released from the Tower. He had pledged himself to be a loyal subject of the Queen in future, but sadly ungrateful he undertook to seize or even murder her, to declare himself a Catholic and to release and marry the Queen of Scots. Ridolfi went off to Madrid with Norfolk's pledges and a long incorrect list of English nobles, who were said to be eager to overthrow their Queen. Philip had no great interest in the list or in the restoration of Mary, but he intended sooner or later to subjugate England. His reply was that he would be prepared to send an army after the conspirators had taken up arms and Elizabeth was either imprisoned or murdered. This Spanish army would have had to come from the Netherlands and the Duke of Alva had informed Philip that Elizabeth was in too strong a position to be deposed. But in 1571, Cecil, now Lord Burghley, was aware of the plot. The new Parliament, entirely Protestant and mainly Puritan, strengthened his hand. It passed a bill with three-fold clauses, aimed at Mary Stuart. The first was that any person refusing to acknowledge Elizabeth's right to the crown could not succeed her; secondly, it was made high treason to deny that the inheritance of the crown could be determined by the Queen and Parliament; thirdly, it was made an offence punishable by life-imprisonment to assert in writing that any particular person might succeed the Queen, other than her issue or some person chosen by Parliament.

Eventually, some of Norfolk's papers fell into Burghley's possession, and the chief conspirators were either arrested or suffered to escape. The Bishop of Ross made abject confession and even vilified the Scottish Queen. The Spanish ambassador was dismissed—Norfolk was sent to the Tower. His offence was too flagrant for inclusion in the clemency with which Elizabeth treated the other nobles involved in the plot. In January, 1572, Norfolk was brought to trial and deservedly found guilty of high treason.

During the spring of this year, Queen Elizabeth had a severe attack of food-poisoning (see The Queen's Medical Case-Sheet, Chapter XV) and was rumoured to be "very sick and in great danger". (John Lee from Antwerp to Burghley.) Illness and recovery always made her inclined to be merciful, and she hesitated for several months to sign Norfolk's death-warrant. In May, she summoned a new Parliament, which voted to proceed with a Bill of Attainder against the Queen of Scots. This meant her immediate execution. Elizabeth vetoed this, and her action shows once more her consideration for her royal captive. The only steps taken were to restrict her out-door recreation, to guard her more strictly and to cut off her communications with the outside world for a time. The casket letters were now permitted to be published by George Buchanan in his "Detection".

Parliament at length gave way to the Queen and ceased to clamour for Mary's execution. As regards the Duke of Norfolk, the Commons repeatedly pressed for the death-penalty. Elizabeth yielded and the Duke was executed on June 2.

In April, Elizabeth had concluded a defensive alliance with Charles IX in which Queen Mary was not mentioned. Elizabeth maintained good relations with France, in spite of the massacre of St. Bartholomew in the following August which was a great blow to the Protestant cause, by encouraging and protracting the courtship of the Duke of Alençon. This year also saw the revolt of the Netherlands and the rise of the Dutch republic.

Consequent upon these events, a wave of enthusiasm for the Dutch struggling to be free swept through Protestant England. Large sums were subscribed and many volunteers went to aid the revolt against the rule of hated Spain. Catherine de Medici and Charles invited Elizabeth to take advantage of the rising and to wage war with them on Spain. On all sides she was pressed to accept the offer. Her Council and Protestant subjects were in favour of it; the French and Dutch alike offered her territorial advantages. Amid all this turmoil and pressure, Elizabeth exercised her wonted sagacity. She saw no advantage in exchanging a Spanish Netherlands for a French one. She was prepared to shut her eyes to the Protestant monies and volunteers that went to the Dutch. The more revolt was kept alive in the Netherlands, the more the French were embroiled in the affair, the less time would be left to Philip to think of his future meditated invasion of England. If she declared war, it might bring disaster on her country and on herself. Besides, as a reigning Queen she never really approved of subjects rebelling against their lawful sovereign.

Elizabeth did not trust the understanding in force at that time between the Valois and the Huguenots, as Burghley and Walsingham did in advising her to join France in attacking Spain. Again she had stood out against them alone. The massacre of St. Bartholomew proved her to be right and that in a country like France, when Catholic resentment against Huguenots was aroused, Queen-Mother and King must participate in bloodshed or be destroyed. Elizabeth, wearing deep mourning, received the French ambassador and expressed her concern at the massacre.

The next thing to be feared was the revival of the Catholic League and a combined attack on England by the forces of France and Spain. All necessary steps were taken for defence. The English Fleet was mobilised; troops were marched to the coast; succour in men and arms was sent to William of Orange; the Huguenots were helped at Rochelle.

The apprehension of a French-Spanish coalition against England renewed the clamour for the execution of the Queen of Scots, who maintained her proud attitude of defiance against Elizabeth. A commission had gone to Sheffield to examine her on her transactions with Ridolfi; Elizabeth at the same time informing her of the Attainder proposed by Parliament. She reassured her that while she had "no intention of revenge", and would persevere in dealing mildly and gently with her, other princes would probably have been less forbearing.

(Elizabeth to the Queen of Scots, June 11, 1572: MSS. *Queen of Scots.* Quoted by Froude.)

The Queen of Scots therefore treated the commission with scorn and gave no thanks to Elizabeth. Shrewsbury reported to Burghley: "It is too plain that her heart is overhardened with deadly hate against the queen's majesty; the more, therefore, her majesty's safety is to be thought upon."

In October, Elizabeth had a severe attack of chicken-pox "so that my Lorde of Leicester did watche with her all night". She had taken pride in the stand she had made to preserve Mary Stuart's life. As she said, "she could not put to death the bird that had flown to her for succour from the hawk". But now her lowered state of health, the importunities of her Council and the Anglican bishops, and the fear of foreign invasion by the Catholic powers made her falter. On pressure from Burghley and Leicester, she agreed to a proposal that Mary should be handed over to the Regent Mar, not to exchange a Scottish prison for an English one, but to be put to death after formal trial for the murder of Darnley. Sir Henry Killigrew was sent to negotiate this, and to stipulate that the demand for Mary's transfer came spontaneously from the Scots. Mar, an honourable man, at first demurred, and then agreed with Morton that the execution was only possible if Elizabeth sent Mary under escort of some high noble, like Bedford or Huntingdon, with three thousand soldiers to overawe the populace. Elizabeth, now restored to health, had already regretted her consent to this unworthy scheme, and at once said the conditions were impossible. Mar died shortly afterwards (October 28, 1572), and with Elizabeth's approval, James, Earl of Morton, a member of the great house of Douglas, became Regent. His main interest was to prevent the restoration of the Queen of Scots, and, as he was not too popular with his peers and the nation, he found the best way to ensure his position was by complete and abject dependence on the Queen of England. To maintain his authority, Elizabeth consented at last to acknowledge James VI as

King of Scotland, his mother being described as the late Queen.

On this recognition by England most of the Queen's party in Scotland laid down their arms. Edinburgh Castle under the command of Grange still held out for Queen Mary, in spite of the money Elizabeth had sent to Morton for the expenses of the siege. It was eventually stormed at the end of May, 1573, by English troops furnished by Elizabeth. The gallant Grange was hanged and the archplotter, Maitland of Lethington, took poison to avoid the same fate. Thus ended the cause of Mary Stuart in Scotland, while, in effect, as long as Morton was in power, Elizabeth was to advise and direct his policy.

The apprehension of a French-Spanish coalition was soon allayed. The defensive alliance of England with France was maintained. King Philip took no active steps. He was occupied with the revolted provinces, with Portugal and with his possessions in the New World. He even made overtures to Elizabeth and signed a commercial treaty with her in 1573. Diplomatic relations were resumed and English prisoners in the Inquisition were set free.

In this same year, Charles IX was obliged to grant the Peace of La Rochelle to the Huguenots and, in 1574, he died of consumption at the age of twenty-four, tormented by his conscience for his share in the massacres of his Protestant subjects. Under his brother Henry III, who fled from his throne in Poland, to assume the crown of France, the religious wars were resumed, and the Holy League for the defence of the Catholic faith was set up under the leadership of the ambitious Henry of Guise. "The Peace of Monsieur" in 1576, initiated by Alençon, had made a temporary peace with the Huguenots and Henry III made another treaty with them, the Peace of Bergerac in 1577. The Guises were, however, always ready to stir up civil war. Elizabeth knew this well and met the situation by encouraging Alençon, secretly aiding the Huguenots, and maintaining the alliance with France to the benefit of English trade.

In 1577, Don John of Austria, the victor of Lepanto, a natural brother of King Philip, became governor of the Netherlands. He found himself unable to rule without a Spanish army and sent for it from Italy. Ambitious and restless, he entered into a plot with Mary Stuart. He was to invade with his army and make himself master of England and Scotland. Mary was to be liberated and they were to be married and reign over a United Kingdom. Mary, as usual was enthusiastic. William of Orange disclosed the plot to Elizabeth who informed Philip that she was compelled to aid the Dutch insurgents as a defence against the designs of his brother, which Philip was unlikely to favour. This plot was dissipated by the death of Don John in 1578, and Escovedo, his confidential secretary, was assassinated in Madrid by King Philip's orders.

Queen Elizabeth also had to keep a watchful eye upon the Guises who were in constant communication with Mary Stuart. Through their efforts another plot against Elizabeth, who had been excommunicated by Pope Pius V in 1570 (see Chapter V), was hatched with Mary's approval. It involved James VI who, at thirteen years of age, was declared of age as King of Scotland. He was to accept the crown of Scotland as a gift from his mother and to rule jointly with her. This at once would antagonise Elizabeth, but before she could act a combined army of French and Scots, led by Henry of Guise, would invade England. The English Catholics would rise, depose Elizabeth, and Mary and James would rule over England, Scotland and Ireland. James considered these offers, but like Philip of Spain, who was consulted, was non-committal. Mary was of course enthusiastic and mother and son entered into secret correspondence on the project. The Jesuits, who were now active in all Mary's plots, began by sending Esmé Stuart, a nephew of the late Earl of Lennox, who had been brought up in France, to Scotland. He speedily ingratiated himself with James and later was created Duke of Lennox. Professing to be a Protestant, he secured the support of the Kirk Ministers and the Protestant Lords of the Congregation, all now enemies of the Regent. He also made an ally of James's other favourite, James Stuart, afterwards made Earl of Arran by the King.

Elizabeth, always well-informed, warned Morton against this new favourite, but in spite of this caution, Morton went unguarded to a council where he was denounced by Stuart before James for the murder of Darnley and arrested. Morton implored the aid of Queen Elizabeth, and her council, so often ready to plunge into war, begged her to invade Scotland and save the man who had served her interests so well. Elizabeth protested and threatened to send an army into Scotland if Morton's life was not spared. But when she saw the Scots were frankly resolved to fight, she did nothing further and Morton was executed by "the Maiden", a form of guillotine which he had invented. The Catholics hoped their plot was succeeding, but in truth Scotland remained after the death of Morton as Protestant as before. Lennox failed to make James a Catholic and had to pretend instead that James's theological arguments had converted him to Protestantism. Guise resisted the entreaties of Queen Mary to invade Scotland, as he could not obtain the approval either of Henry III or of Philip II. Lennox meditated assuming power in Scotland in the name of Queen Mary, seizing James and sending him, a prisoner, to France or Spain. But while he hesitated, the Protestant nobles, with Elizabeth's secret approval, seized the King in the famous Raid of Ruthven in August, 1582. Lennox escaped to France where soon afterwards he died of a fever. On November 8, Mary Stuart wrote in her own hand to Elizabeth a bitter letter upbraiding her for the support which she had afforded to the rebels who had kidnapped her son, and arraigning her before the judgment seat of God for the succession of wrongs she had inflicted on her nearest kinswoman. To this letter Elizabeth, after some delay, returned a dignified reply, pointing out that as Mary deeply charged her conscience, "we think ourselves bound in conscience to let her know that if anything towards her ward may justly breed in us remorse, it is the care we have had for the safety of such an one, whose preservation has since brought the ruin and overthrow of infinite numbers in both realms". It was only too true.

At this time many Catholic plots were afoot for the assassination of Elizabeth, a plan approved by the Pope and Philip II and much recommended by the Duke of Alva. A half-crazed gentleman, named John Somerville, with others was arrested for intending this crime in 1583. He strangled himself in prison and Arden, his fellow-conspirator, was hanged. Another would-be assassin, William Parry, confessed at his trial that he was about to stab her, but was appalled by her likeness to Henry VIII.

The Catholic plotters with Mendoza now planned with Queen Mary for a Spanish invasion of England with the Duke of Guise in command. One of the intermediaries by which Morgan, Mary's agent in Paris, communicated with the Queen of Scots, and the Queen of Scots with Mendoza was Thomas Throckmorton, a nephew of Sir Nicholas Throckmorton. Walsingham's secret police discovered him and, though he found time to send his compromising letters to the Spanish ambassador, under torture of the rack he betrayed the Spanish plot. He broke his pledged word, betrayed Mary Stuart, his associates and Mendoza, and stricken with remorse, welcomed his hanging. The Earls of Arundel and Northumberland who were implicated in the plot were sent to the Tower. Northumberland shot himself in prison; Arundel was released, but on attempting to go abroad, was brought back and ended his days in prison. Mendoza was expelled and diplomatic relations broken off with Spain. Again the English fleet guarded the coast, forts and harbours were repaired and the Queen's loyal subjects mustered and drilled to repel the Spanish invasion. A perquisition was made through the country and Romish priests and Catholics were executed, not on account of their religion but for treason, as Burghley pointed out in his defence of the Queen's government.

In 1584, also, a Bond of Association for the protection

of Elizabeth was drawn up by the English Government which pledged all Englishmen to prosecute to the death all those who conspired against the Queen. It declared further that all those on whose behalf such a conspiracy was made were consequently deprived of all claim to the succession. Elizabeth's important loyal subjects, Catholic and Protestant, readily signed the Bond. As a warning it was shown to the Queen of Scots, who offered to sign it herself! Parliament was summoned and gave the association the authority of law. The association and the edict were clear intimations to the Queen of Scots and her friends that she could not obtain the crown of England by way of assassination.

In 1583 James had escaped from his captors and now ruled Scotland with his favourite, the Earl of Arran. At first he inclined towards the Catholics, invited the Duke of Guise to Scotland, communicated with Philip II and even wrote a letter to the Pope. He also encouraged his mother in the belief that he was active in her interests and rebuffed Walsingham, who had been sent to him by Elizabeth to admonish him.

James was also concerned in the Spanish plot, which the arrest of Throckmorton had revealed. While the Duke of Guise landed in England with an army of French and Spaniards, James consented simultaneously to invade from Scotland. The Queen of Scots, who knew that a formidable attempt of this kind would be the signal for her death, endeavoured to persuade Elizabeth to treat with France for her release on safe terms. Elizabeth, wishing to spite James, entered into tentative negotiations, but broke them off on hearing of the meditated invasion, for the justifiable reason that once at liberty Mary would ignore her pledges and ally herself with France and Spain to the great peril of England.

James and Arran, seeing that no help came from Philip II, became staunch Protestants again. James entered into friendly relations with Elizabeth, became her pensioner, and in a cruel and unfilial letter bade Mary remember that she was only the queen-mother and enjoyed no authority in Scotland. He told her to be ruled by Elizabeth's wishes. She had already been removed from the care of Sir Ralph Sadler and consigned to the custody of Sir Amyas Paulet, a dependent of Leicester's, an honourable man but a rigid gaoler, who kept her in strict ward at Tutbury. Mary now appealed to Elizabeth to release her on any conditions she pleased, but the requests went unheeded, except that Elizabeth warned her cousin from further plotting.

The warning was vain. Elizabeth had so often spared her captive that Mary believed that she did not dare to put her to death. Yet times had changed. The Jesuits and other Catholic emissaries were active. A Spanish invasion was threatened and in these critical times a fertile source of danger and disunion like the Queen of Scots, in the opinion of Burghley and Walsingham, could not be allowed to exist. Queen Mary was removed early in 1585 to Chartley Castle in Staffordshire, and Sir Amyas Paulet was instructed to relax his surveillance. Immediately, a plot was on foot for the murder of Elizabeth, and a rebellion in favour of the Queen of Scots. The chief persons involved were a young Papist, a Derbyshire gentleman of fortune, named Anthony Babington, and his associates Ballard, a Jesuit, Savage, Donne, Barnewell, Tichbourne and Thomas Salusbury. When their plans had ripened, they were arrested, taken to the Tower, tried and executed in Lincoln's Inn Fields. Mary's papers were seized and there was ample evidence of her participation in the plot. "When all is ready," she wrote, "the six gentlemen must be set to work."

Elizabeth could no longer shelter her captive. Queen Mary was removed to Fotheringay Castle in Northampton-shire, and on October 14, 1586, Commissioners, including the Lord Chancellor Bromley, the Lord Treasurer Burghley, and other peers, privy councillors and judges, held a court to try the Scottish Queen. She was charged first with conspiring with traitors and foreigners to invade the realm, and secondly, to compass the death of the Queen. She acknowledged the first charge but repudiated the second. Her defence was spirited but not convincing. After hearing her, the Commissioners adjourned to the Star Chamber at Westminster, where they pronounced her condemnation on October 25. On October 29, Parliament met and both Lords and Commons petitioned Elizabeth to carry out the sentence without delay. Elizabeth sent a message to the two Houses to know whether they could not devise some means of sparing Mary's life. Both Houses said this was impossible. She then returned an ambiguous reply in these words:

"If I should say that I meant not to grant your petition, by my faith, I should say unto you more perhaps than I mean. And if I should say that I mean to grant it, I should tell you more than it is fit for you to know. Thus I must deliver to you an answer answerless."

The lonely Queen at this juncture was desperately unhappy. Averse at all times to shedding blood, she was especially reluctant to have her cousin executed, in spite of the fact that her captive enemy had repeatedly encouraged her own assassination. She had assured her Council that outside representations would not influence her, yet she listened to associated remonstrances from Scotland and France which pleaded for Mary's life. As regards Scotland the protests were not altogether sincere on the part of James. The deputation consisted of Sir Robert Melville and the Master of Gray. Melville was true to Mary Stuart and his purpose as honest as Gray's was false and treacherous. Gray had privately intimated to Walsingham that James only protested for the sake of appearances and if he were assured of the succession to the crown of England, Elizabeth might do what she would with his mother. Knowing the ignoble and base character of the Scottish King, who was willing to drive a bargain for acquiescing in his mother's death, Elizabeth assumed a haughty attitude towards the deputation and abruptly broke off the conference. When Melville followed her, pleading for some delay of the execution, she sternly replied, "No, not an hour".

Henry III intervened with more sincerity. He sent over M. Belièvre, as a special envoy. Elizabeth received him at Richmond on November 27. She sat in her chair of state, with Leicester, Burghley, Hatton and others of the Council standing beside her. Belièvre made an eloquent oration on behalf of the Scottish Queen. He ended with the words:

"Honour points clearly towards clemency. Interest is at least equally balanced. Think of the judgment of posterity and of the name which you will leave behind you. Spare this lady and you will lay my master under an eternal obligation, and you will earn immortal renown for yourself."

The Queen in reply deeply regretted M. Belièvre should have come hither on so bad an errand. The Queen of Scots had sought shelter in her realm, had received nothing but kindness there, and in recompense had three times sought her life. This was naturally valuable to her, and she was not safe in her own realm. She was "a poor lone woman", surrounded by secret enemies who were perpetually seeking to kill her. But she delayed giving the envoy a definite reply. Soon afterwards the sentence on the Queen of Scots was published and was received by the people of England with acclamation. London was illuminated. Joy bells pealed from every church steeple and bonfires blazed in town and village. The nation felt the death of the Queen of Scots would not only safeguard their beloved Queen, but also deliver them from the threat of civil war.

Belièvre communicated with Paris and Henry undertook on behalf of himself and the Guises that if the Queen of Scots' life was spared she should relinquish her claims on the succession for ever, and never trouble England more. He bade Chasteauneuf bribe members of the Council if necessary. If nothing availed and if the queen persisted, he said that France could not pass it over. (The King of France to Chasteauneuf and Belièvre, December 14–24, 1586: *Egerton Papers*. Quoted by Froude.)

Belièvre had not an opportunity of conveying his King's message to Elizabeth until January 6, 1587. She discussed the question with him for two hours showing signs of great irresolution. A week later he went back to France bearing a letter of complaint from the Queen to Henry III that she must not be threatened, but again giving no decision.

In fact, she had decided to convey to Queen Mary a possibility of pardon. Before the sentence was published, she sent Lord Buckhurst and Mr. Secretary Beale to Fotheringay with a copy of it, and to inform Queen Mary that the court had re-examined her sentence and found her guilty in spite of her denials; that Parliament had ratified the verdict and demanded her execution; and that Elizabeth was urged on all sides to sign the death-warrant. It was intimated, however, that if she would confess her crimes, express regret for them and sue for pardon, the Queen of England might forgive her. It was the only way Elizabeth could see out of her dilemma. For if Mary confessed and became a suppliant, Elizabeth would be justified in the eyes of all her subjects and Europe, and Mary herself, a confessed criminal, would no longer be a rallying centre of conspiracies, and her life might well be spared. As might have been anticipated, Mary rejected the terms and prepared for death as a Catholic martyr. She wrote to Elizabeth, thanking God that her tedious pilgrimage was at an end, asking that her execution might be public, affirming that she was a Catholic and wished to be buried by her mother's side in France. She wrote to Philip II and to Guise that she was dying for the sake of the Catholic faith, and to the Pope to the same effect, asking also for his absolution. She commended her son to the Pope; if he did not become a Catholic, she bequeathed her rights in the English crown to the King of Spain.

Although Elizabeth realized that the Queen of Scots had rebuffed her overtures, she remained still irresolute.

She even showed disfavour to Walsingham, perhaps because he had been too zealous in implicating Mary in the Babington plot. Although Walsingham was in financial difficulties for debts incurred in the Queen's service, she refused to grant him any recompense and bestowed the forfeited Babington estates on Sir Walter Raleigh. Walsingham withdrew to his house at Barnelms, and only his sense of loyalty and Burghley's persuasion made him return in a few weeks to the Queen's service.

In his absence and to avoid further intercession from the French King, Elizabeth pretended to believe that the French ambassador was concerned in a pretended plot against herself for which Walsingham afterwards apologized to him.

The fate of Mary Stuart could no longer be delayed. On February 1, Lord Howard of Effingham told Elizabeth that the national feeling was so clamorous for the execution of Mary's sentence that she must make a decision. The Queen was much perturbed and asked Howard to send Davison, who acted as Secretary in Walsingham's absence, to come to her with the warrant. When he came, she talked at first of irrelevant subjects, then asked him for the documents in his hand and took them from him. She carelessly signed the sheets, including Mary's death warrant, and threw them one after the other on the floor. It seemed she would pretend she had not noticed the warrant. If so, she changed her mind and asked Davison if he was not sorry to see the paper she had signed. Davison replied that he was sorry the guilt of the Queen of Scots had made it necessary. She then bade him take the warrant to the Chancellor, get it sealed unobtrusively, saying nothing to anyone, and then send it to those entrusted with the execution. She expressed a wish to be troubled no further till all was over. She appointed the great hall of Fotheringay Castle for the execution, "misliking the court or green". On Davison's way to the Chancellor, she told him to visit Walsingham at his house, and tell him of the matter, "because the grief thereof would go near", as she said ironically, "to kill him outright". Then, as Davison was about to leave, she complained of Sir Amyas Paulet and others, that might have eased her of this burden, wishing that Walsingham and Davison would yet write to Paulet and Sir Drew Drury to sound their dispositions on this behalf. (*Davison's statement.*)

While Elizabeth was thus distraught and hysterical, it is alleged therefore that she sought a base and treacherous way out of her terrible responsibility. If true, it is an indelible stain on her character. Great as she was, in that after-thought she was untrue to her honour and her royal dignity. Davison said it was a useless request, but Elizabeth insisted.

The perplexed Davison consulted the Lord Treasurer (Burghley) and then went to London. On the way he related to Walsingham all that had transpired, drafted the letters to Paulet and Drury, and then had the warrant sealed by the Lord Chancellor. On his return to Walsingham's house, the letters were ready. Walsingham and Davison signed them and they were sent off. In substance they suggested that the recipients should find out some way of shortening the life of the Scots' queen as a token of their love to Queen Elizabeth. They have been held to be tantamount to an incitement to secret murder.

The originals of these letters no longer exist. The supposed copies of them, first given to the world in 1722 by Dr. George Mackenzie are "impudent forgeries", probably fabricated in the reign of George I by some Oxford Jacobite. Professor Beesly considers it quite consistent with Davison's statements that Elizabeth only desired Paulet and Drury to arrange the public execution of the Queen of Scots without delivery of the warrant (*Queen Elizabeth*, pp. 186, 187.)

Both Paulet and Drury were men of integrity and refused to make away with Mary Stuart without warrant. Paulet pointed out that as the Act of Parliament interpreted the "association bond" (to which reference had been made) the Queen's command was required and this she had not given. Elizabeth was angry. She said Paulet was a precise fellow, who professed zeal for her safety, but when the time came would do nothing.

On the morning following the sealing of the warrant, Elizabeth sent a note to Davison bidding him to hold his hand until she had spoken with him again. He saw her at once. She seemed displeased that he had carried out her instructions so promptly, as he had been ordered, so much so that Davison asked if she had changed her mind. She said she had not, but again complained of the burden thrust upon her.

It was obvious to Davison and her chief advisers that she felt as a Queen it was necessary for Mary's sentence to be followed by execution, but as a woman she shrank from the responsibility of shedding her kinswoman's blood. Davison dared not take upon himself to make the necessary arrangements, in case his Queen might disavow her previous commands. He consulted Hatton, the Lord Chancellor, and they spoke with Burghley, who was in bed with an attack of gout. Ignoring the Queen's injunctions of secrecy, Burghley summoned to his sickroom the members of the Privy Council then in London. They were Leicester, Howard, Hunsdon, Cobham, Sir Francis Knollys and Lord Derby. Walsingham, Hatton and Davison also attended. Burghley laid the situation before them. The Council were unanimous that the sentence should be carried out, and approved Burghley's suggestion that they should share the responsibility of the deed without troubling the Queen further, which was her desire at heart. Lord Shrewsbury and Lord Kent were the commissioners named to see the warrant executed. Secretary Beale was sent forthwith to them with the warrant and the Council's instructions.

Queen Elizabeth made no further inquiries, except that she remarked to Davison that she had had a dream in which the Queen of Scots was executed, and was so incensed at hearing of it that if a sword had been at hand she would have run him through the body. She evidently wished to create the impression that she knew nothing of what was going on.

On February 8, 1587, Mary died bravely and heroically as a Queen. At the end of her sad and chequered pilgrimage she must have welcomed death. The trial and the manner of her death created an awful precedent for the arraignment of sovereigns before a tribunal for their misdeeds. It gave tragic sanction to the executions of Charles I, and of Louis XVI and of Marie Antoinette in years to come. It was a peril which Elizabeth herself foresaw, but Mary's own conduct and the political necessities of the times were too strong for her.

X

The Denial of Responsibility

WITH the execution of the Queen of Scots a feeling of relief was experienced by the loyal subjects of Queen Elizabeth. The focus of discord and of threatened internecine strife had been removed. Henceforth, a united nation of Protestants and Catholics would face the hostility of Spain. Froude, Creighton and Beesly are in complete agreement that the elimination of Mary Stuart was a dire necessity, regrettable for many reasons, but justified by the danger to the Queen and the nation of the international situation. Froude wrote: "The political wisdom of a critical and difficult act has never in the world's history been more signally justified".

On the morning following Mary's death (February 9) intelligence of it came to Burghley at Greenwich. He hesitated to inform the Queen, but the news soon leaked out and joy-bells pealed and bonfires blazed again. The Queen learned the news on returning from her morning ride. Outwardly she appeared calm, but in her letter to King James she said that "she fell into such deep grief of mind, accompanied with unfeigned weeping, as the like had never been seen for any accident in her life".

As in her interviews with Davison she had shown signs of irresolution, and as she had decided that she would never give an official order under her own hand for the execution, which the Council fully realized, she became convinced in her own mind that she never intended the sentence to be carried out. The full explanation of this attitude has a medical aspect which will be discussed later.

161

On February 10 she summoned Hatton. Horror-stricken and indignant she told him that Davison had betrayed her. Davison and the Council expected some such exhibition "to cast it from herself", but they were ill-prepared for the invective and anger she displayed on the following day, when she called the Council together. Not one of them escaped the lash of her displeasure. Burghley, as the leader of the resolution, she attacked bitterly and then ordered Davison to the Tower. Her ministers, headed by Burghley, fell on their knees and begged her to delay. She only stormed at them and ordered Burghley out of her presence. It was an exhibition of royal Tudor rage which made all quake. Davison was tried before a special commission. He refused to take the sole blame and told his judges exactly what had transpired. He was acquitted of evil intention, but censured for neglect and precipitancy. His imprisonment continued for some time, he was fined ten thousand marks and his career was ruined. Burghley was in deep disgrace for two months and when he resumed his attendance at the Council was roundly abused by the Queen for his treachery.

The affront of Mary's execution for a brief space excited great anger in Scotland and clamour for war against England. James had received an exculpatory letter from Elizabeth and was not at all inclined to wage war with the country whose future king he hoped to be. He had to bend to the storm, nevertheless, and told the Queen that if she was innocent she must prove it by chastising the guilty persons. This she complied with by making Davison the scapegoat. James secretly intimated that he was ready to be paid for remaining quiet; and meanwhile encouraged border raids and pretended that if Philip sent a Spanish army to Scotland he would invade England to exact retribution for his mother's death. But the façade of protest soon wore thin.

As early as April 11–21, 1587, Walsingham was writing to Stafford as follows:

"The part of your letter where you say the King of

Scots excuses her the blame of the late execution, and lays the same upon her council, did wonderfully content her majesty, who desires nothing more than to have it generally conceived that she had least part in the action."

France was also indignant at the news that a former Queen of France had been executed by a headsman. The Holy League and the Guises clamoured for war, but the enmity which Henry III had for the House of Guise and the need to maintain his alliance with Elizabeth only resulted in a formal protest against his sister-in-law's death.

Elizabeth after the execution reversed all the hostility she had previously shown to M. de Chasteauneuf, the French ambassador. She first sent for M. Roger, a gentlemen of the privy chamber of the King of France, attached to the embassy, and told him "that she was deeply afflicted for the death of the Queen of Scots; that it had never been her intention to put her to death, although she had refused the request of M. de Belièvre." She put the blame on Davison, who would now have to answer for his conduct and charged M. Roger to inform his majesty of France to this effect. Her explanation was of course received with derision in France. On March 6, she invited M. de Chasteauneuf to dine with her at the Archbishop of Canterbury's palace at Croydon. She received him most graciously and promised men, money and munitions to assist Henry III against the League, an offer which the ambassador declined. She then made a lame apology for her previous accusation of the ambassador, saying she had been misled. In spite of Chasteauneuf's reluctance to enter on the subject, she insisted on her innocence concerning the death of Mary Stuart. She had indeed signed the warrant, but it was only to satisfy her subjects. It was to be held in readiness in case of foreign invasion or a formidable insurrection in England of disloyal persons. "She swore by her Maker's name that but for her ministers' long services, and for the supposition that they had acted out of consideration for the welfare and safety of her person and State, they should all have lost their heads".

The Queen detained the ambassador for three hours with her protestations and assertions of the damage she had inflicted on Philip of Spain, ignoring his offers of peace and friendship, out of regard for the King of France and to assist him against the League.

Chasteauneuf, however, made it sufficiently clear that it was an insult to his intelligence that she should expect him even to pretend to credit her with her good intentions.

Elizabeth, consistent in her inconsistency, continued to maintain the pose of injured innocence to the end of the tragedy. She immediately went into mourning for her victim. For six months she allowed Mary Stuart's body to lie neglected and unburied. Then she ordered it to be buried with royal honours, in Peterborough Cathedral. The chief nobles and ladies of the court formed the funeral train, headed by the Countess of Bedford, who acted as proxy for the Queen of England, the chief mourner. Pope Sextus V was moved to bitter irony and amazement at this stupendous act. "What a glorious princess!" he cried. "It is a pity that Elizabeth and I cannot marry—our children would have mastered the whole world".

On another occasion the Pope said:

"There are but three sovereigns in Europe who understand the art of governing, namely, myself, the King of Navarre and the Queen of England. Of all the princes in Christendom there are but two, Henry and Elizabeth, to whom I desire to communicate the mighty things that are revolving in my mind, and as they are heretics I cannot do it."

After James I came to the throne, he had his mother's remains transferred to Westminster Abbey. There she rests near Elizabeth under a monument, like to that of the Virgin Queen, but, as Dean Stanley wrote (*Memorials of Westminster Abbey,* Chapter III): "on a grander scale, as if to indicate the superiority of the mother to the predecessor, of the victim to the vanquisher". According to Demster, her bones were resplendent with miracles, which is probably, adds Dean Stanley, "the latest instance of a miracle working tomb in England, and it invests the question of Queen Mary's character with a theological as well as an historical interest".

Round the memory of the Scottish Queen, that hapless daughter of the Renaissance, has ever raged controversy. Many of the accusations levelled against her are doubtful, and perhaps the real truth of her unhappy life of plots and intrigues will never be clearly revealed. Some will always regard her as an innocent, beautiful and persecuted prisoner. Others as an embodiment of wickedness, deceit and folly. One has only attempted here to record facts as impartially as possible, and to note afresh the fact that Elizabeth saved her life from the Scots, resisted putting her to death for nineteen years, and regretted the deed bitterly when at length it was done.

Elizabeth's behaviour after Mary's execution has frequently been stigmatized as deceitful, undignified, cowardly, unjust and stupid in that it deceived nobody. Archibald Douglas, who came at this time as James's ambassador, in a letter to Burghley of date April 9, 1587 (*MSS. Scotland*) advised that the Queen should defend the execution on public grounds—"so it would be more able to be justified, and have greater appearance of princely dealing". Subterfuge and denials, he thought would "bring her reputation into doubtful terms"; she could not throw the blame on the Council in such a matter without punishing them. It might have been expected that a Queen of Elizabeth's heroic qualities would have adopted this advice. No one believed her protests and denials except herself. As Froude wrote: "She had convinced herself of her innocence by the violence of her assertion of it". There is a medical explanation of her conduct.

Elizabeth's relations with Mary, Queen of Scots, have been described in this book at some length, because they are relevant in this connexion. For nearly twenty years the care of her dangerous captive had preyed incessantly upon Elizabeth's mind. She detested having such a focus of intrigue and danger in her kingdom, but equally she dared not let her go for fear she would bring about foreign invasion. Even when writing lines on the valour of her people, she could not help her thoughts turning to "the daughter of debate that eke discord doth sow".

The Queen's Medical Case-Sheet (Chapter XV) shows that in the course of her life she was sometimes subject to hysterical attacks, though she was far from being a hysterical woman, as a general rule. When these attacks occurred they might be very severe. For instance, on June 30, 1586, at the time when Walsingham was watching the Babington plot, Mendoza wrote to Madrid from Paris as follows:

"Since I wrote last about England (on February 1) the Queen-Mother (Catherine de Medici) has received news from there that the Queen had been for four hours speechless, and as if dead, in a swoon, this being an indisposition to which she is occasionally liable."

This appears to have been a prolonged hysterical fit although the unconsciousness that appears to accompany such a fit is seldom as complete as it looks. Although the critic may demand further proofs, it is a tenable medical surmise that after Mary Queen of Scots' death, Elizabeth worked herself up into a state of hysteria, as can readily be imagined when the prolonged mental strain to which she had been subjected in her youth and for so many years is remembered. Hysterics often gain their ends by forgetting what it would be painful to remember. The onlooker, as in Elizabeth's case, may find it hard to tell how genuine or complete is this forgetfulness. In spite of all that her advisers could say, Elizabeth was convinced in her own mind that she had never intended the death warrant to be used except in dire emergency, and that she had never ordered her cousin's execution. The scene with the

French ambassador, the letter to James, the mourning and her representation at the funeral ceremony, the rating of the Council and the imprisonment of Davison, have all been regarded as manifestations of deepest hypocrisy. Is it not more consonant with Elizabeth's character that they were in reality the genuine expressions of an unhappy woman's grief who had deceived herself? In this distraught state, which fortunately did not endure long, one should pity Elizabeth rather than condemn her.

XI

Elizabeth and England

PERHAPS only now, after passing through years of anxiety and strife in which our island was again threatened by invasion from a ruthless enemy, can we begin to recognise the greatness of the years in which Elizabeth Tudor ruled as Queen.

The Elizabethan leaders, endowed with the culture and learning of the Renaissance, have left their heritage to the people of England. Through the generosity of their descendants, we can visit the mansions in which the nobility and gentry lived, like Hardwick Hall in Derbyshire built by "Bess of Hardwick", Lord Shrewsbury's turbulent spouse, and Hatfield, the home of the Cecils. We can see their painted monuments in the churches, father and mother lying in state under a stone canopy and a numerous family of be-ruffed children with hands clasped in prayer kneeling beside them. Their written words survive, either in clerkly penmanship or in beautiful Italian script, as penned by Elizabeth herself.

They bequeathed to us a wonderful literature. If, as Professor Trevelyan remarks, the social historian of today can only point out some of the conditions under which the people of the past lived, and is unable to show what our ancestors were like, Shakespeare can. In his pages the men and women of those times can be studied, their feelings, their very words and their attitude towards life. Their paintings and statuary show what manner of men and women these Elizabethans were.

Pride in their nationality and in "this blessed plot, this earth, this realm, this England," was fostered by the powerful influences of the English Renaissance and the Reformation. It was a time when, as men saw the world was wide, their minds grew wider. Avid curiosity was one of their chief characteristics. It was the motive power of expeditions oversea, which brought wealth and commerce to the country. It led men like Gilbert and Caius to delve into science, and induced Francis Bacon to find his recreation in science and philosophy. Moreover, it inspired the Elizabethans with a zeal to study their own country and its past history. To this end it bred a goodly company of chroniclers, topographers, antiquarians, surveyors and map-makers. The knowledge thus garnered both enriched their contemporaries and has been most valuable to posterity. Otherwise much information must have been lost, had it not then been recorded. The writings of men like Leland (1506–1552), Laurence Nowell, who studied Anglo-Saxon, and his pupil, William Lambarde, the county historians, who met at the house of Sir Robert Cotton, William Harrison, Camden, Holinshed, Stow and others, revealed the history and topography of their country. To William Camden (1551–1623), headmaster of Westminster School, we owe the famous *Britannia* (1586), a survey of the British Isles, "the common sun, whereat our modern writers have all lighted their torches," said Bishop Nicholson (1655–1727).

Education was no longer the privilege of the cloistered monk and student bred at Oxford or Cambridge, but through the grammar-schools gave the middle classes from the squire to the tradesman a tincture of classical learning and acquaintance with the writers of Greece and Rome. Translations, like Chapman's version of Homer, helped to diffuse this knowledge. The Universities, which after the inspiration of the Humanists had undergone a period of decay in the storm of the Reformation, revived during Elizabeth's reign largely owing to her personal encouragement of their learning and to the efforts of their Chancellors, Leicester at Oxford and Burghley at Cambridge. It was fortunate that England possessed an intellectual and scholarly queen acquainted with letters. As late as 1593, being troubled at the apostasy of Henry IV of France, to divert her mind she renewed her theological studies, collating the writings of the ancient fathers with the Scriptures. Finally, she made an excellent English translation of the five first books of *Boethius on the Consolations of Philosophy*.

In August, 1564, Elizabeth visited Cambridge and stayed in King's College. To the Latin speech of the public orator she listened, at times deprecating his praises in good Latin. When he praised celibacy she said: "God's blessing of thine heart; there continue." On Sunday she attended service at the University Church, and in the evening witnessed the "Aulularia" of Plautus which was acted in King's College Chapel. Next day she listened to lectures and disputations and attended a play on "Dido" in the evening. On the fourth day she visited the Colleges, being greeted at each by a Latin speech and receiving a volume of Greek and Latin verses composed by members of the College in her praise. "As Her Grace rode through the street, she talked much with divers scholars in Latin". On the last day of her stay after hearing more disputations, she was prevailed upon to deliver an oration in Latin which delighted all hearers. At first she asked William Cecil to speak for her, "because the Chancellor was the Queen's mouth". Cecil replied that in Cambridge "he was Chancellor of the University not hers."

In 1566 the Queen honoured Oxford with a visit, being received by Leicester with similar ceremonies to those of the sister University. She gave a caustic word to the Vice-Chancellor, Lawrence Humphreys, a noted Puritan, saying: "Mr. Doctor that loose gown becomes you mighty well; I wonder your notions should be so narrow." She spoke Greek at Carfax in reply to the oration in that tongue of the Professor of Greek, and then proceeded to Christ Church where she stayed for five days. Here also she listened to disputations, visited the Colleges, received orations and volumes of verses, and attended Latin and

English plays which were acted by the undergraduates. Finally, she addressed the University in Latin. The Mayor and Corporation of Oxford, on her departure, accompanied her to Magdalen Bridge; the University representatives went as far as Shotover. After a final address in Latin, the Queen waved her hand and said: "Farewell, famous University; farewell, my faithful subjects; farewell, dear scholars; and may God bless your studies. Farewell, farewell." Could Universities be more encouraged by royal favour?

Much has already been said in this book of the Queen's preoccupation with foreign affairs and intrigues, but at the same time she ably administered England. In 1560 she restored the English currency to sterling value, which was most beneficial to English trade and commerce. Camden terms it "a matter indeed, weighty and great," and stigmatizes Henry VIII's mingling of copper with silver as a great disgrace of the kingdom and damage of his successors and people. She employed Sir Thomas Gresham, "that prince of English merchants," in restoring the financial credit of England at home and abroad. His negotiations with the Antwerp merchants were most remunerative in this respect. In 1571 she honoured Sir Thomas by dining in state with him in Cornhill, and by opening the new *Bourse* to which she gave the name of the Royal Exchange. In the public departments of the State the Queen introduced a careful system of control and audit which checked extravagance, waste and peculation. This irked, as we shall see, warriors like Lord Howard of Effingham, who preferred to pay a questioned war expenditure or pension out of his own pocket rather than argue the matter with the Queen's civil servants; but in peace-time it had a salutary effect and made for integrity in public affairs.

Queen Elizabeth's rule was a personal one. She governed the kingdom with the advice of her Privy Council. Parliament, as Professor J. E. Neale has shown in his books, based on many years' work on the sources and discoveries of fresh documents, particularly early

Parliamentary diaries, was a growing force in the country. Professor Neale has made it clear that the independent spirit of the House of Commons and its growing opposition to the despotic control of the Crown, was not a seventeenth-century development of Stuart rule, but arose in the time of the Tudors. Young Thomas More fell under Henry VII's displeasure for opposing the grant of a subsidy in the Commons, and later when Speaker opposed the entrance of Cardinal Wolsey into debate, and further secured freedom of speech from Henry VIII for members of the House of Commons. Elizabeth did not like Parliaments, but followed her father in always knowing when it was politic to give way to them.

In her reign of forty-five years there were only thirteen sessions of Parliament. It was summoned when she wanted subsidies for war or defence or to make laws against her political and religious opponents. As Professor Beesly wrote: "In fact to do without Parliament was distinctly popular, because it meant doing without subsidies." The English people of that age very much resented taxation, although during the Queen's reign many of them had become wealthy and prosperous. In the first thirty years of her reign, in which there were nine sessions of Parliament, the Queen asked eight times for money grants and allowed one to be reduced. All the expenses of government, including loans to her Scottish, Dutch and French allies were paid chiefly out of her Crown revenues, which only amounted to £300,000 a year towards the end of her reign. With this she also succeeded in paying off her father's long-standing debts and accumulating a small reserve for emergency. Such was the fruit of the years of peace, of her economies and of her shares in ventures oversea. No wonder she was keen on money. On one occasion when presented with a covered cup by a loyal corporation at Norwich, she lifted the lid and beheld the contents. Handing the cup to a retainer, she said: "Look carefully to it; there is an hundred pounds!" They smiled at her "avarice" but it was for England that she hoarded.

The war with Spain dissipated her reserves and though she received twelve subsidies from Parliament in the remaining years of her reign she obtained them with difficulty. To pacify the grumblers, she condescended to explain to Parliament the large sums she had expended in the Spanish and Irish wars and in subsidizing her allies. She had sold crown lands (in order to raise £372,000) and her jewels. All this was for the benefit of the State. Her personal expenditure was on a modest scale, except in dress. She was fond of jewels, but these she regarded as a good investment, and the cost of her entertainments were partly defrayed by her wealthy subjects when she visited them.

In her last Parliament the Commons debated the subject of her monopolies. They were dissatisfied with the abuses exercised by some of the individuals to whom they were granted, but they did not attack her royal prerogative in granting them. The Queen sent a message that she had been unaware of these abuses, that she shared their indignation and that she would stop those which were injurious. The Commons were more than placated.

Parliament in Queen Elizabeth's reign enlarged its privileges, maintained its rights to freedom of speech, control of taxation and legislation. In theory, said J. R. Green, Elizabeth and her ministers regarded three cardinal subjects—matters of trade, matters of religion, and matters of State—as being exclusively within the competence of the Crown. Her Parliaments interfered with all these matters as previous Parliaments had done. On these three subjects Elizabeth opposed them, not aggressively but with tact and evasion. For example, repeatedly they asked her to marry and to name her successor. Marriage she always promised to consider; the question of her successor she forbade them to raise, but told them later, "she did not mean to prejudice any part of the liberties heretofore granted them." The Commons were won in this way to a loyal assent to her wishes. It has been noted in Chapter V how she resisted the ecclesiastical bills, which, nevertheless, were presented to her in every Parliament. Throughout her reign the Queen fought a conciliatory battle against the encroachments of Parliament on the sway of the Crown, which the obstinacy of her immediate successors brought to a tragic issue.

Justice for the age was more evenly administered than before. It was still rough and ready, and the accused was often either convicted and hanged, or acquitted. The State trials though weighted for the prosecution were more fair than in previous reigns. After conviction the Queen often interposed with her clemency, and she was always reluctant to sign a death-warrant. Able judges and lawyers adorned her reign; and a legal training in the Inns of Court was much valued.

In local government under the Tudors the influence of the Crown was far-reaching. The principal officer was the Lord-Lieutenant, an office created in 1549 which provided direct communication between the government and the provinces. He was usually a peer and often a privy councillor, and in control of a county or group of counties in which he held estates. Some of them had other responsibilities which kept them in London, like Burghley who was Lord-Lieutenant of Lincoln, Essex and Hertfordshire and Hatton of Northamptonshire, so in such cases the Queen appointed deputies for them. These were chosen from the most influential persons in each county. The Lords-Lieutenant or their deputies had chiefly military duties. They had to raise local bodies of men for military service, provide them with equipment, call for mounted men from the gentlefolk; they also administered county finances, settled questions of precedence, regulated markets and corn supplies, and hunted out spies and recusants.

The Tudor statesmen reorganized local government on the basis of the parish with the unpaid local magistrates, the justices of the peace, as representatives of the Crown. One of their important duties concerned unemployment and destitution in their areas. The dissolution of the monasteries increased the numbers of beggars and vagrants, for those, who formerly relied on the monastic doles locally, were drawn far afield to seek their sustenance. The soldiers discharged at the end of the brief campaigns of the period, the men "broken in the warres", further swelled the numbers of the destitute.

After the Reformation, poverty became a crime and these unfortunate persons were harried from town to parish. Stern legislation imposing penalties of whipping, forced labour, mutilation and death failed to diminish their numbers. Many of them became vagabonds, thieves and murderers, a menace to travellers and to society. Social discontent was a subject of concern to the Queen, and as early as 1561 she appointed a commission to inquire into it and the best remedial measures. The Poor Law legislation of Henry VIII and Edward VI put the onus of relief on the charity of local districts. A beginning towards statutory local responsibility for the poor was made in a statute of 1572, which required justices in country districts and mayors and other officers in towns to register the impotent poor, to settle them in fitting habitations and to assess all inhabitants for their support. It was not, however, until the celebrated Poor Law Act of 1601, forty-third of Elizabeth, which made the maintenance of the aged and invalid poor and the provision of work for the able-bodied a statutory burden on the parishes through the levying of rates, that the problems of unemployment and destitution began to be handled effectively. Hence it was in Elizabeth's reign that the State began to realize its social responsibilities.

For the promotion of commerce the parish was also responsible for road maintenance (Statute of Highways, 1555). The executive duties of the parish vestries were performed by the constable and the churchwardens or by newly appointed officers, such as the overseers of the poor and the surveyor of highways. These officers received no remuneration, but acceptance of appointments was compulsory. The administrative work of the parish vestries and the duties of their officers were authorized and controlled by the justices, who might be appealed to by the parishes in their area, either individually or at quarter sessions. Quarter sessions could also deal with problems affecting the whole county, and thus gradually became the county local authority and entirely replaced the sheriff and his county court.

This organization on paper was an approach to democratic local government, but in reality the powers of the parish vestries were extremely limited, as the justices exercised the main control. The justices of the peace were appointed by the Crown, usually on the nomination of the Lord-Lieutenant, could be dismissed at the royal pleasure, and were directed in their duties by the Privy Council and its judical committee, the Star Chamber. In other words they were the instruments of central authority, which in Elizabeth's time had the control of local government in its hands more effectively than at any other period of English history.

Other conditions of the reign favoured the reduction of poverty and unemployment. More attention was paid to agriculture, more money was spent on the land, the breed of horses and cattle improved and more agricultural labourers employed.

Manufactures were developed and were an important means of employment. The linen trade and silk weaving were small concerns, but woollen manufacture, including the spinning of yarn, weaving, fulling and dyeing of cloth, occupied large towns like Norwich and the countryside. In farms and villages housewives spun sheep's wool into clothing. The industrial skill of French and Dutch refugees helped with many manufactures and brought in new looms and stocking frames. England also began to take the lead in industrial technology and heavy industry. Fresh industries were begun, equipped with new machinery and a host of new inventions.

Iron was smelted in Kent and Sussex though less wood was now available from forests for feeding the furnaces. This scarcity of wood favoured coal mining and the use of "sea-coal", so-called from its manner of transport to London and coastal towns. Cornwall exported tin and copper. The printing presses increased; there were now blast furnaces, furnaces for separating silver from copper ore, for using coal for treating iron; bricks were made; brewing flourished; new mines were opened up and old workings deepened. A word of praise is due to the much maligned Earl of Leicester for his encouragement of mining and other industries. The fisheries were developed, and their hardy crews furnished seamen for Drake and for the repulse of the Armada.

Above all, English commerce expanded. After the capture of Antwerp by Parma, a third of the city's merchants and manufacturers sought refuge in London, which grew into the chief mart of Europe, "where the gold and sugar of the New World were found side by side with the cotton of India, the silks of the East, and the woollen stuffs of England itself" (J. R. Green).

Elizabeth encouraged commerce by preserving peace, by sharing in its speculations, and by giving her sanction to the great Merchant Companies which protected the trader in his ventures overseas. The most important of these were the Merchant Adventurers of London which had received a charter from Henry VII, the Russian or Muscovy Company (1554), the Turkey Company (1581) and the East India Company (1600). English merchant ships were seen in the far distant seas of India, China and Japan. Wealth poured into the country, the land grew prosperous and social troubles and dangers receded. The Queen's government controlled wages and prices, apprenticeship by the Statute of Artificers (1563), which enacted that every craftsman had for seven years to learn his craft under a master, the right to set up trade and the conditions of trading.

The Wars of the Roses, as Robert Burton tells us, were not forgotten, but the peers of the realm, diminished in numbers, had lost the military and political power which challenged the Crown's authority. Their last attempt was the rebellion of the Northern Earls which was swiftly subdued. Elizabeth kept her peers manageable and select by making few creations. The middle classes increased in wealth and prosperity; they owned lands and built manor-houses with glass windows, tall chimneys, oak panelling or tapestries on the walls, carpets on the floor and other luxuries. The advantage of this class was that in origin it was representative of the nation and embraced nearly all social classes. The top men might rise to be nobles; the merchants, lawyers and yeomen who made their fortunes bought estates and lands and became squires and gentle-folk. Their younger sons might be apprentices to trade and industry. Then came the yeomen, "the backbone of England". They farmed their own land, often a small plot, were often, as Harrison said, "farmers to gentlemen", and many prospered, buying the lands of unthrifty gentlemen, "and often setting their sons to the Universities and to the Inns of Court." After the merchants and yeomen freeholders came the wage-earners, frequently as Shakespeare displays them, able to read and write, independent, loyal and fond of a jest and merry-making. "As for slaves and bondmen we have none," said Harrison.

Nutrition was good except among the very poor. More meat was eaten and less salt-fish consumed. The increase of industries, of shipping and commerce also brought about the enlargement of existing towns and the building of new ones. The urban population began to grow at the expense of the rural one. London increased enormously. Stated to have a population of some 60,000 at the time of the Reformation, it had grown to over 300,000 by early Stuart times.

Queen Elizabeth, herself an author, encouraged litera-ture and the drama. In her golden reign, the English Renaissance, as is well known, flowered in a wonderful literature, the second half of the reign fertile in imperish-able names—Shakespeare, Francis Bacon, Edmund Spenser, Sir Philip Sidney, Marlowe, Ben Jonson, Hooker—to mention the greatest out of many. There were countless masques, pageants, interludes and plays written to celebrate every important ceremonial, as whenever the Queen made a progress or visited one of her nobles or the Universities, or desired an entertainment at court. These literary pastimes had to be well phrased, for she was no mean critic. In this way and through printed books a tincture of letters was diffused among her subjects, and every courtier knew how to write verses or a love-sonnet.

The popular *Euphues* of John Lyly, poet and dramatist, published in 1579, in its extravagances and conceits and classical metaphors reflected the life and talk and dress of the Court. The Queen, it has been said, was the most affected of Euphuists, and her fantastic phraseology can sometimes be traced in her ambiguous letters and even in a prayer which she wrote. Shakespeare satirizes this affectation in *Love's Labour's Lost*.

Such in brief outline was the golden age of Queen Elizabeth, Gloriana, Empress of the West. Not all the credit can be ascribed to her for steering the Ship of State from storm-tossed waters into placid seas. She had able and good men in authority under her, and she chose her ministers and officers wisely. The greater part of the good work was wrought by them and her free people. She, nevertheless, was the steadying influence at the helm of the Ship of State. For the most part she loved tolerance and intervened when extremists threatened to get the upper hand. She always desired to see her people united, at peace, contented and prosperous, and she did what she could to bring this to pass and saw success crown her efforts.

XII

The Prelude to the Spanish Armada

THE march of events gradually forced Queen Elizabeth from veiled into open hostility with Spain. She had resisted becoming King Philip's declared enemy and the Champion of Protestantism in Europe for many years. In the first place because she disliked war. Repeatedly when her Council urged her to bellicose decisions, she would rap the table impatiently with her hands, exclaiming: "Gentlemen, no War, no War!" Secondly, because she knew in the early years of her reign that England was in no state to wage a continental war or to repel foreign invasion.

Elizabeth realized however from the beginning of her reign that war might one day come. To meet this contingency she saved money, she built up a navy, which since her father's day had shrunk almost to nothing, she strengthened the coastal defences and established a militia for defence of the realm. The union of Spain, France and Scotland against England would have been deadly. Fortunately, Philip of Spain's zeal for the Catholic faith was subordinated to his political interests. He had no more desire to see England, France and Scotland united under Mary, Queen of Scots than had Elizabeth. Being of a painstaking mind he hoped eventually to make Elizabeth a Catholic and from time to time she and Leicester encouraged him in this aspiration. In that event England might become an appanage of Spain. Philip was also aware of the value to the Netherlands of trade with England; and that war with England would threaten his sea communications with that country. For all these reasons during the greater part of Elizabeth's reign Philip remained on amicable terms with her in spite of much provocation.

Elizabeth for her part took further precautions. The chapters of this book dealing with Scottish affairs have shown how she protected England from a northern invasion, how she supported the Scottish Protestants and how fate played into her hands by giving her the custody of Queen Mary. It has also been shown how she used the offers of foreign suitors as instruments of policy and brought forward one after another in order to gain time, to strengthen her position, to preserve the continental balance of power and to avert the threat of war. She secretly assisted the Huguenots in order to keep Catherine de Medici, Charles IX and Henry III so embroiled in civil war that they were unable to support the adherents of Mary, Queen of Scots either in England or Scotland. Above all, she always knew that Spain was her chief enemy, and she employed every means in her power to damage that country short of open warfare.

When Philip II became King of Spain, he appointed Margaret, Duchess of Parma, natural daughter of Charles V by a Flemish mistress, to govern on his behalf the seventeen provinces of the Netherlands. She spoke Flemish, was kindly and intelligent and with the help of the Dutch nobility might have ruled well and wisely. Philip, however, through his agent Cardinal Granvelle shackled her with instructions to institute religious persecution; and told her to rely for her government on the advice of Granvelle and other Spaniards and to enforce his wishes through Spanish troops.

The Dutch, who under his more politic father, had been given a greater share in administration, were indignant at being treated as a subject race, at the institution of the Spanish Inquisition, and at the continued presence of Spanish troops. The moderating influences among them were William of Nassau, Prince of Orange, Egmont and Count Horn. Protests against the Inquisition and the heresy edicts were laid before Philip and when they were ignored, an association of Dutch young leaders was formed, known as *les Gueux*, "the Beggars," to resist the enforcement of Spanish oppression.

The incensed Philip then sent the ferocious Alva at the head of an army of Spanish and Italian troops to the Netherlands to stamp out heresy. Egmont and Horn were treacherously captured and beheaded at Brussels. Orange was outlawed. He was joined by many insurgents and with their help and that of volunteers from Germany and England and supplies of money and munitions from Elizabeth, he maintained incessant warfare against Alva by land and sea. On land the Dutch were often defeated by Alva's trained troops; on the coast the "sea-beggars" were more successful and captured Brill. After this the Northern provinces rose and the splendid campaign of sieges began—Haarlem, Alkmaar and Leyden.

Elizabeth never approved of rebellions, and if Philip had granted his Protestant subjects the same freedom of conscience as she allowed to her Catholic subjects, and had withdrawn his Spanish armies, which were a perpetual menace to England, she would have ceased supporting the insurgent Dutch. Her aid to them was another means of defence. She wisely refused to accept the sovereignty of the Northern provinces which Orange offered her. After Philip had recalled Alva, and Requesens, his successor, had died, the Spanish army being unpaid mutinied, seized Alost and sacked Antwerp so terribly that the deed was known as the "Spanish Fury". So great was the indignation in the Catholic southern provinces, that in 1576 they made common cause with Holland and Zealand in the Pacification of Ghent. The new governor, Don John of Austria, had to agree to the departure of the Spanish troops and to maintain the charters and liberties of the Dutch. This gave a further respite to Elizabeth. She lent the allied states the large sum of £40,000, and, as has been related, disclosed Don John's plots against England and his project of marrying Mary Stuart, to the jealous Philip, with whom she remained on friendly terms, in spite of his incitement to bravos to assassinate her.

Peace in the Netherlands was of short duration. Religious hostility sowed dissension between the Northern and Southern provinces. In 1578, Don John's nephew, Alexander Farnese, the Duke of Parma, by his victory at Gembloux brought back Belgium to the rule of Spain. Orange in 1579 consented to the Union of Utrecht which consolidated the Protestant resistance in the Northern provinces. To obtain foreign aid he invited the aid of the Duke of Anjou (Alençon), the suitor of Queen Elizabeth and the heir to the French Crown. In Chapter VI, it has already been related how Elizabeth befooled Alençon and encouraged him in his Netherlands enterprise, although she was less successful in deluding his brother, the King of France.

In 1584 William of Orange was assassinated by Balthazar Gérard, but the state that he had created, a federation of six free republics, endured and the house of Orange continued to guide its destinies.

The loyalty and adventurous spirits of the great mariners of England, unofficially, gave Queen Elizabeth another means of injuring Spain both in European waters and in Spanish possessions in the New World. Exploration of unknown lands and oceans went hand-in-hand with privateering, sacking of Spanish towns and capture of Spanish merchant vessels and treasure ships. These intrepid mariners are often termed pirates, but that is to judge them by the standards of a different age. They were privateers, merchant adventurers who were extending and promoting the influence of England and gaining wealth in so doing. Their guiding beliefs were legitimate pride in England and in their Queen, and on her behalf they challenged the dominant power of Spain in unacknowledged warfare.

So they sailed from England in their wooden ships, built, launched, armed and equipped out of private funds, and invaded the trade monopoly of Spain and Portugal in the South Seas. In 1567 at San del Ulloa, a port of Mexico, John Hawkins with his kinsman, Francis Drake, with his five ships lay alongside a Spanish fleet, when they were treacherously attacked by the Spaniards. In spite of superior numbers, after a stubborn and heroic fight, Hawkins managed to escape with two ships. When this was known, "Military and seafaring men all over England fretted and desired war with Spain. But the Queen shut her ears against them."

Young Francis Drake went voyaging again in Spanish waters. In 1568 he fitted out two ships, the *Dragon* and the *Swan* with which he sailed to the Spanish Main and in 1568 he went to explore those seas; on both occasions he captured "not a few goodly barks laden with merchandise". In 1572 he sailed to America in the *Pacha*, his brother John being captain of the *Swan*, and in company of his trusty follower, John Oxenham. In Panama he took much treasure, and on seeing the Pacific from the top of a high tree prayed Almighty God of his goodness to give him life and leave to sail once in an English ship on that sea. On his return voyage he surprised and burnt Venta Cruz and obtained more booty. Drake's dramatic home-coming to Plymouth on August 9, 1573, when the people in church, hearing of his arrival, rushed out to welcome him, is well known.

In 1577 Drake planned another expedition of five ships and through the patronage of Sir Christopher Hatton informed the Queen of the project. She, with Leicester, agreed to take the largest share in the venture. The conditions of her support, Drake knew full well. If he failed and was hanged by the Spaniards, she would disavow him; if he succeeded she would share in the plunder. This was Francis Drake's memorable voyage in which he circumnavigated the globe. The first English-man to sail through the Straits of Magellan, he seized gold, silver and other treasure assembled for shipment to Spain, and captured a ship richly laden. He then crossed the Pacific, reached the Moluccas, sailed on to Java, thence across the Indian Ocean, rounded the Cape of Good Hope, touched at Sierra Leone, and reached Plymouth in the *Golden Hind* on September 25, 1580, with Spanish booty in value nearly £750,000. King Philip was greatly incensed and had already sent indignant protests to the Queen through Mendoza, his ambassador. Elizabeth cautiously delayed any recognition of Drake until she had ascertained that Philip was too occupied with an expedition to claim the crown of Portugal to have time to make reprisals on England. When she decided to express her admiration of Drake's success, she did so right royally. The *Golden Hind* having been brought up to Deptford on April 4th. 1581, the Queen went aboard in state and was entertained at a splendid banquet. As a compliment to her learning, copies of Latin verses written by Winchester scholars, praising the Queen, the *Golden Hind* and her captain were nailed to the mast. After the feast the Queen dubbed Drake a knight, and issued orders that his ship should be preserved as a monument of the nation's glory and of the famous navigator. She was characteristically eager about the treasure. She gave £10,000 to Drake, and took a good share for herself. The remainder was removed to the Tower for safety and an inventory of it was supplied to the Spanish ambassador. Some writers assert that he was appeased by a share of the spoils. Froude states that he refused it. Ultimately, those who took shares in the enterprise received a dividend of 100 per cent. and the Queen kept the residue.

Soon afterwards Elizabeth caused further inconvenience to Philip. He had annexed Portugal to his dominions in 1580, and Don Antonio, prior of Crato, the Portuguese pretender fled to France carrying with him the Braganza crown jewels. Catherine de Medici and King Henry III suggested that Terceira, one of the Azores, should be occupied by a joint expedition of French and English. There the Spanish treasure ships voyaging from Panama to Cadiz might easily be intercepted. Elizabeth was inclined to wink at Drake and Hawkins going with the expedition under Don Antonio's flag. The scheme was betrayed to Mendoza by Sir James Crofts, who was in Philip's pay. Mendoza protested to the Queen and when Don Antonio came to London, she refused at first to see him as a rebel to his sovereign. But she was fond of jewels and took the Braganza diamonds to set beside those of the House of Burgundy, which she already possessed. In return Don Antonio received a sum of money, with which he purchased ships to join the Terceira expedition, although Elizabeth had evaded giving him permission to do so. He went to Plymouth to join Drake.

By this time, Elizabeth on second thoughts saw that the fitting out in one of her ports of a portion of a hostile expedition intended to seize a Spanish possession might well be taken by Philip as a declaration of war. She sent Walsingham to Paris with instructions to embroil France with Spain and to make it clear to Queen Catherine and Henry that she would neither join the Terceira expedition nor marry Alençon. Walsingham told her he would rather she sent him to the Tower. She was giving him an impossible task. It was made even more difficult by the contradictory instructions she afterwards sent him especially in regard to her marriage. Henry was much annoyed, but Elizabeth's policy had so far succeeded that a squadron flying the French flag was already at Terceira. She stopped Don Antonio's ships from sailing and said Drake and Hawkins were not to go on the expedition. The Queen had to send Alençon privately two hundred thousand crowns (see Chapter VI); Henry III renewed with her the defensive alliance; Alençon went into the Netherlands on his own responsibility; King Henry disavowed the ships at Terceira. Elizabeth, pressed by Don Antonio for the return of the pledged jewels, in the end first allowed four and afterwards six of the ships to escape out of harbour. They arrived at Terceira too late to avert defeat of the whole expedition by the Spaniards. Don Antonio remained an exile in England.

Don Bernardino Mendoza bearing a sharp letter of protest from Philip to Elizabeth with some difficulty presented it to her at Richmond. She sat still instead of rising to receive him, as was her wont, on the excuse that she had rheumatism. She read King Philip's letter in which his grievances were set out with additions from the ambassador—the seizure and plunder of his towns and ships, the expedition of Drake, her interference in the

Netherlands, and lastly the support she had given to Don Antonio, who had sailed down the Thames flying the Portuguese flag and subsidized with loans from London merchants. Elizabeth said she believed Don Antonio had left the country, which the ambassador knew was not the case, and that she had prevented his ships sailing, otherwise, the treasure-fleet would not have reached Spain. At this Mendoza angrily exclaimed: "If your majesty will not hear words, we must come to the cannon and see if you will hear them!" Very quietly Elizabeth replied: "If you use threats of that kind I will fling you into a dungeon." Mendoza said more respectfully that he was only giving his master's message. The Queen then repeated Mendoza's threat to her lords in attendance, adding: "I told him he need not think to frighten me." Here Mendoza interposed to say that he was not so foolish . . . "and the queen being a lady also, and so beautiful a lady might well throw me to the lions." Her countenance cleared at the compliment and she related the kind things she had done for King Philip. She had saved the Netherlands from France for him, and he in return had invaded Ireland and pensioned her rebels. One of his previous ambassadors, Don Guerau de Espes, had fomented disaffection in England; and Mendoza, himself, had tried to get Don Antonio assassinated. Mendoza denied all her contentions and the audience became stormy again, Elizabeth declaring she could do nothing about Drake's treasure until she had received full satisfaction from the King about Ireland. She emphasized that she had been the first offended, and would have the first satisfaction, and ended the audience. As she turned away Mendoza heard her say, with a deep sigh, "Would to God we could each have our own and be at peace."

Mendoza gained nothing, Philip took no action and Elizabeth made no concessions. After the discovery of the Throckmorton plot (see Chapter IX) in November, 1583, Mendoza was expelled, but being transferred to Paris he was hand-in-glove with the Guises and brought the financial aid of Spain to the Holy League. By 1585 Alençon and

William of Orange were dead, Henry III, though wishful to acknowledge Henry of Navarre as his heir, was forced by the treaty of Nemours to pledge himself to extirpate heresy in France and to lead an army against Henry of Navarre in alliance with Henry of Guise. "The War of the Three Henrys", the last great war of religion, was to last until Henry of Navarre secured the French crown. The League's army was defeated by Navarre at the Battle of Coutras (1587), but Guise overcame his German and Swiss allies. Guise on the day of the barricades (1588) became "King of Paris". Henry III retreated to Blois, made terms with Guise, and appointed him Lieutenant-General of the kingdom. Then Henry had Guise assassinated at Blois and in 1589 was himself fatally stabbed by the monk, Jacques Clément.

Thus in 1585 after the Treaty of Nemours, Queen Elizabeth was deprived of the French alliance which had so greatly strengthened her since 1572, and had to face the aggression of Spain alone. At long last she was driven into the position of being the Protestant champion, which Burghley and Walsingham had urged her in vain for many years to assume. These precious years had been employed through her wise statesmanship in bringing the blessings of peace and prosperity to her people and in building up the naval and military might of England.

The Queen now considered the best use she could make of the Anglo-Dutch Alliance. Again the Dutch offered to become her subjects; again she firmly refused. They had previously offered the sovereignty to Henry III, after his brother's death, and he had eventually refused for fear of the Guises, who were on friendly terms with Philip. Elizabeth told the States they must put more men in the field and be more active against their Spanish foes. She would send them an army and money which must be repaid when victory was achieved. For security she would take Flushing and Brill. The Dutch disliked giving these towns in pledge and while they were bargaining on the subject, Antwerp was captured by Parma. It was a great blow, for the city was of paramount importance.

"If we get Antwerp," said the Spanish soldiers, "you shall all go to Mass with us; if you save Antwerp, we will all go to conventicle with you." This catastrophe made the Dutch envoys agree to the Queen's conditions. General Sir John Norris was already in the Netherlands with two thousand men; and the Earl of Leicester was appointed Commander-in-Chief of Her Majesty's forces in the Netherlands and representative of her authority in these countries.

Leicester was still dear to Elizabeth as her friend and adviser. He was long trained in affairs, he had served in the wars and his appointment was approved by Burghley, Walsingham, the rest of the Queen's Council, and by public opinion. In challenging the might of Spain it was highly desirable that one of the chief noblemen of England should command the Queen's forces. Furthermore, and this weighed heavily with the thrifty Queen, this commander must defray his personal heavy expenses and contribute largely to the cost of the campaign. Leicester in this respect did all he could to fulfil the Queen's wishes. He raised money by mortgaging his estates and gave large sums towards necessary military expenditure which Elizabeth dispensed without any idea of repaying; indeed, before Leicester left England she insisted on his repaying a considerable sum of money which he owed her. Leicester both before and during the campaign protested to the Queen and to Walsingham that he was not given adequate resources in men or money to make successful war against Parma. In this he spoke truly and Elizabeth has often been blamed for her parsimony. But she had no intention of waging the grand war of Protestant liberation which Leicester and Walsingham desired. In her "Declaration of the Causes moving the Queen of England to give aid to the defence of the people of the Low Countries", she stated that she intended "a deliverance of them from war by the Spaniards and foreigners with a restitution of their ancient liberties and government by some Christian peace". She always desired a peaceful issue and hoped that this "demonstration" in force, for it was little more, would induce King Philip to restore his Dutch subjects their "ancient liberties". The Duke of Parma, a much more enlightened person than his sovereign, fully realised this and advised King Philip to accept Elizabeth's terms and to withdraw the Spanish troops. The bureaucratic king penning endless memoranda and minutes in the Escorial, hampering Parma with insufficient resources and instructions that were out of date by the time they reached him, was implacable. Another reason for Elizabeth's inadequate support of the Netherlands campaign was her statesmanlike evaluation of England's resources. Parma had the highest reputation as a general. If she squandered her fighting men and treasure in an unsuccessful war oversea, and Philip then invaded England, the country would be unable to put up a successful resistance. England was first and last in her thoughts. Her aim, it must be repeated, was peace, but she stood alone among her hot-headed nobles in trying to ensue it. To this end with Burghley's reluctant assistance, she entered into secret negotiations for peace with Parma, at first without the knowledge of Leicester and Walsingham, almost at the beginning of the campaign. Her Commissioners continued the negotiations at Bourg, near Calais, up to the time when the Armada reached the Channel.

On the other hand, Leicester, whose head was turned by his new dignity, excited her deep anger by his acceptance of the title of Governor-General of the States which was offered to him in January 1586 on his arrival in the Netherlands. Elizabeth had expressly forbidden him to accept any title which implied that she was ruler of the country. She stormed at her Ministers, at the States, who imagined they were pleasing her, and at Leicester. To the latter she wrote:

"We could never have imagined, had we not seen it fall out in experience, that a man raised up by ourself and extraordinarily favoured by us above any other subject of this land would have in so contemptible a sort, broken our commandment, in a cause that so greatly toucheth us in honour."

Her first intention was to compel him to resign the title and to recall him in disgrace. She even thought of sending him to the Tower. It was not until June that her anger abated and, on the advice of Burghley, she allowed Leicester to remain and to keep the title. Leicester's letters of contrition and adoration helped her to relent. Elizabeth's displeasure diminished Leicester's prestige in the eyes of the Dutch. Furthermore, he was not a tactful administrator and they resented his arrogance. The Queen's negotiations for a peace of compromise, which the Dutch by now would not entertain, leaked out by the means of Parma's agents, and rendered the States un-co-operative. Parma's army was almost as ill-supplied from Spain as that of Leicester from England. The war on both sides consisted of the siege of a few towns, predatory raids and some minor battles of which the best known is Zutphen, where the gallant Sir Philip Sidney was killed.

As a further means of exercising pressure on King Philip to restore peace to the Netherlands, the Queen commissioned Sir Francis Drake and sent him out as her Admiral against Spain. In 1585 he sacked Vigo on the Spanish coast and then sailed to the West Indies with his fleet of twenty-one ships. Here he burned the town of St. Iago and plundered Carthagena and St. Domingo. In 1586 Thomas Cavendish reached the Spanish Main, wrought much destruction there, and on his return in 1587 captured a Spanish merchantman laden with treasure.

Soon it became known in London that Philip was preparing in the ports of Spain and at Lisbon a mighty force and fleet for the invasion of England. Elizabeth and Drake had finally worn out the patience which had endured for some thirty years. The heretic Queen was to be over-thrown. Elizabeth renewed her peaceful overtures which were rejected. Then she sent Drake with thirty ships to examine the harbours of Spain. In this "singeing of the King of Spain's beard", Drake first attacked and sank upwards of eighty vessels in the roads of Cadiz. He then sailed along the coast as far as Cape St. Vincent, destroying above a hundred ships and battering down four forts. In the Tagus he seized a great ship, the *St. Philip*, laden with rich merchandise, under the mortified eyes of the Grand Admiral of Spain, Santa Cruz, who was bound by instructions to avoid encountering the English raider. Santa Cruz had been intended to lead the Great Armada, but died soon afterwards. This exploit did so much damage and so greatly disorganised the Spanish Armada that its sailing had to be postponed for another year. Drake on his return to England was received as a popular hero, but the Queen for whom he had done such doughty deeds was alarmed by the magnitude of his success which she rightly estimated would make King Philip an even more inveterate enemy. She gave no thanks to Drake and even apologised to Parma for his deeds; she had only sent him "out for her own protection". Farnese politely accepted her explanation, saying he could well believe anything of a man bred as a pirate and professed himself ready to continue peace negotiations. Elizabeth was not deceived by this pacific answer. She knew that Philip was pressing on with his preparations; that Catholic volunteers from various countries of Europe were enrolling under his standard as if for another crusade; that at his request the Pope had issued a new bull of excommunication against her, and had lent money to Philip in order that the heretic countries of England and Scotland might once more become fiefs of the Holy See.

The conquest of England was to be an important step in Philip's plan to secure the hegemony of Europe and the restoration of Roman Catholicism in its recreant lands. France stood aloof and the League was almost co-belligerent with Spain. James in Scotland was waiting to see which way the cat would jump. England stood alone to combat the aggressor.

XIII

Her Greatest Hour

KING PHILIP II since 1558 had received many
injuries and slights from Queen Elizabeth. She had
refused to marry him; for many years she had encouraged
his rebellious subjects in the Netherlands, allowed English
volunteers to aid them, supplied the rebels first secretly
then openly with money and munitions, and finally
appointed the great Earl of Leicester to lead an English
army against him and practically to assume the position of
her viceroy in his own dominions. Englishmen with her
tacit approval had sailed to the Spanish Main to attack and
plunder his colonies, seize his treasure ships and merchant-
men and inflict crushing blows on Spanish commerce. As
a devout Roman Catholic, Philip regarded the English
Queen's apostasy from the true faith as an additional
injury. She had conformed to it in Mary's reign. She had
allowed the dreadful heresy of Protestantism to become
the religion of her country, and had put to death the Queen
of Scots, the champion and martyr of the true faith. All
these wrongs had finally determined the deliberate Philip
to settle matters by seizing England, Scotland and Ireland
for himself. He considered he had a double right to the
two crowns both through his descent from John of Gaunt,
who married Constance, daughter of Peter the Cruel of
Castile, from whom the Emperor Charles V was descended,
and by virtue of the fact that the Queen of Scots had
made him her heir.

The preparations for the Armada were on a colossal
scale. The chief centre of activity was at Lisbon where
the ships assembled under the command of the Grand

Admiral of Spain, but every ship-building yard in the ports of Spain was active. The dockyards of Antwerp, Nieuport, Gravelines and Dunkirk had long been busy with the building of flat-bottomed boats for which the forest of Waes had been felled to supply timber. These were intended to convey Spanish troops from the Netherlands for the invasion of England. Parma in addition to his garrison forces had mustered 30,000 infantry and 1,800 cavalry for the expedition. The Spanish fleet amounted to 135 men-of war, which conveyed 8,766 seamen and 21,855 soldiers.

In the valuable years of preparation for the struggle, secured by Elizabeth's delaying policy which so fretted her Protestant subjects, England had built up a small but powerful navy. Her shipwrights were excellent, and her ships were superior to those of other nations. They were smaller than the Spanish vessels, could tack, alter course and sail closer to the wind, and were manned by good seamen, many of them well experienced in home waters and on the Spanish Main. The Elizabethan Royal Navy was virtually the Queen's creation and though in 1588 it only consisted of 34 ships of 100 tons and over, it was well equipped, in good condition and kept in the Medway when not in commission. In contradistinction to Froude, who did not like Elizabeth and tends to be sometimes unfair to her, Beesly observes that the fleet could be fitted out for sea at very short notice, that economy was enforced in the Admiralty as in other departments but not at the expense of efficiency. The wages of officers and men were increased. He admits, however, that some of the Queen's economies especially in victualling, which were reasonable in peacetime, were not well adapted to the extra stress of warfare. As to the small size of the Royal Navy, as compared with the 135 war vessels of King Philip, it must be remembered that there was a large commercial and privateer navy in reserve which the Queen could call upon in a time of crisis like the present. The number of ships belonging to private owners which augmented the English fleet numbered 163. The Queen like her royal father had always seen to her ordnance, and her ships' guns were much heavier metal—some thirty-three pounders and even sixty-pounders—than the Spanish guns and out-ranged them. Lord Howard of Effingham was Lord High Admiral, whose father, Lord William Howard, and whose grandfather, Thomas, Duke of Norfolk, had filled the same office. Sir Francis Drake was her Vice-Admiral. It was a notable fact contributing to the English victory, that all the Queen's veteran seamen—Drake, Hawkins, Fro-bisher, Grenville, Cavendish—were then serving in the Fleet and not voyaging on the Spanish Main. They knew the Spaniards and their warfare.

> "Now all the youth of England are on fire,
> And silken dalliance in the wardrobe lies;
> Now thrive the armourers, and honour's thought
> Reigns solely in the breast of every man."

Henry V appeared about 1599. In writing these memorable lines Shakespeare must have recalled the wave of enthusiasm that swept through England to prepare to meet the Spanish invader, and the gallant bearing of the volunteers and newly-raised militia as they marched to the muster at Tilbury. "At every rumour of the approach of the foe and the prospect of doing battle with him they rejoiced," says Stow, "like lusty giants about to run a race."

Queen Elizabeth herself became the nominal general-issimo of two armies. The first she gave to Leicester and appointed him her Lieutenant-General. He had as his Chief of Staff, that veteran and able soldier, Sir John Norris. This army of some 23,000 men was stationed at Tilbury; the second army for the defence of London was called the Army Royal or Queen's Body-Guard and was commanded by Lord Hunsdon.

As we have seen in our own time when the country was in peril, all were at one. Protestants and Catholics alike flocked to the Queen's Standard and Elizabeth proudly surveyed a united nation. Viscount Montague, his son

195

and grandson, appeared before the Queen with 200 horse which he had raised to defend her, while the very prisoners for their religion in Ely signed a memorial that they were ready to fight to the death for her against all her enemies—Pope, priests, kings or any power.

The women were as loyal and enthusiastic as their menfolk. One worked so hard in the national effort that Elizabeth, according to Miss Strickland, bestowed upon her the honour of knighthood. This female knight was Mary, the wife of Sir Hugh Cholmondely of Vale Royal known as "the bold lady of Cheshire".

The Duke of Medina Sidonia, a grandee inexperienced in naval warfare, was appointed by King Philip to command the Armada. On May 29, 1588, the mighty fleet of tall ships sailed from Lisbon. Hardly had it reached the open sea when the elements intervened for the defence of England. A gale from the west off Cape Finisterre broke up the serried ranks of the fleet, and the Admiral had to run into Corunna to repair his damaged ships. Rumour exaggerated this disaster as the complete destruction of the Armada, and Elizabeth believing it sent orders to Lord Howard of Effingham to lay up the four largest of her men-of-war. The prudent Lord High Admiral promised to maintain them at his own cost and the event justified his foresight. On July 19 the Armada was seen off the Lizard and Howard at once put to sea with the English fleet. Camden thus described the first sight of the enemy:

"The next day, the English descried the Spanish ships, with lofty turrets, like castles, in front like a half-moon, the wings thereof spreading out about the length of seven miles, sailing very slowly, though with full sails, the wind being as it were, tired of carrying them, and the ocean groaning with the weight of them."

On the 21st Howard endeavoured to come to grips with the invaders, leading the van in his flag-ship the *Ark Royal* or *Raleigh*, while Drake, Hawkins and Frobisher attacked the hindmost squadron. The quick-sailing English ships circled round the heavy Spanish galleons, while their heavy artillery wrought much havoc.

The Duke of Medina Sidonia's instructions from King Philip were not to fight the English, until he had joined forces with Parma's invading forces in Flanders. These harassing tactics of the English fleet threw the Armada into confusion and depressed the morale of the Spaniards. Every Spanish vessel was crippled in one way or another by the English fire and there were many casualties among the crews. Only a few ships were lost, as Howard had prudently ordered his captains not to grapple and board the galleons. Sir Walter Raleigh, who appears to have been engaged in the action with other gentlemen volunteers, in his *History of the World* praises Howard for his judgment in these words:

"In like sort had Lord Charles Howard, Admiral of England been lost in the year 1588, if he had not been better advised than a great many malignant fools were that found fault with his demeanour. The Spaniards had an army aboard them, and he had none; they had more ships than he had, and of higher building and charging; so that had he entangled himself with these great and powerful vessels, he had greatly endangered this kingdom of England. For twenty men upon the defences are equal to a hundred that board and enter; whereas then the Spaniards, contrariwise, had a hundred for twenty of ours to defend themselves withal. But our admiral knew his advantage and held it; which had he not done he had not been worthy to have held his head."

The Council probably received this explanation when they sent Richard Drake to inquire of the Lord High Admiral why he had not boarded the Spanish ships.

For a whole week the "Invincible Armada" was beset and harried, until on August 6, it limped into Calais Roads and anchored there followed by the English fleet,

197

which in turn anchored two miles astern. The Duke of Medina Sidonia communicated with the French governor, M. Gourdain, requesting the hospitality of the port and sent a dispatch to Parma, saying he was helpless against the enemy's repeated attacks and asking for thirty or forty flyboats or gunboats to keep the English at bay. The reply was most disappointing. Parma had no gunboats. The States acting as faithful allies of England had blockaded the Dutch ports under his control rendering it hazardous to bring out his transports, and in any case it would be certain destruction to come out until the English fleet was dispersed. The Armada must first clear the Channel. Farnese also sent a special messenger to Philip to say that it would be madness to risk his invasion barges in a naval engagement or in stormy weather.

When these unwelcome tidings arrived, the Spaniards found themselves hemmed in by 140 English sail, for Winter and Lord Henry Howard had joined the Lord Admiral's fleet with the squadron of the Straits. A Council of War was held by Howard in his cabin, attended by Sheffield, Seymour, Southwell, Palmer, Drake, Hawkins, Frobisher, Winter and Fenner to decide the fate of England. According to Camden "the foresight of Queen Elizabeth" had suggested the course they followed to throw the enemy into confusion.

Eight fire-ships were hastily prepared and the wind being inshore Captains Young and Prouse took them at midnight to the Spanish lines, and then took to their boats. Then the vessels now fully ablaze, exploding their charges, bore down on the Armada. There was a cry throughout the fleet, "The fire-ships of Antwerp, the fire-ships of Antwerp," as the Spaniards recalled with horror those floating volcanoes of the Mantuan engineer, Gianibelli, now in England, which had shattered the bridge and floating forts of Parma. Forthwith every cable was cut and each galleon and galeasse was put in motion to escape destruction. In the pitch-black darkness all was confusion and panic. Ships ran foul of each other and two were utterly consumed by the flaming ships. When these were burnt out, the Duke of Medina fired a gun to recall his flying vessels, but few heard it. They had fled in fear and scattered along the coast from Calais to Ostend. To add to the terrors of the night a tempest had set in, a furious gale blew from the south-west, while thunder and lightning raged to be followed by heavy rain. Some vessels ran ashore on the French coast, others were cut off by the enemy, some foundered at sea. A final battle off Gravelines, August 8–9, so shattered the Armada, that Medina Sidonia had no recourse left but to retreat to Spain through the North Sea and by rounding the north of Scotland. Of the proud and gallant Armada only isolated battered ships remained, each fleeing from the enemy as best it could. The English fleet, short of provisions and of ammunition, were unable to follow up their victory, and many have accused Elizabeth both then and since of short-sighted parsimony in not supplying Lord Howard's urgent demands for further supplies. Of the historians, Froude and Motley are most severe on this question. Walsingham wrote: "I am sorry the Lord Admiral was forced to leave the prosecution of the enemy through the want he sustains. Our half doings doth breed dishonour and leaveth the disease uncured."

But Elizabeth, when the demands were received, had no knowledge that the success of the English fleet had been so overwhelming. Her great care was the defence of the realm, to guard against Parma's invasion, supported possibly by the Armada refitted in some Scottish port. She had to envisage these contingencies and so she kept her gunpowder in the Tower of London. It is easy to be a critic after the event.

The weather, which before, then and since has so often protected England, intervened anew to complete the Armada's destruction. Unpiloted, in unknown and storm-tossed seas many ships went to destruction on the rocky shores of the Orkneys, the Hebrides, Connaught and Kerry. Many of the crews were drowned or killed after landing. Out of King Philip's 135 ships which had sailed from Lisbon only some 53 struggled back to the ports of

northern Spain. Of the 30,000 men who sailed in the
fleet it is probable that not more than 10,000 ever saw
their native land again (Motley). Most of the leaders of
the expedition perished, but Medina Sidonia reached
Santander in October. Through the over-optimistic Don
Bernardino Mendoza wild rumours had circulated in
France of the Armada's complete success; some of these
he had conveyed to King Philip. When the King heard
the dismal truth, as he sat at his desk in the Escorial, he
received it with composure, saying he could easily if he
chose place another fleet on the seas, and then continued
with his letter-writing.

For the sake of a consecutive narrative the vanquishing
of the Armada at sea has briefly been related, and we must
now return to the effect which it produced on land. On
the night of July 19, as soon as the news of the Armada off
the Lizard was reported, the chain of beacons set throughout the length and breadth of England to give warning of
the threatened invasion were kindled one by one from
south to north.

> "Till the proud Peak unfurled the flag o'er Darwin's
> rocky dales,
> Till like volcanoes flared to heaven the stormy hills of
> Wales,
>
> . . . .
>
> Till Skiddaw saw the fire that burned on Gaunt's
> embattled pile,
> And the red glare on Skiddaw roused the burghers of
> Carlisle."

Forthwith Leicester's army mustered at Tilbury, the
militia of the midland counties marched to London; those
of the south and east stood in readiness to meet a descent
on either shore. Had Parma landed he would have been
opposed by a force greater than his own, many of them
raw recruits, but stiffened by men who had already fought
with his trained infantry in Flanders. Parma knew the
difficulties of the task. "I must fight battle after battle,"

he warned King Philip. "I shall lose men by wounds and disease." He was doubtful of the issue unless a rising of English Catholics aided him, and they would have continued loyal to their Queen and country.

Elizabeth had now reigned for thirty years. She was aged fifty-five years, an old woman for those days, but her eye was not dim nor her natural force abated. She ardently desired to emulate her father's action of 1545 when he went to the coast to repel foreign invasion, and only the strong remonstrances of her council prevented her. Instead during the crisis she made her headquarters at Havering Bower, near London and close to the main army of defence. When as yet she knew not how the naval battle between her fleet and the Armada would end, she made that famous visit to Tilbury to review her troops which will live for ever in history. Midway between the fort and the camp she was met by Sir Roger Williams, with two thousand horse and two thousand foot. He escorted her to the house of one Master Rich, about three miles from the camp, where she spent the night. On the following morning she rode to the camp, attended only by the Earl of Leicester and the Earl of Ormond, who bore the Sword of State before her; behind walked her page bearing her white-plumed regal helmet.

"She wore a polished steel corslet on her breast, and below this warlike bodice descended a fardingale of such monstrous amplitude that it is wonderful how her mettled war-horse submitted to carry a lady encumbered with a gaberdine of so strange a fashion; but in this veritable array the royal heroine rode, bare-headed, between the lines, with a courageous but smiling countenance."

The serried ranks past which she slowly rode cheered her madly and vociferously again and again. There she appeared before them not now as Diana, the imperial huntress, seeking peace and ensuing it, but as Bellona, the goddess of battle armed and arrayed to fight for her people. She was Gloriana, Queen of England, the personification of the England that under her rule had become so strong and great that it was challenged today by the dominant world power of Spain. Queen of half an island, she and her people stood alone to resist the invader and already the omens were propitious as more hopeful news came from the fleet and the sound of gunfire came booming from the Channel.

Then, when the cheering subsided, in her deep voice she spoke her famous speech, so often quoted, which ended with the words, "not doubting but by your obediance to my General, by your concord in the camp, and your valour in the field, we shall shortly have a famous victory over these enemies of my God, of my kingdom and of my people."

Again and again the cheers broke forth as she rode from the camp, proud and smiling, a royal Queen confident of victory, inspiring men to live or die for her. It was her greatest hour.

She told her subjects that under God she had always placed her chiefest strength and safeguard in their loyal hearts and good will. She was justified, for tidings soon came of the great victory achieved by the courage and bravery of her seamen. At St. James's Palace she watched warlike exercises, tilts and tourneys day after day, for the fear that the Armada might return and Parma invade from the Spanish Netherlands endured for some time.

To celebrate the victory medals were struck, some showing a fleet flying under full sail with the inscription, "*Venit, vidit, fugit*", "It came, it saw, it fled"; others represented the fire-ships scattering the Armada, with the legend, "*Dux femina facti*", "It was done by a woman", in compliment to the Queen. Whenever she appeared in public, the crowds greeted her with demonstrations of affection and gratitude.

Elizabeth's honour lists were always brief and not even the national triumph impelled her to a lavish distribution of honours and awards. She bestowed a pension on Lord Howard and made provision for the wounded seamen.

She told the Lord Admiral "that she considered him and his officers as persons born for the preservation of their country," and she always recognized the captains and commanders who had fought for her and greeted them by name. That in her view was ample reward and involved no expenditure. Leicester, who had resumed his old ascendancy over her, she deemed worthy of high distinction. For him she would have created the office of Lord Lieutenant of England and Ireland, a dignity which would have given him unprecedented power as her viceroy. The patent was made out and only the earnest protests of Burghley and of Hatton prevented her from carrying out her intention. Leicester is said to have been resentful, but his last letter to her breathes only sentiments of affection and loyalty. He disbanded his army and died on September 4, at Cornbury Park in Oxfordshire, not far from Cumnor, on his way to Kenilworth, of "the continual fever" or "cold rheums" which had troubled him since the beginning of the year. It was possibly a malignant form of malaria. His body was examined *post-mortem* and the death was held to be natural. Parsons has a story that Leicester, wishing to dispose of his second wife, had given her a poison which he said was an excellent cordial in sickness. She innocently administered it to the Earl in his illness with fatal results. Another version says that her action was not so innocent and the fact that soon afterwards the Countess married young Sir Christopher Blount, Leicester's equerry, lent colour to the scandal. In his will Leicester left costly jewels with many expressions of gratitude to Elizabeth, but he was already in debt for considerable sums to her, although the money had been chiefly expended in her service and to maintain the dignity of his offices. The Queen received the news of her favourite's death with tears, but the business instincts of Henry VII were so strong in her, that she forthwith ordered the dead earl's effects to be seized and sold by public auction to repay the debts. It was a sordid epilogue to Elizabeth's prolonged love and friendship.

It was not until the autumn that the full story of the Armada's destruction was known and that Parma no longer threatened invasion. On November 24, the Queen attended a thanksgiving service at St. Paul's Cathedral to celebrate the national deliverance. Dr. Pierce, the Bishop of Salisbury arrayed in full pontificals preached the sermon from the appropriate text, "Thou didst blow with thy winds, and they were scattered". Banners and other trophies from the Armada were displayed in the Cathedral.

Thus culminated the mighty epic of the Armada, in which Elizabeth rose to her greatest height as the leader and defender of her people, and in their affection, courage and allegiance reaped the reward of years of patience, of tortuous policy, of combat with short-sighted ministers and Parliament and, above all, of her whole-hearted devotion to her people's prosperity and well-being. For this she had given up Leicester; she had renounced being a wife and mother in order that no conflicting interests should interfere with her rule of England.

With Leicester dead, she was more than ever lonely, but she had received the full price of her renunciation. She had made England great, she had overcome the Spanish menace and now stood forth, the Queen of a united nation in which the seeds of greatness were once more growing and thriving. She was, even more than her great sire had been, a power to be reckoned with in European affairs.

XIV

Young England : Elizabeth and Essex

THERE are spots on the sun, flaws in beautiful marble, flies in the ointment and defects in noble characters. Elizabeth was not devoid of faults. We have just seen how when the challenge came she could rise to heights which only a great and patriotic queen could have ascended. She could not always live on this heroic plane and there are traits in her character—undignified and even ignoble— which every student of her life must deplore.

It is, nevertheless, a part of her enigmatic conduct that her very extravagances and weaknesses often became instruments of her policy, while her prudent ministers, Burghley, Walsingham and Hatton stood apprehensive of the risks she was incurring. She played with fire and sometimes burnt her fingers, but, on the whole, the knowledge that she was so wonderful a queen atoned for her many imperfections.

Her Majesty, the late Queen Mary, is said to have remarked of the altered society of today, "We must move with the times," and Queen Elizabeth was far-sighted in this respect for her day and generation. Bishop Creighton and others have emphasized that by the time of the Armada a new and different generation had grown up. In contrast to the men who had surrounded the Queen when she came to the throne the men of the new epoch were "outspoken, adventurous, and turbulent, overflowing with life and energy."

Elizabeth ruled the cautious, silent, prudent and self-restrained men of the older generation by her personal ascendancy and authority. She had kept her ministers in their place by exalting her favourites, more especially the Earl of Leicester, who in reality had never influenced her policy for long, although, as in the old negotiations with Philip of Spain, he had sometimes appeared to do so. She adapted this policy of making favourites to the new generation. She always liked handsome young men around her, and to have them dependent on her smiles and frowns; she encouraged their rivalry which made them disinclined to form factions against her authority. At the same time, she kept the older courtiers like Christopher Hatton, her Chancellor, dancing attendance upon her. Though she neared sixty years of age, all had as a matter of convention to profess to be dying for love of the Queen with her rouged, raddled face, her jaded eyes and her red wig. They penned sonnets to her eyebrows, they professed to be desolated and heart-broken when they were out of favour. They intrigued for money, grants of monopolies, place and estates; they quarrelled with one another for her good graces; and in her absence they made love to her maids-of-honour and sometimes married them secretly to the Queen's high displeasure.*

There were many of these young adventurous spirits, including Charles Blount, "Of stature tall and very comely proportion", and Walter Raleigh, who may or may not have laid his cloak on a muddy path for the Queen to walk upon. He was noticed for his "good presence, in a handsome and well-compacted person, a strong natural wit, and a bold and plausible tongue."

The chief favourites in the Queen's good graces was her distant young relative, Robert Devereux, the Earl of Essex (see Table, Appendix III). His stepfather, the Earl of Leicester, had recommended him to the Queen and her thwarted maternal instincts found satisfaction in treating

---

* For instance, she was annoyed when Thomas Shirley, the son of her treasurer for the wars in the Netherlands, married one of her ladies-in-waiting, Frances Vavasour. She sent Raleigh to the Tower for wedding another of her ladies, the fair Elizabeth Throckmorton, daughter of Sir Nicholas Throckmorton. She was highly displeased when Essex was found to have married Frances, the daughter of Sir Francis Walsingham and widow of Sir Philip Sidney, but she forgave him.

this good-looking youth of twenty as a favourite son. By
May, 1587, it was reported: "When the Queen is abroad
nobody is near her but my Lord of Essex; and at night, my
Lord is at cards, or one game or another with her that he
cometh not to his own lodging till the birds sing in the
morning." Desirous to win fame in the Wars he attempted
to embark to join Leicester in Flanders, but Elizabeth
sent in pursuit and compelled him to return. He was
wounded in a duel with Charles Blount because the Queen
had given him a favour. Elizabeth insisted on a reconciliation between the two young men and reproved them.

After the defeat of the Armada, the adventurous spirits
of the new generation, some of whom had either served
with Drake on the Spanish Main or were fired with tales of
the riches of Mexico and Peru, desired to strike a deva-
stating blow at Spain by conquering the Spanish possessions in the New World, or to make English colonies in
other parts of the American continent. Through the
inspiration of Sir Walter Raleigh a beginning had been
made. His half-brother, Sir Humphrey Gilbert, had
taken possession of Newfoundland for the English crown
in 1583, but he and his brave little company were lost at
sea on the return voyage. In 1584 Raleigh sent an
expedition of reconnaissance under Philip Amadas and
Arthur Barlow which took a new dominion in North
America for the Queen, which she herself called Virginia.
Sir Richard Grenville took colonists there in 1585, but
they were not successful and only too glad to be taken
home in Drake's fleet in the following year when he
visited the settlement. These deserters appear to have
introduced the habit of smoking tobacco into England,
which Raleigh made fashionable at Court, though at first
it met with much opposition. The learned Thomas Hariot
spoke enthusiastically of its medical virtues, and in his
account of Virginia—perhaps the first statistical survey
of a country ever published in English—spoke favourably
of the potentialities of the soil and prospects of colonisation.
It was not until seventeen years later that the Virginia
colony was definitely established. Raleigh appreciated

the good that would accrue to England from establishing colonies oversea, but his contemporaries were more eager to find gold in the New Indies and to return home to buy estates or to spend it. The Queen was not impressed by the reports of the returning colonists and in any case was too cautious to spend men, money and ships in conquering the Spanish possessions in South America and the West Indies. She was, however, still at war with Spain and allowed some marauding expeditions.

The first of these of importance was organized by Drake and Norris, the chief shareholders in the venture, in 1589. The Queen contributed six ships and £20,000. It was intended to conquer Portugal for the pretender, Don Antonio. The members of the expedition landed at Corunna, defeated a large Spanish force and did much damage. They then sailed to Lisbon, being joined by the Earl of Essex, who had succeeded in escaping from England. The expedition failed, because the Portuguese did not rise in Don Antonio's favour, as had been expected, and there was much sickness among the troops and sea-men. On the way back Vigo was burnt and plundered.

Essex on his return was forgiven by the Queen, although for trying to leave England without her permission the less fortunate Earl of Arundel, son of the beheaded Duke of Norfolk, was kept a prisoner in the Tower until his death. It is only fair to add that he had been supposed to favour the cause of the Queen of Scots and while in the Tower was accused of praying for the success of the Armada.

In 1589 Henry of Navarre had become King of France as Henry IV, but the League under the Duke of Mayenne, uncle of the young Duke of Guise, refused to accept him and civil war still raged in France although many of the moderate Catholics supported Henry. Philip II also coveted the French crown and had a faction in the Holy League in his pay, who supported in defiance of the Salic Law, the claim of Philip's daughter to be Queen of France, as she was grand-daughter by her mother of Henry II.

Queen Elizabeth after her usual indirect fashion at first supported Henry IV in his warfare with money, and attacked Spain by sea. In 1589 she sent Henry 4,000 troops under "the brave Lord Willoughby." In 1590 Henry defeated Mayenne at Ivry in one of the most famous of cavalry battles, but after a protracted siege had to withdraw from Paris to meet Alexander Farnese in the field. For King Philip had told the reluctant Parma that he must proceed to France, raise the siege of Paris and occupy Calais and Boulogne in order to prevent English intervention. It was in vain that Farnese protested that he had neither sufficient money nor supplies for this task and that the Netherlands were still in revolt. The Duke of Parma was to talk no more of difficulties but to conquer them (*Simancas MS.*).

On hearing of Parma's intervention, Elizabeth decided to send an English force to France to aid King Henry. Essex sought the command, but the Queen entrusted it to Sir John Norris. Later she allowed Essex to take an additional 4,000 men to besiege Rouen which was garrisoned by the League. Parma relieved the town but received a wound at Caudebec. While he lay ill, Henry defeated his army at Yvetot, and Parma arranged for the retreat of his forces to the Low Countries, but died at Arras. After the death of Philip's best general, Prince Maurice of Nassau gradually gained a military ascendancy which ultimately secured the independence of the United Netherlands.

Essex was recalled from France in 1592, but Elizabeth continued to aid Henry in his war against Spain and the League, which was already showing signs of disintegration. Henry being an astute diplomatist as well as a great general used the English forces in any part of France where he wanted them, and met Elizabeth's protests and her demand for Calais, Boulogne or some other French port as security for her assistance with a compliment, a jest, or an insincere promise.

The French people were weary of civil war and apprehensive of the designs of King Philip. In 1593 Henry

14

consolidated his sovereignty by becoming a Roman Catholic. Elizabeth took him severely to task for this apostasy, the worldly wisdom of which she must have recognized, but continued the Anglo-French alliance. She was even more indignant in 1598 when King Henry made an independent peace with King Philip, "his ambition thwarted and his monarchy like himself worn out and dying," by the Treaty of Vervins. By then Henry was sufficiently strong to do without English support.

Sir Francis Walsingham died in 1590. He had served Elizabeth well and had protected her from plots and assassination by organizing a most successful secret service, initiated by Burghley, at home and in the chief Courts of Europe. While Essex was in France, Burghley persuaded the Queen to appoint his son Robert Cecil as secretary. Essex's nominee had been either William Davison, the scapegoat for Mary Stuart's execution, or Sir Thomas Bodley.

Essex, who was regarded as a sort of leader of young England, was always presuming on the Queen's affection for him and attempting to control state affairs with which she would not allow him to meddle. Then he sulked, was rude and impertinent and behaved like a spoilt child. He had the best of counsellors in Francis Bacon, who advised him to imitate Leicester and Hatton, to apologize for past indiscretions, to seek civil rather than military preferment, "for Her Majesty loveth peace; next she loveth not change." Also Essex should not appear to seek popularity. But Essex would not heed good advice or be discreet in his behaviour.

In 1596, the Archduke Cardinal Albert, ex-Archbishop of Toledo, a brother of the Emperor Rudolph, was appointed by Philip II Governor-General of the Spanish Netherlands. In March he attacked Calais, and took the outlying forts. As Elizabeth was one Sunday at church at Greenwich, she heard the distant report of the Archduke's cannonade on the walls of Calais. She sprang up in the midst of the service and vowed that she would rescue the town. But when Henry asked for aid she made an impossible condition that Calais should be garrisoned with an English army. In the end she sent 2,000 troops to garrison Boulogne.

There were preparations in the ports of Spain for the launching of another Armada, and Elizabeth and her Government could not spare many men for France. Both the Queen's great sailors, Drake and Hawkins, had died in their disastrous last predatory expedition to the West Indies. Lord Howard of Effingham and Essex urged that a naval expedition should be sent to Spain to attack the invasion ships in port. It was decided to fit out a fleet of ninety-six sail which were joined by twenty-four Dutch ships, the total number of men being 16,600. Howard was to command at sea and Essex on land. Sir Walter Raleigh was Vice-Admiral.

The expedition sailed from Plymouth Sound in June. Cadiz, the rich port and arsenal of Spain, was taken by surprise, the sea defences overcome, men-of-war and merchant ships in the harbour captured or destroyed and much booty secured. Essex wished to hold Cadiz, but Howard and his Council of War knew the Queen's wishes and would not allow this. Once more it was shown to the world, as Raleigh declared, that English ships and English seamen were more than a match for all the Spaniards afloat.

There were many squabbles between Elizabeth and Essex over the distribution of the spoils of Cadiz, for the Queen as was her wont took the chief share. In 1597 Essex led the unfortunate expedition to the Azores. His rival Raleigh was with him and captured Fayal without orders, which Essex resented. Advised to bring Raleigh before a court-martial, he chivalrously replied, "So I would had he been one of my friends."

The expedition took several ships, but missed its main object, the capture of the Spanish treasure-fleet from America. This annoyed Elizabeth who received Essex coldly and rebuked him for insulting Raleigh. A further cause of offence to Essex was the bestowal of the Chancellorship of the Duchy of Lancaster on Robert Cecil and the elevation of Lord Howard to be Earl of Nottingham. In order to pacify the spoilt favourite Elizabeth had to make him Earl Marshal which regained his precedence over Nottingham. She even at his repeated request consented to receive his mother, the Countess of Leicester, but only on one occasion.

After the Treaty of Vervins, the aged Burghley advocated peace with Spain. The hot-headed Essex, ignoring the Queen's wishes, argued for war, whereupon Burghley, who had been the Earl's guardian, put a bible into his hands and pointed to the text: "Men of blood shall not live out half their days." It was prophetic of the Earl's fate.

Soon afterwards a scene occurred in the Council. The question of a new Lord Deputy for Ireland was under discussion, the Cecils proposing Sir William Knollys and Essex Sir George Carew, somewhat intemperately. The Queen made a sarcastic comment on Essex's advocacy. He retorted with a contemptuous expression, whereupon Elizabeth gave the impertinent young man a sound box on the ear; the Earl in a fury clapped his hand to his sword. The Lord Admiral threw himself between Essex and his indignant sovereign, after which Essex exclaiming that "it was an insult which he would not have taken from her father, much less from a king in petticoats," rushed out of the Council chamber.

So rash and imprudent was Essex's conduct to the elderly Queen, who had loaded him with benefits, that Bishop Goodman hints that it was the effects of disease for which Lopez had treated him. He had contracted malaria in his campaigns and although some of his absences from Court were due to offended dignity he often suffered from severe attacks of fever and ague. From a boy, however, he was spoilt, arrogant and hot-headed and these traits may have been accentuated by illness.

The quarrel between Essex and the Queen occurred in June, 1598, and it was not until November that a reconciliation took place. In the meantime two persons whose lives had been closely linked with that of Elizabeth had died—Burghley, her faithful prime minister and King Philip of Spain. Much to Essex's indignation, Sir Robert Cecil succeeded his father in the Queen's counsels and pursued the same cautious policy.

In 1599 Essex, supported by Cecil, who was anxious to remove him from Court, prevailed on Elizabeth to send him to restore order in Ireland. He went with the title of Lieutenant and Governor-General of Ireland; he was given money, an army of 21,000 men, many of them veteran troops who had fought in the Netherlands, and with the fullest powers ever conferred upon an Irish Deputy. He had full authority to continue the war or to make peace; to pardon such crimes and treasons as he thought fit and to make his own appointments. Elizabeth gave him her personal instructions before he left. He was to march straight into Ulster and attack Hugh O'Neil, Earl of Tyrone, who had rebelled and was styling himself Earl of Ulster. He was not to make the Earl of Southampton, his friend and the friend of Shakespeare, commander of the cavalry, and he was to be chary of confirming knighthoods on her behalf.

All these instructions the arrogant, spoilt young earl disobeyed on arriving in Ireland. He had marched out of London on March 27, 1599, accompanied by the flower of the young English nobility and followed by the acclamations and good wishes of the people. This homage went to his head and he seems to have imagined that his popularity with the nation and the past favours of the Queen made him virtually independent of her. He created a large number of knights; he appointed Southampton General of horse; he did not march against Tyrone, but went south into depopulated districts, squandering his forces on small undertakings in which he met with reverses. Under direction he might have done good service; alone, he was a poor strategist and a bad administrator. When the Queen upbraided him in her letters for his disobedience and maladministration, he sent back impertinent replies and complained of the favour she showed to his ill-wishers, Cecil, Raleigh and Cobham. The troops were decimated by sickness, the provisions supplied by the English contractors were unwholesome, and Essex meditated returning to England at the head of his troops to remove the Queen's advisers. Something of this reached Elizabeth and she wrote; "We do charge you, as you tender our pleasure, that you adventure not to come out of that Kingdom."

Essex's army was now reduced to less than 5,000 men. With some difficulty he obtained from the Queen a reinforcement of 2,000 men and marched into Ulster. On September 5 he met Tyrone encamped with a large army in the County of Louth. Instead of a battle he held a conference with Tyrone, for whom he was no match in war or diplomacy, and arranged an armistice with the promise of large concessions. A few days afterwards he received another angry letter from the Queen explicitly forbidding him to grant any terms without her permission. Thereupon Essex deserted his post and reached London on September 28.

Essex's gross insubordination in leaving Ireland, when affairs were so disordered, together with his other faults could not be passed over. He was placed under arrest and confined to his room. Next day he was examined by the Council. He was asked to explain why he had left Ireland without leave; why he had made so many idle knights there, contrary to the express desire of the queen; why he had written such presumptuous letters to Her Majesty; and how he had dared to enter Her Majesty's bedroom. The last offence was not the least. Miss Strickland pointed out that this impertinence was unlikely to be forgiven by "a royal coquette of sixty-eight, who had been surprised by Essex at her private morning toilet, undighted and uncoifed, in the most mortifying state of disarray, with her thin grey locks dishevelled and hanging about her haggard countenance, ere she had time to deliberate in which of her eighty wigs of various hues it would please her to receive the homage of her deceitful courtiers that day."

Angry though the Queen was—she never saw Essex

again after the first day of his return from Ireland—she showed the hot-headed Earl as much consideration as was compatible with the gravity of his offence.

While a State prisoner Essex had been dangerously ill. The French ambassador, M. Boississe, at King Henry's request had interceded with the Queen for him, and she had so far relented that she desired his eight doctors should hold a consultation on his health, and send her their opinion. On receiving a grave report, the Queen sent her own physician, Dr. James, to the Earl with a kindly message. Her attitude subsequently became sterner towards him; and it is conjectured that this was due to Cecil informing her of Essex's secret correspondence through his sister Lady Rich with the King of Scots. Nothing could have incensed the Queen more than Essex's salutations to King James and proffered advice to claim the succession to the English Crown. Yet through the mediation of Francis Bacon, the Queen altered her first intention to have Essex tried by the Star Chamber.

She delayed his trial until June, 1600, allowing him in the meantime a certain amount of freedom, and then the court of eighteen commissioners were empowered to pass "censure", but not judgment. The court condemned Essex to forfeit the offices which he held by patent from the Crown and to remain a prisoner at Her Majesty's pleasure. The Queen hoped that this sentence would humble his arrogant spirit and that he would sue for her forgiveness. Essex, being self-willed and obstinate, only begged to be dismissed and professed himself willing to live in retirement with his wife, his friends and his books in the country, a peaceful mirage which his restless mind could only have contemplated for a day or two. Even so, the Queen ordered his release from custody on August 26, but he was forbidden to appear at Court.

Essex could never be wise. If he had kept quiet and shown submission, he would probably have been forgiven and might even have been taken into favour again.

The Queen spent the summer of 1600 chiefly at Oatlands and Nonsuch. In September she was hawking, sometimes at Hanworth and sometimes in the New Forest. In spite of her advancing age she struggled to keep continually active and to go through all the fatigues of state visits and ceremonies. Sir Robert Sidney speaks of this struggle and her calling for a staff to support her, in a letter to Sir John Harrington and adds:

> "I do see the Queen often; she doth wax weak through the late troubles, and Burghley's death doth often draw tears down her goodly cheeks. She walketh out but little, meditates much alone, and sometimes writes in private to her best friends."

Francis Bacon continued to intercede on behalf of his friend Essex, but was one day informed by the Queen that she had received some dutiful letters from the Earl, which at first had made her relent towards him. On reading further she found that they only amounted to a petition for a continuation of his patent for a monopoly of sweet wines. She looked into the matter and found the value of the privilege was £50,000 per annum. She refused the request, which Essex deeply in debt unwisely renewed, and took the revenue from sweet wines for her treasury, remarking that when horses became unmanageable it was necessary to stint them in their corn. After this she received Bacon's pleas on behalf of the Earl with coldness, and he made no further effort in this direction. Indeed it was now dangerous to do so for Harrington, who presented one of the Earl's petitions to the Queen remarked "that he had nearly been wrecked on the Essex coast."

As for Essex, instead of retiring to the country, he went down the path of his tragic destiny. His language about the Queen, who had shown him so much consideration was unpardonable and ungrateful. He spoke of her as an "old woman, crooked both in body and mind." He made a secret league with King James, who when he became King of England always spoke of him as "my martyr, Essex." His house in the Strand became the meeting-place of malcontents and desperadoes with whom he discussed his grievances. Trusting in his popularity, he plotted to seize Whitehall Palace and the Tower, to coerce the Queen into dismissing his enemies, notably Cecil, Raleigh and Cobham, and to favour the succession of the King of Scots with himself as Lieutenant-General of the Kingdom. The chief men associated with this rash scheme were the Earl of Southampton, Sir Christopher Blount, Essex's stepfather, Sir John Davis and Sir Charles Danvers.

And here for a tantalizing moment the figure of William Shakespeare may have emerged on the stage of high and dangerous politics. For Shakespeare had the Earl of Southampton for his patron and one of Essex's adherents, Sir Gilly Merrick, paid for *King Richard II* to be played as useful propaganda on the afternoon before the Earl's conspiracy came to a head. Professor E. Dowden considered it was very unlikely that this play was Shakespeare's, but Rowse and others refer to it as "Shakespeare's play". Inasmuch as the play concerned the deposing of a king, Essex, or some of his fellow conspirators may have contemplated deposing Queen Elizabeth in favour of King James. Elizabeth herself had no doubts of Essex's intention. When subsequently William Lambarde presented his *Pandecta*, written in Latin, of the documents in the Tower to the Queen, she cast her eye down the list of reigns of the kings and said, "I am Richard II. Know ye not that?"

All the plans of the conspirators were known to Cecil through his excellent secret service, and as the plot neared fruition Essex received a summons to attend the Council, while the guard was redoubled at the palace. He pleaded illness as an excuse for not obeying the summons and decided to act immediately. On Sunday, February 8, 1601, his friends to the number of 300 assembled at his house, and the Lord Keeper Egerton, the Earl of Worcester, the Lord Chief Justice and others soon afterwards came to know the meaning of this gathering. Essex said he was defending his life, and without listening to their expostulations hustled them into a room where they were kept prisoners. Sword in hand, he then rushed into the street, followed by Southampton, Rutland, Sandys, Mounteagle and most of his adherents. They were joined on the way by the Earl of Bedford and Lord Cromwell with 200 men.

This improvised band reached the City. Here Essex expected as the popular hero to be joined by the citizens, but the streets were comparatively empty, the Lord Mayor and Corporation kept away and only a few of the common folk cried "God bless your honour." Essex rode along shouting in vain "For the Queen, my mistress, a plot is laid for my life." Crestfallen he returned to his house, where shortly afterwards he was besieged by the Queen's forces.

At night Essex and Southampton with their followers surrendered to Sir Robert Sidney on promise of a fair trial and after a night spent at Lambeth Palace the two ringleaders went to the Tower. Their trial followed and Essex was found guilty of high treason and condemned to death. It was a bitter blow to Essex to see his former friend, Francis Bacon rise to refute his defence at the trial. Essex declined to sue to the Queen for his life, which she afterwards told Biron, the envoy of Henry IV she might have granted him, "but that neither his friends nor relations could prevail on him to ask it." The story of the ring which the Countess of Nottingham failed to deliver to the Queen is unauthentic. Biron also was to lose his head through plotting against his sovereign.

On February 25, 1601, Essex was executed acknowledging the justice of his punishment. Southampton was kept in prison, and on March 17, Sir Christopher Blount and Sir Charles Danvers were beheaded.

During the revolt, when all around her were apprehensive, Queen Elizabeth was sustained by her splendid courage. She even wished to go and oppose the insurgents saying "that not one of them would dare to meet a single glance of her eye. They would flee at the very notice of her approach." On the day when Essex was executed she sat unconcernedly playing the virginals. She had no doubt that Essex had received the due punishment for his presumptuous crime, for when her "good and honest Lambarde" said: "such a wicked imagination was determined by a most unkind gentleman, the most adorned creature that ever your Majesty made," she replied, "He that will forget God will also forget his benefactors."

Elizabeth sorrowed for Essex, but it was not, as many have thought, because she had signed his death-warrant. She never doubted the justice of her decision. It was because once more her craving for affection had been made a thing of nought. In her lonely old age with Leicester, Burghley and Hatton dead, she had hoped to make of Essex an adopted son who would love and respect her and who, if unfitted for the highest offices of State, would nevertheless be her confidant and faithful servant. It was not to be. Essex had taken everything she had given him, he had been rude and arrogant, regarded her as a doting old woman, whose wishes could be disregarded, and in the end had risen in rebellion. He had mistaken her forbearance for weakness and imagined he could overthrow one of the greatest and most popular of Queens. In the heyday of his favour he was sometimes all she could have wished, but when he was absent she could not help wondering whether he was playing a part. Their personal relationship was always a most difficult one and was bound to end in disaster, for Elizabeth would not be the instrument of her favourite's ambition against the best interests of the country, and he would not be schooled into submission.

Now in the declining years of her life Elizabeth was more than ever the lonely Queen.

XV

The Queen's Medical Case-Sheet

THIS chapter is devoted to consideration of Queen Elizabeth's health. First, a general account is given of her appearance and qualities. Next comes her family history. Afterwards the question of congenital defect is discussed at some length, because its existence or non-existence is of supreme importance. The fourth section of the chapter treats of the illnesses and minor ailments from which the Queen suffered in the course of her long life. The chapter concludes with a general commentary upon her health.

The Queen's Appearance and Qualities

How Elizabeth looked to her subjects is gathered from contemporary portraits and accounts. As regards portraits, Elizabethan portraiture until recently has been regarded as mediocre. The portraits are flat and without shadows. The dresses of the sitters ornamented and decorative. The Art Critic of *The Times* observes (August 24, 1953);

> "Hilliard, in his treatise on limning, constantly refers to his dislike of shading and of those artists who 'smut' their work with shadows. No doubt he meant his precepts to be applied to his own art of the miniature rather than to painting in general, but in the larger Elizabethan portraits his rule is nevertheless almost always obeyed."

Horace Walpole regarded Elizabeth as a creature made by her clothes. He said:

THE QUEEN'S MEDICAL CASE-SHEET

"A pale Roman nose, a head of hair loaded with crowns and powdered with diamonds, a vast ruff, a vaster farthingale, and a bushel of pearls are the features by which everybody knows at once the portraits of Queen Elizabeth."

It has also been noted that the Queen issued a proclamation commanding that her portraits should in future all be copied from one approved portrait. This proclamation was clearly never strictly enforced for we have a diversity of portraits of the Queen, some looking right, some full face, etc. As Mr. Rowse has pointed out, the two portraits of her in the National Gallery are quite different, and there are a number of other different portraits of her. One may quote as examples, the gaily-hued portrait at Hatfield, the Coronation portrait at Warwick Castle, the Woburn portrait and the portrait at Hardwick in which traditionally the Queen was painted in a dress presented to her by Bess of Hardwick. The majority of the portraits were painted when Elizabeth had become Queen, including the beautiful miniatures by Nicholas Hilliard, and represent her in the late twenties or early thirties, in middle age and in old age. There is one portrait in the Royal Collection at Windsor Castle which represents her when she was eighteen or twenty years of age. It shows her slender well-shaped hands, of which she was proud, clasping a book and depicts a sedate, good-featured young woman.

Elizabeth was of middle height, about 5 feet, 3 inches. Her figure in youth was slender and upright, but she was thin to the verge of emaciation and bent in late life. She probably was often undernourished, for she took a good deal of exercise and ate little, sometimes refusing food altogether, as she did in her last illness. Her face was long, her lips thin, her nose straight and in old age "a little hooked". Hentzner, the German traveller who saw her in 1598, says that her eyes were small, yet black and pleasant. Her teeth were yellow and black through dental caries from which she suffered ("a defect the English seem subject to from their too great use of sugar".) In old age many of her teeth were missing, so that her speech was indistinct when she spoke quickly. She always had a natural dignity and usually spoke graciously to her subjects. Her voice was deep and sometimes gruff. Her hair was auburn inclining to red. When she was about 31 years old, she seems to have become bald after her severe attack of smallpox, for in subsequent references her red wigs are mentioned. Previously to 1565 she had her own hair, as Melville, the Scottish ambassador relates in his memoirs. She inherited her red hair from Henry VIII and her pale complexion and black eyes from her mother, Anne Boleyn. From her father too, she inherited a love of learning and scholarship, intellectual gifts, statecraft, autocracy tempered with the knowledge that she must secure popularity with her subjects, and those outbursts of invective and anger in which she sometimes indulged; it is alleged she threw her shoe at Walsingham! From her mother she inherited her vanity, her coquetry and her liking to be admired and wooed, redeemed in her case by an admixture of prudence.

Elizabeth greatly admired her father and from her infancy strove to model herself upon him. As she said in her famous speech at Tilbury: "I know I have but the body of a weak and feeble woman; but I have the heart and stomach of a King and of a King of England too."

M. Hurault de Maisse, special French envoy from King Henry IV, gives a picturesque and detailed account of the Queen in old age. (See *De Maisse's Journal*, translated and edited by G. B. Harrison and R. A. Jones, London, 1931.)

Family History

The Tudors appear to have had an hereditary predisposition to tuberculosis. (For a detailed account of this question, see *Henry VIII: A Difficult Patient*, Chap. II 25.) Henry VII apparently had tuberculosis which affected his joints and "wasted his lungs". It was associated with asthma, as not infrequently happens. Prince Arthur, his eldest son, was subject to repeated attacks of fever and coughing and was probably infected with tuberculosis by his father. Arthur died at the age of sixteen during an epidemic of sweating sickness from which his young bride, Catherine of Aragon, also suffered, but recovered. Prince Arthur's frame, debilitated by consumption, lacked sufficient resisting power to cope with the disease.

Although Henry VIII was free from active tuberculosis, two of his sons died of this disease. Henry, Duke of Richmond, a natural son by Elizabeth Blount, lady-in-waiting to Catherine of Aragon, died of "rapid consumption at the age of 17." Edward VI, Henry's legitimate son by Jane Seymour, from four years of age when he had a quartan fever, was a delicate child, thin and weakly. In April, 1552, the boy king wrote in his journal: "I fell sike of the mesels and the small pokkes," The two diseases, measles and smallpox were often confused, and King Edward probably had a severe attack of measles. The infectious malady, at all events, caused the seeds of tuberculosis to break out in his frail body. He suffered from fever, nights-sweats, "a racking cough", with sputum occasionally tinged with blood, and died in 1553, aged fifteen years and nine months. It appears that pulmonary tuberculosis was accompanied by Raynaud's disease, for the King's fingers and toes fell off.

Mary and Elizabeth seem to have resisted tuberculosis. Queen Mary was always delicate and subject to indigestion and "stomach attacks". Her strength was reduced by the frequent bleedings ordered by her physicians. The actual cause of her death, in the opinion of Sir Spencer Wells, was an ovarian cyst and dropsy. Dr. James Rae notes that a strange fever was prevalent in the last two years of her reign. This was apparently an epidemic of influenza from which, he considers, the Queen died after two months of illness. It has been suggested that Elizabeth's terminal illness, which was some disease of the throat, attended with swelling and sputum which made speaking difficult, was tuberculous laryngitis, and that she suffered from a

fibrotic form of pulmonary tuberculosis. As stated subsequently, streptococcal infection of the tonsils with
quinsy followed by an attack of influenza would better
explain her terminal illness. "If she had the Tudor
hereditary predisposition to tuberculosis, it did not
appreciably limit her activities or shorten her days."

From Henry VIII, her father, Queen Elizabeth inherited her strong constitution and her intellectual powers.
"He was a man of fine physique, a famous athlete and
healthy and robust up to middle life. At 22 years of age,
the King contracted a severe attack of smallpox from
which he made a good recovery." Elizabeth at the age of
29 also suffered severely from smallpox and recovered.
"At 29, he had malaria (benign tertian) and thereafter, or
at all events up to 50 years of age, he had recurrent attacks
of the disease." Elizabeth sometimes suffered from
febrile attacks and agues which may have been malaria.
"He was subject to catarrhs and severe headaches . . ."
Elizabeth had catarrh sometimes and Henry's headaches
may like hers have been due to migraine as well as to the
effects of a head injury at a tournament in 1524. King
Henry suffered from varicose ulcers of the leg. (See
Henry VIII: A Difficult Patient, Chap. X.) Elizabeth
probably inherited his tendency to varicose veins, for, as
stated later, she suffered for nine years from an ulcer of
the leg (*vide infra*).

Elizabeth's mother, Anne Boleyn, appears to have been
a healthy young woman. She was greedy in her diet. On
one occasion, she told Thomas Heneage at supper that
"she wished she had some of Wolsey's meat as carps,
shrimps and others," which hint was duly conveyed to
the Cardinal. Elizabeth, on the other hand, was most
abstemious.

Henry VIII secretly married Anne Boleyn at the end of
January or beginning of February, 1533. On September
7 she gave birth to Elizabeth. In 1534 Queen Anne had a
miscarriage, probably at six months, and again in 1535.
In January, 1536, she aborted of a male foetus "about
three and a half months old". This she assigned to the

shock of being abruptly informed of a severe accident to her husband at a tournament. In the opinion of Sir Eardley Holland and two other eminent obstetricians, Queen Anne's still-births can be ascribed to a condition such as recurrent toxaemia of pregnancy.

The Question of Congenital Defect

Because Queen Elizabeth never married, it has been asserted both by some contemporaries and subsequently, that she had some bodily defect which rendered her incapable of marriage. Ben Jonson (1572–1637), in his conversations with William Drummond of Hawthornden (1618–19), alluded to this rumour and added that "at the coming over of Monsieur (the Duke of Alençon), there was a French chirurgeon who offered to operate on her, yett fear stayed her and his death." Ben Jonson, either in his cups or out of them, is no reliable authority, while there is plenty of evidence that Elizabeth was a fully and completely formed woman and regarded as eligible for marriage. Henry VIII, Somerset, Northumberland and Queen Mary all contemplated marrying her off to some foreign prince, and one can be sure that in those days the subject of her physical fitness for marriage was duly considered. King Philip II, who must have heard many intimate details about Elizabeth from his wife, Queen Mary, desired in his wife's lifetime to marry Elizabeth to his friend, Philibert, Duke of Savoy, and after Mary's death proposed to wed her himself. No student of the State papers of the reign should entertain doubt on this question. In 1566, for instance, when the Archduke Charles was again a candidate for Elizabeth's hand and the Earl of Leicester was again the difficulty, Cecil in a careful minute (*Hatfield MSS.*) drew up a table of the necessary points to be considered, and contrasted the merits of the two suitors. One of his headings relates to the likelihood to bear children, most important for the succession to the throne. Of the Archduke he writes: "His father, Ferdinando, hath therein been blessed with multitude of children. His brother, Maximilian, hath plenty. His sisters of Bavaria, Cleves, Mantua and Poland have already many children." The comment on Leicester is "*Nuptae steriles. . . .* Himself married and no children." The minute implies that there was no doubt in Cecil's mind that if Elizabeth married the Archduke, the marriage was likely to be fruitful. He, as the Queen's confidential chief minister, would have medical assurance on this point.

It is true that de Feria, the Spanish ambassador, writing to Philip II about the Archduke's marriage in 1559, said he had discovered that the Queen was not likely to have children. He was using this supposed discovery as an inducement to the match, suggesting that Charles or his brother, Ferdinand, if married to Elizabeth, might make himself master of the kingdom at her death; but he qualifies the statement by the words: *Si las espias no mi mientes quo no creo*, "if the spies do not lie, which I do not believe." (April 29, 1579. *MS. Simancas.*) They were only repeating the tittle-tattle of the courtiers, who supposed, as others have done after them, it was Elizabeth's knowledge that she would be childless that made her so averse to marriage.

Elizabeth, herself, never doubted her physical capacity for marriage. On two occasions, at least, she seriously contemplated matrimony. She would have married the Lord Admiral, Thomas Seymour, if the Privy Council's consent had been obtained. She earnestly desired to marry Lord Robert Dudley and only abandoned the project when she saw her people were strongly opposed to the match. Also, the hint dropped by Cecil in the sense of his minute of 1566 may have influenced her, for it was not until after Leicester's marriage to his second wife that he had a legitimate son.

More than once, in speeches to Parliament on the subject of her marriage, the Queen spoke of having children as its likely result.

In 1579, when the conditions of the Queen's alliance with the Duke of Alençon were seriously entered upon, as a preliminary, Elizabeth consulted a physician (probably

Dr. Robert Jacob) on the subject of having children and received a favourable answer (*Decifrada de Don Bernardino*, January 15, 1579: *MS. Simancas.*) Queen Catherine de Medici on each occasion when negotiating an alliance with Elizabeth, firstly for Charles IX, secondly for the Duke of Anjou (afterwards Henry III), and thirdly for the Duke of Alençon, made careful inquiries not only as to Elizabeth's morals, but also as to her fitness for marriage, and was reassured by the French ambassadors at the English Court and by her unofficial envoy, Cavalcanti, on both points. On several occasions, while Elizabeth was still of marriageable age, French and Spanish ambassadors consulted the Queen's physicians as to her capacity for bearing children and were fully assured in this respect.

A number of additional instances might be extracted from State Papers. Elizabeth could not have used the possibility of her marriage as a diplomatic card of trumps, if any physical defect had existed, or even if there had been serious doubts on the question.

Illnesses

Queen Elizabeth, except for the illnesses and indispositions now to be recorded, up to 1602 always enjoyed good health "thanks to her exact temperance both as to wine and diet, which she used to say was the noblest part of physic." The first references to illness in the State Papers are obtained from Mrs. Ashley, Elizabeth's governess, and relate to the year 1548 when Elizabeth was nearly fifteen years of age.

"She was furst syk about mydsomer." This is dated February 4 1549 and refers to the midsummer of 1548 (*S. P. Dom. Edw. VI*, Vol. VI, No. 20). Other references by Mrs. Ashley relate to September, 1548. One is: "Sche beyng seke yn hyr bed." We do not know the nature of this illness, but it was evidently of some severity for in October, the Princess wrote to Somerset as follows:

"Many lines will not serve to render the least part of the thanks that your grace hath deserved of me, most especially for that you have been careful of my health; and sending unto me not only your comfortable letters, but also physicians, as Doctor Bill, whose diligence and pain has been a great part of my recovery." (*S. P. Dom. Edw. VI*, Vol. VI.)

The physician especially mentioned here was Thomas Bille, M.D. Cantab. (1534) and Pavia, F.R.C.P. He was physician to Henry VIII and after that King's death, became physician to Edward VI, from whom, in 1546–47, he received a grant of £100 per annum. He was also specially summoned to attend the Princess at Cheshunt in 1549 (*Athenae Cantab.*).

The years 1548 and the early part of 1549 were the times when Elizabeth was accused of being concerned in the Lord Admiral Seymour's plot. From the *Domestic State Papers of Edward VI*, Vol. VI, it would seem that the illness of the Princess in these years helped to exculpate both her and Mrs. Ashley from the more serious charges, as the latter was in constant attention on the invalid.

Attacks of Migraine

In letters to her brother, Edward VI, during the years 1549 to 1550, Elizabeth on several occasions complains of pains in the head which have prevented her from writing regularly. Thus in an undated letter she writes: "O King . . . the reason that you have not for so long a time seen any letters from me is . . . because the pain in my head precluded all modes of writing. . . . Truly, I am both ashamed and grieved that I must so often make excuses of this kind . . . I am somewhat restored to health."

In September, 1550, Thomas Parry writing to Cecil at Elizabeth's command says: "Her Grace has long been troubled with rheums (colds or catarrhs), but now thanks to the Lord! meetly well again, and shortly ye shall hear from Her Grace again."

The Princess herself wrote on April 21, 1552, to King Edward:

"I commit your Majesty to His hands, most humbly craving pardon of your Grace that I did write no sooner; desiring you to attribute the fault to my evil head, and not to my slothful hand." Wood: *Letters of Royal and Illustrious Ladies*, Vol. IV, p. 225.)

Another undated letter from Elizabeth to the King stated:

". . . A disease of the head and eyes has come upon me, which has so grievously troubled me ever since my coming to this abode, that, although I often attempted to write to your majesty, I have, even to this day, ever been recalled from my purpose and resolution. As this affection, by the aid of the great and good God, has now somewhat abated, I have considered that I ought no longer to defer the duty of writing." (Wood: *Ibid*, Vol. III, p. 234.)

On September 20, 1554, Sir Henry Bedingfield reported to the Council that Elizabeth said she had such pain in her head that she could not write more that day. On the following morning she washed her head.

Elizabeth suffered from time to time from these severe attacks of headache. On April 22, 1580, de Castelnau wrote to Paris from London:

"The Queen . . . has also been a little ill and has always kept to her chamber since I saw her, because of a headache and a nervous headache."

Most physicians are of opinion that these headaches associated with disturbances of vision, like those of the first Duke of Marlborough, were probably attacks of migraine. The word migraine is a contraction of *hemi-crania*, the intense attacks of headache being usually localized to one half of the head. The malady is sometimes hereditary and Henry VIII suffered from headaches which as stated may have been migraine. It is usually seen in intellectual people, and Elizabeth's studious youth and life predisposed to the condition. Commonest in young adults and middle life, the attacks often diminish in frequency and severity in later life or cease entirely. This was apparently the case with the Queen's headaches, for after 1580, when she was 46 years of age, they seem to have ceased. The cause of migraine is unknown, but may be due to some disturbance of the brain's blood supply, or of the endocrine system. Except for short periods of temporary incapacity, migraine is quite compatible with an active and often highly intellectual life.

Acute Nephritis

Miss Strickland in her life of Elizabeth (p. 66, ed. of 1842) states that the Princess was ill in 1553. On December 6 of the same year, Elizabeth was travelling to Ashridge, but on the way became so ill that Queen Mary had to send her horse litter to convey her thither. (Letter of Simon Renard to Charles V of date, December 17, 1553). The illness may have been an attack of scarlet fever, for, as already related in Chapter III, in January, 1554, at the time of Sir Thomas Wyatt's rebellion, she was suffering from swelling of the face and dropsy. This was almost certainly an attack of acute nephritis (inflammation of the kidneys) which may arise independently but was frequently a complication of scarlet fever. The malady prevented her obeying Mary's command to come to London conveyed in a letter of date January 26. She sent her sister a message "that she was too ill at present to travel and prayed her majesty's forbearance for a few days." (See Strype, *Mem*. iii, Part I, p. 127). The officials of her household, at the same time, sent a letter to the Lord Chancellor saying:

"We attend on my Lady Elizabeth's Grace our mistress, in hope of her amendment to repair towards the Queen's Highness, whereof we have as yet no apparent likelihood of health."

At Elizabeth's request and to verify that her illness was not feigned, Queen Mary sent two of her physicians, Dr. George Owen and Dr. Thomas Wendy to prescribe for her and to report on her condition. They were both men with high medical reputations and well known to Elizabeth as royal physicians, first to her father and afterwards to Edward VI and Mary.

George Owen, M.D., Oxon, F.R.C.P., was born in the diocese of Worcester. He became probationer fellow of Merton College in 1519. Soon after 1527 he was appointed physician to Henry VIII. He practised obstetrics as well as medicine, and is believed to have brought Edward VI into the world by caesarean section. He was one of the witnesses to Henry VIII's will. The King left him a legacy of £100. Owen also had lands and houses near Oxford including Cumnor Hall. He was President of the Royal College of Physicians in 1553 and 1554, and he helped to obtain the Act, 1 Mary, for the confirmation and enlargement of the powers of the College. He wrote a medical treatise entitled, "A Meet Diet for the New Ague set forth by Mr. Owen," Fol. Lond. 1558. He died in 1558, the year of Elizabeth's accession and was buried in St. Stephen's Church, Walbrook.

Thomas Wendy, M.D., Cantab., F.R.C.P., was educated at Gonville Hall, Cambridge. He took a degree of M.D. abroad and was incorporated thereon at Cambridge in 1527. Henry VIII granted him the manor and rectory of Haslingfield, Cambridgeshire, part of the possessions of the dissolved monastery of St. Mary of York. Together with Dr. George Owen and Dr. Robert Huicke he attested the King's will, receiving a legacy of £100. He received the same sum annually as physician to Edward VI. On November 11, 1548, he was appointed one of the Commissioners to visit Cambridge and Eton. Admitted Fellow in 1551, he became an Elect of the College of Physicians in 1552. *The College Annals* describe him as "a learned, wise and prudent doctor." He died in his sixtieth year in 1560 and was buried in the Church of Haslingfield.

The physicians arrived at Ashridge on January 28. They found Elizabeth ill in bed, but reported to the Queen's Commissioners, Lord Admiral William Howard, Sir Edward Hastings and Sir Thomas Cornwallis, who came on February 11, "the state of her body to be such, that without danger to her person" the Commissioners might require her to make the journey. Elizabeth, weak and ill, desired some longer respite, but was persuaded to travel in the Queen's litter. On February 13 "they had her forth as she was, verie faint and feeble, and in such case that she was ready to swound three or four times between them. . . ." She was sick in the litter. At Highgate, as previously mentioned, her limbs were so swollen that she remained there a week. She entered London on February 22. De Noailles, the French ambassador, stated: "she is so swollen and weakened that she is a pitiful sight," and on February 24 wrote to Paris:

"Madame Elizabeth, sister of the said lady, arrived Thursday in this city, so ill with dropsy or some swelling which has attacked her whole body and even her face, that those who have seen her do not promise her long to live. I believe that on account of this illness she will not be able to accompany her sister, but will remain here, if she live that long." (*De Noailles*, Vol. III, 86, 87.)

Simon Renard's report of her pallor, due to the anaemia of nephritis has already been cited. On March 12, de Noailles reports:

"They tell me that Madame Elizabeth, sister of the Queen, will be soon thrust into the Tower, no matter how ill she may be; and she almost entirely swollen." (*De Noailles*, Vol. III, 125.)

She was so thrust and the damp conditions of her

imprisonment favoured the continuance or recurrence of the nephritis when she went to Woodstock under Sir Henry Bedingfield's charge. Reference to this condition may be found in the *Bedingfield Papers*. For instance:

"My lady Elizabeth's grace continually in helthe accustomed with thonlye swellyng in the visage at certain times excepted." (June 9, 1554. *Bedingfield Papers*, p. 174.)

The Council on this report consulted Dr. Owen; he gave a medical report on her case to Sir Henry Bedingfield as follows:

"Plesyth yt that I have understonde by my l. off the quenys highnes most honorabyll counsell that my ladye Elizabeths grace ys trobled with ye swellyng In hir face & also of her armes and hands. Syr, the occasion off theis affects ys off that hyr graces bodye ys replenyshed with mannye colde and waterysh humors, wch wyll not be taken awaye but by pergacons mete and convenient for that prpose. But for as moche as thys tyme off the yere, and specially the distemperaunce off the wether, does not permit to minister purgacons, her grace must have some pacience untyll the tyme off the yere shall bee more meter for medisyns . . ." (June 20, 1554. *Bedingfield Papers*.)

In this same month of June, Sir Henry forwarded Elizabeth's request to the Council for a "phesician" to be sent to her:

"First . . . that my l. Elizabeth's grace ys daylye vexed with the swelling in the face and other parts of her bodye, and graunte that shee may have doctour Huycke, accompanied with doctour Wendye or doctour Owen, the quenes maiesties phesicons, immediatlye to repare unto hir, whoese counsell she velouslye desyreth, to devise remedie for swellyng in her face and other parts of hir bodye, wch I dooe see hir grace often vexed with all . . . ' (Bedingfield to Gage, June 29, 1554.)

Presumably the request was complied with. On July 16, Bedingfield reports to the Council that her face on Saturday was somewhat swollen, and on the same night she said she was very ill at ease.

On October 21, Elizabeth through Sir Henry asks again for the Queen's physicians, "for to mynister to hir physike, bryninge of their owne chose oon exparte Surgion to let hir gracs blode, yf the said doctours or twoe of them shall thinke yt so good, uppon the vewe of hyr sewte at their comynge. . . . Hyr grace desyerethe that thys hyr sewte may have spede answer whereby she maye inioye thys tyme of the yere apte for thys purpose afforesaide. . . . (Sir Henry Bedingfield to the Council.)

On October 29, the physicians arrived at Woodstock with a surgeon, who bled Elizabeth next morning through the arm, and in the afternoon through the foot, after which, Sir Henry reports: "as far as I see or here, she doethe reasonablye well." In the following year (1555) she was again ill, and the Queen's physicians again came and had her bled.

After this, the nephritis seems to have cleared, although in 1556 the French ambassador in a letter to the King of France reports that the poor Dame Elizabeth is unlikely to live long as she is suffering from "jaundice and the yellow sickness", as well as from a shortness of breath, which she has been suffering from "ever since the time when her sister began to maltreat her" (d'Acqs to King of France). She may have had an attack of catarrhal jaundice this year. The shortness of breath was probably due to some asthmatical complication, aggravated by the damp conditions of her imprisonment. It may be observed that both Dr. Owen and Dr. Wendy knew that damp was prejudicial to her disease, for in the Commissioners' report from Ashridge to Queen Mary occurs the following:

"Her Grace much desireth that she may have a

lodging, at her coming to court, somewhat farther from the water than she had at her last being there; which your physicians, considering the state of her body, thinketh very meet, who have travailed very earnestly with her grace, both before our coming and after in this matter."

In spite of this medical advice, Queen Mary sent her sister to a prison on the Thames.

The only reference to a further possible recurrence of nephritis is in a dispatch from de Quadra, the Spanish ambassador in London, to King Philip of date September 23, 1561, to this effect:

"What is of most importance now is that the Queen (according to what I hear) is becoming dropsical, and has already begun to swell extraordinarily. I have been advised of this from three different sources and by a person who has the opportunity of being an eye witness. To all appearances she is failing and is extremely thin and the colour of a corpse." De Quadra then adds that "both the Marchioness of Northampton and Lady Cobham consider the Queen is in a dangerous condition, beyond doubt, and if they are mistaken he is mistaken also. He can obtain no more precise intelligence."

This is only hearsay and was probably untrue. Mary Queen of Scots heard that the Queen's Majesty had been "for a space evle disposed". (Randolph to Cecil, July 15, 1562). At all events, Elizabeth's good constitution triumphed over recurrences of the nephritis. As sometimes happens, there was a prolonged period of convalescence. She never showed symptoms of the chronic form of nephritis.

Acute Infectious Diseases

Owing to the sheltered life which Elizabeth led in early youth, she does not seem to have had the common infectious diseases until later in life, although, presumably, she had measles as a child. At the age of 29, she was attacked by smallpox at Kingston in October, 1562. The attack was a serious one, and it was expected she would die. De Quadra wrote to the Duchess of Parma (October 16, 1562):

"The Queen has been ill of fever at Kingston, and the malady has now turned to smallpox. The eruption cannot come out and she is in great danger." On the following day he wrote to the Duchess: "she was all but gone."

For three days it was doubtful whether the Queen would recover. At the crisis of the attack she was unconscious and speechless for two hours. During this time of uncertainty, the Council was in constant session, and twice debated the question of the succession without coming to any conclusion, opinions differing greatly. On the third day, Her Majesty was somewhat better. Martin Kyernbeck, *Medicus*, apparently a Swedish doctor, in London, informed Nicholas Guildenstiern, the Swedish Chancellor on October 20, that the Queen was not free from symptomatic fever, as part of the poisonous matter was still between the flesh and the skin. De Quadra on October 25 told the Duchess of Parma:

"She is now out of bed and is only attending to the marks on her face to avoid disfigurement."

As a result of the smallpox, the Queen became bald soon after her thirtieth year, and thereafter wore a wig. On her recovery she was much annoyed to hear the question of the succession had been debated by the Council, although it was a contingency they were bound to consider. Her grave illness also caused the matter to be raised in Parliament.

Ten years later, when Elizabeth was 39 years old, she had another acute infectious disease while staying at Hampton Court. This was diagnosed as a second attack of smallpox, for Cecil writes in his diary (October 4, 1572):

"The Queen's Majesty appeared to have the Small-poxs at Hampton-court; but she recovered spedely."

Fénélon, the French ambassador, reports on October 13: "Elizabeth ill with chicken- or small-pox." The attack was in all probability one of chicken-pox, a disease which is severe and even today mistaken sometimes for smallpox when arising in older persons. On October 15, Sir Thomas Smith wrote to Lord Burghley:

"Her majestie hathe bene very sick this last night, so that my Lord of Leicester did watche with her all night. This morning, thanks be to God! she is very well. It was but a soden pang. I pray God long to preserve her. These be shrewde alarmes."

Finally, we have the Queen's own account of her illness as set out in a letter to the Earl of Shrewsbury of date, October 22, 1572:

"We perceave that you had heard of som late siknes wherewith we were visited. True it is that we were about XIII days paste distempered as commonly happenith in the begynning of a fever; but after twoo or three daies, without any great inward siknes, ther began to appere certain red spotts in som parte of our face, likely to prove the small pox; but thanked be God, contrary to the expectation of our phisycians & all others about us, the same so vanished awaye as within foure or fyve dayes passed no token almost appered: and at this day, we thank God, we are so free from any token or marke of any suche disease that none can conjecture any suche thing. So as by this you may perceave what war our sikness, and in what good estate we be."

Mauvissière, the French ambassador, recorded that when Queen Elizabeth was 46, about July, 1580, she had an attack of whooping cough, accompanied with high fever. She must have contracted it from some child. Possibly, she herself had not had the disease as a child, or if she had, her immunity had lapsed as often happens with elderly people.

Ulcer in the Leg

King Henry VIII suffered from an ulcer on the thigh which Thomas Vicary, his surgeon, cured. Afterwards, the condition recurred and both legs were affected. The ulcer, in the opinion of Sir D'Arcy Power, Mr. Alban Doran and other authorities was a varicose ulcer associated with varicose veins. The persistence of the ulcers was favoured by the wearing of garters and thigh armour.

Probably, Elizabeth inherited her father's tendency to varicose veins, for on July 27, 1569, Fénélon reported that with bad health and an affliction which she has in her legs she will not be long-lived. The Duke of Anjou, afterwards King Henry III of France, in 1570 told his mother, Catherine de Medici, "that he would not marry her (Elizabeth), for she was not only an old creature, but had a sore leg." In June of this same year, Cecil told Fénélon that the Queen must not overdo herself because she was ill in her leg. A few days afterwards Fénélon had an audience of the Queen and found her "dressed like an invalid, having her leg *en repoz*." She told the ambassador about her affliction and lameness. De Espes in a dispatch to Madrid stated: "The illness of the Queen is caused by an open ulcer above the ankle which prevents her walking."

In July and August, on account of the ulcer, Elizabeth made her progress through Buckinghamshire and Oxfordshire in a coach. During this progress the leg was so painful that she had to rest it for a fortnight or more at Chenies, Lord Bedford's house.

In May, 1571, Elizabeth heard of the Duke of Anjou's remark about her leg and complained to Fénélon. On May 10 she told him, "that notwithstanding the evil report that had been made of her leg, she had not neglected to dance, on the preceding Sunday, at the Marquis of Northampton's wedding, so she hoped that

Monsieur would not find himself cheated in marrying a cripple, instead of a lady of proper paces."

What suffering this dance cost her is not recorded; it is only another proof of her determination not to be regarded as an invalid. She was better in June, for Leicester told Fénélon, "that he had never seen her in better health or spirits; and that she would not go out in her coach any more to the chase, but on a fine large horse."

Although usually repudiating invalidism, Elizabeth sometimes used her state of health for diplomatic purposes, as when she told Fénélon in July of this year "that she very much feared that this young prince (the Duke of Alençon) would dislike her and, that she would not find herself sufficiently healthy or suitable for a young husband, and that she would like to postpone the proposal until she felt better."

During the Queen's attack of chicken-pox in 1572, de Guaras writing to the Duke of Alva said: "As she has an issue in the leg there is always some fear of her health."

It was then good treatment to keep an ulcer discharging. In 1578 this discharging ulcer in Queen Elizabeth's leg was said to be drying up, "nor know the physicians how to find a remedy for this mishap." (Salviati, Papal Nuncio in France to the Cardinal of Como, January 6, 1578.) Mary Queen of Scots, who had no cause to love "Bess of Hardwick", the wife of the Earl of Shrewsbury, wrote to Queen Elizabeth in November 1584, "that four or five years ago, when both Queens were ill, the Countess of Shrewsbury told her that Elizabeth's malady "came from the closing of a fistula she had in one leg."

Previously, on August 30, 1566, de Silva wrote to King Philip II that the Queen was so troubled with her indisposition which is an issue on the shoulder, that she could not go to the chase. He also said that she had been previously indisposed; the issue in her shoulder may therefore have been due to a seton being inserted there as part of medical treatment. Alternatively, she may have had a pustule, carbuncle or abscess there which was discharging. The ulcer of the leg seems to have lasted about nine years. Like her father, for a long time Elizabeth would not give it the complete rest which would have cured it, and which her surgeons no doubt recommended.

Minor Ailments

Elizabeth suffered from occasional catarrhs, digestive disturbances and attacks of breathlessness and faintness, probably due to tight lacing and faulty corsets which unduly compressed the heart, lungs and upper abdomen. Elizabethan ladies of fashion were liable to these little derangements. Her meal times were irregular, for she ate when she was hungry and drank when she was thirsty. As a rule, she was abstemious in her diet to which contemporary writers attribute her longevity, but on occasions she had to partake of rich food at lengthy banquets. Fénélon states she could not see him in October, 1572, because she had a bad stomach owing to her having taken a little mithridate."* In March of the same year she had an attack of food-poisoning, ascribed to eating fish, though she herself ascribed it to neglecting regular purgation and venesection for three of four years which strict discipline her physicians had advised. The attack was a serious one, for both Leicester and Burghley watched for three entire nights at her bedside (Fénélon).

The Queen often complained of toothache. Her teeth were yellow, carious and black. Probably she had pyrrhoea. On several occasions she had to cancel audiences on account of toothache. In October, 1578, by the Queen's command, "Dr. Dee conferred with Dr. Bayley concerning her majesty's grievous pangs and pains caused by toothache and the rheum." Dr. Dee was an exceptional empiric, and, no doubt, Dr. Baily felt ethically justified in meeting him.

The Queen had attacks of "Mother", which was a term

* An antidote against poison, named from Mithridates, King of Pontus. It was also taken as a precaution against poisoning.

for hysteria. Leicester writing to Walsingham in November, 1572 states that the Queen, it was reported, was "troubled with a spice or show of Mother, but indeed not so: the fits that she hath had hath not been above a quarter of an hour, but yet this little thing in her hath bred strange brutes (*bruits*, rumours) at home." The short duration of the fits does not exclude hysteria as Leicester imagined. Dr. Needham in *Medela Medicinae*, 1665, speaks of "*Hysterica-passio* or the *Mother*, because it seizeth upon women, though men too have something like it."

According to Catherine de Medici's information (see Chapter X), Elizabeth occasionally went into trances which were possibly cataleptic. It has been argued that these obscure attacks may have been epileptic, but it is unlikely that her nervous system was diseased. It must be remembered that Elizabeth was a consummate actress, and used an hysterical attack or swoon to get out of awkward situations. She often slept badly, especially in her later years.

As is the case with many women, the Queen suffered from time to time from feminine ailments. We know that she did so suffer, because when Ivan the Terrible asked her to send an English physician to attend his wife in 1581, she selected Dr. Robert Jacob, and informed the Czar that Dr. Jacob was well skilled in female complaints and that she herself had often benefited by his advice. She would not willingly have parted with him if it had not been for the need of her beloved sister, the Czarina. She assured the Czarina that Dr. Jacob knew more about the situation of lying-in women than even the midwives themselves. (*Annals R.C.P.* in which the Queen's letters in her physician's favour are entered at length.)

Like her sister, Mary, Elizabeth was short-sighted, as the result of straining her eyes over black-letter volumes. This condition, uncorrected by glasses, helped to aggravate her migraine. From time to time she had attacks of fever and ague, possibly benign tertian malaria. In her later years she had rheumatism or fibrositis in her arm, which interfered with her riding on horseback, as M. de

Beaumont, the French ambassador, reported in 1602 to Henry IV. She also stooped a good deal, for Essex was unwise enough to say, "she being an old woman, was no less crooked in mind than in body."

Last Illness

By 1602, in spite of a brave attempt to carry on with her accustomed activities, Queen Elizabeth, aged 68, was a very old woman for those days. As J. R. Green wrote: "Death crept on, her face became haggard, and her frame shrank almost to a skeleton." Like Henry VIII in his last days, she was subject to fits of melancholy, which could no longer be dissipated, as in times past, by playing the virginals.

On January 12, 1603, she "sickened of a cold", and two days later removed from Whitehall to the Palace of Richmond "where she was well amended of the cold." From February 20 to March 7 she was ill with tonsillitis. Baker's *Chronicle* states: "At the beginning of her sickness the almonds of her jaws began to swell and her appetite failed her." An abscess or quinsy formed in her throat, and she experienced great difficulty in swallowing or speaking. The bursting of the abscess relieved her. The throat condition has been ascribed to Vincent's angina and even to tuberculous laryngitis on account of the Tudor family history, but it seems more probable that it can be explained by a septic infection of the throat, probably streptococcal and favoured by dental sepsis. Her mind was somewhat disordered, perhaps through fever, for she refused to go to bed. Dr. James Rae considers that influenza supervened, for "the 18th of March following, being Friday, she began to be very ill . . . and continued till Wednesday the 24th of March about three of the clock in the morning at which time she died." (*Somers Tracts*, XIV, 359.)

Strype in his life of Archbishop Whitgift observed that one of the Queen's physicians wrote about her mortal sickness. It would be interesting to read this report, for the medical details of Elizabeth's end are scanty. She left careful instructions that her body was not to be examined and that she was not to be embalmed. These expressed wishes were disregarded, for the surgeons cered (embalmed) the body.

The remains of the great Queen were brought by water from Richmond to Westminster and thence to Whitehall. Camden describes in a couplet the universal grief:

"The queen did come by water to Whitehall,
The oars at every stroke did tears let fall."

Stow records the lamentations of the crowd at the funeral as the multitude beheld her wax effigy lying upon the coffin, set forth in royal robes, having a crown upon the head thereof, and a ball and sceptre in either hand. From the palace the coffin was carried in procession to Westminster Abbey and laid on that of Queen Mary in the north aisle of Henry VII's chapel. Here by Elizabeth's desire, the royal sisters rest in the same tomb in the stately monument, erected by James I, and paid for by the citizens of London. One of the inscriptions on the tomb reads: *Regno consortes et urnâ, hic obdormimus Elizabetha et Maria sorores in spe resurrectionis.* "Partners alike in throne and grave, we sisters Elizabeth and Mary sleep in the hope of the resurrection." The Queen's heart was removed and placed in an urn which stood beside an urn containing Mary's heart in the Abbey.

General Commentary

From this detailed inquiry into Queen Elizabeth's medical history, the following conclusions seem justifiable.

Physically, Queen Elizabeth was a perfectly well-formed woman, normal and without any congenital defect which would have prevented her from having children if she had married. She showed no signs of the Tudor predisposition to tuberculosis. She inherited her father's robust constitution, and, except for occasional illnesses and indispositions, up to 1602 she always enjoyed reasonably good health.

The Queen herself was an amateur of medicine and a patron thereof. She listened attentively to the disputes in the Physic Act at both Oxford and Cambridge Universities, sometimes made comments thereon, and jested with Dr. Huicke, her physician when he was incorporated M.D. at Oxford.

When a princess, she seems to have had confidence in medical treatment, for she asked Somerset and later Queen Mary to send physicians to prescribe for her, especially during her attacks of nephritis. When she became Queen, she continued to consult her physicians in her illnesses like smallpox, chicken-pox and ulcer of the leg. As we have seen, she highly valued Dr. Jacob's advice and treatment for her gynaecological troubles. In her minor ailments she often neglected to follow her physicians' orders, and preferred the advice of the empiric, Dr. Dee, or even that of the herbalist, Margaret Kenwix. In 1572 after her attack of food-poisoning, she told Fénélon, the French ambassador:

> "that she believed the attack had not come from eating fish, as some said, for she often ate it, but rather had come from the fact, that for three or four years, she had found herself so well that she had disregarded all the strict discipline which her physicians formerly had been accustomed to impose upon her by purging her and drawing a lot of her blood from time to time."

Her good health was in fact probably maintained by discontinuance of the purging and bleeding.

The Queen's serious illnesses were as follows:

I. An unknown illness of some severity during 1548 and 1549, when she was fifteen years of age, for which Dr. Bille attended her. This may have been the onset of her attacks of migraine, brought on by intellectual overstrain and which at first may have been frequent and severe. In letters to her brother, undated but relating to these years, she speaks of the pain in her head precluding all manner of writing; and of "some ill-health of body, especially headache . . ." Her headaches appear to have ceased after 1580, when she was 46.

II. *Acute Nephritis.* Elizabeth had an illness in 1553 when she was 19-20 years of age. This was probably scarlet fever, for by January 1554, she was ill with acute nephritis, being attended by Dr. George Owen and Dr. Thomas Wendy at Queen Mary's command. She was in danger of her life on account of Wyatt's rebellion, and strain and anxiety must have aggravated her illness. So also did her imprisonment in the damp Tower of London. It is not surprising to learn that her convalescence at Woodstock was protracted and that she had relapses apparently up to the year 1556. In 1561, according to de Quadra, Elizabeth had another attack of nephritis. She never showed symptoms of the chronic form of the disease.

III. *Smallpox.* In October, 1562, aged 29, the Queen suffered from a severe attack of smallpox from which she nearly died. The Council even considered nominating the Earl of Huntingdon, a descendant of the Duke of Clarence, as her successor. The illness from which she suffered in 1572 was almost certainly chicken-pox.

IV. *Varicose Ulcer of the Leg.* The Queen suffered from a varicose ulcer of the leg for about nine years (1569–1578). If she had rested the leg, as her surgeons must have advised her, the ulcer would not have lasted so long.

V. *Influenza.* Though ageing, the Queen was active and energetic up to 1602, when she was 68 years of age. Her terminal illness was probably influenza.

Minor Ailments. The Queen's minor ailments were migraine, catarrhal jaundice, whooping cough, occasional colds, rheumatism, febrile attacks (probably benign tertian malaria), occasional gastro-intestinal upsets and some gynaecological troubles. When overwrought and overstrained, she sometimes worked herself up into a state of hysteria, as after the execution of Mary Queen of Scots (see Chapter X).

Professor E. S. Beesly observed that "in capacity for resisting bodily fatigue and freedom from nervous ailments she was like a man." She continued hunting and dancing up to the last year of her life and her mental faculties were unimpaired almost up to the end.

"No frail, anaemic, weak woman," a nervous wreck, as some have suggested, could have successfully ruled England in the perilous circumstances of her reign as she did. The whole history of her life is opposed to such a view. She did, however, suffer in the course of her long life from certain maladies like everybody else, and like other rulers and statesmen she used her indispositions, when occasion arose, for diplomatic purposes. From her serious illnesses she made a complete recovery which testifies to the soundness of her constitution. Her maladies, as a whole, spread over a life of nearly seventy years are nothing out of the way, considering the time she lived in when plague and other infectious diseases were rife. She lived to an advanced age in spite of her active and strenuous life.

XVI

The End of the Pilgrimage

NOEL DE CARON, Envoy of the States-General of the Netherlands, on a hot afternoon in April, 1600, was seeking to know from Queen Elizabeth her intentions regarding making peace with Spain. He protested against the negotiations which she was conducting at Brussels and Madrid with the representatives of King Philip III, and her neglect to inform the States on a matter that concerned their national independence, for deprived of English aid they might be crushed by Spain. Oppressed by the heat of the day and the arguments, the Queen, accompanied by de Caron, wandered from room to room of the palace seeking a cooler atmosphere. Suddenly she turned to the envoy and said: "We are travelling about like pilgrims, but what is life but a pilgrimage?" When she spoke, she was nearing the end of the hard path she had trodden for the glory of England.

Her days still passed with wonted regularity. She usually spent the winter in London, or at the Tudor Palace of Placentia at Greenwich, her birth-place, or Richmond; in spring, summer and autumn at Oatlands, Nonsuch, Hampton Court, or on progress, staying at the mansions of her nobles. In September, 1601, she invited the Duke de Biron, Henry IV's envoy, to accompany her on a progress in Hampshire, staying as the guest of the Marquis and Marchioness of Winchester at Basing. She enjoyed her visit so much that she remained there for thirteen days, which was a more costly visit than her host had bargained for, and created ten knights, which for her was most exceptional. She boasted, "that she had done more than any of her ancestors had done, or any other prince in Christendom was able to do—namely in her Hampshire progress this year entertained a royal ambassador royally in her subjects' houses."

In her progresses she was easy of approach, and greeted affably all comers, rich, poor, gentle and simple. She took with her own hand petitions, read them and spoke kindly to the petitioners, assuring the people of her care for them. She never appeared tired, out of temper or annoyed in public, though in private, says Bohun, "she would chide her familiar servants so loud that they who stood afar off might sometimes hear her voice; and it was reported that for small offences she would strike her maids-of-honour." Seeing an unfortunate lady-in-waiting clad in a gown which she considered unsuitable, she is said to have torn it off with her own royal hands. These outbursts of Tudor rage, although alarming, were soon over.

The Queen rose early; her toilet and choice of dress occupied some time, as can be gathered from the fact that her wardrobe contained over 3,000 dresses, many embroidered with pearls and other jewels. Incidentally, it may be mentioned that on economical grounds it is said that Anne of Denmark, James I's consort, had to wear out these dresses, which is the reason why fashions did not change with the new reign! Despite an elaborate toilet, often before daybreak Elizabeth was at work with her secretaries of State and masters of requests. She had orders in council, proclamations and State documents read to her, and then either minuted them herself or instructed her secretaries concerning them. Doubtful matters referred to her she discussed with her ministers weighing the *pros* and *cons* before coming to a decision. If the day were fine, after this she walked in her garden, or when the weather was wet or cold in her long galleries, usually with one of her courtiers with whom she discussed some intellectual subject. Every day, as a rule, in the company of some learned man, she devoted three hours to reading history, the classics, theology or some other study.

She liked fresh air, keeping her windows wide open in summer. She always ate moderately and in her declining years very little. She drank ale and little wine. Fast days were strictly observed, no meat being served. She preferred to dine in private, but her State banquets were sumptuous, the side tables being covered with costly plate; she was always served on the knee, while songs were sung and music played during the feast.

After dining in private, in summer she took a noon-day rest, but not in winter. Supper was a more informal meal to which she would invite her favourite courtiers and her ladies and converse with them. After supper there might be music, singing or dancing. Occasionally, the Queen played at cards, of which like her father she was very fond, or at tables (backgammon). When she won, she demanded her winnings promptly. It was often politic to lose to the Queen at cards, and Robert Cecil ruefully expended large sums in this way to keep in favour. She was also fond of chess, and gave her patronage to the game by appointing Burghley and Leicester her "Chess Keepers". It was after supper too that Tarleton, the comedian, and her jesters were sometimes bidden to amuse her with droll stories and merry quips. Carried away by the applause of the audience, they often overstepped the mark by making too much fun of Leicester, Raleigh, Hatton or Essex. Then they were banished from the royal presence for a time. Later in the evening, attended by the ladies of her household, the Queen withdrew to her bed-chamber to which only, as a rule, such noblemen as Leicester, Hatton, Essex, Nottingham, and Raleigh had the *entrée*. After talking awhile, she dismissed them and went to bed—one of her ladies always sleeping in the same room; her pages and some of her gentlemen were on duty in the adjoining room and her guards kept the doors.

The Queen granted numerous audiences during the day to high and low. She especially enjoyed conversing with divines, men of letters, inventors and travellers in distant countries. By meeting them she kept in touch with the numerous advances in her realm and oversea, and assured the pioneers of her interest in their discoveries. She also honoured doughty deeds. After the Armada, for instance, she received that heroic Welsh mariner, David Gwynn, who as a prisoner of war had toiled in the Spanish galleys for over eleven years. In the Armada, Gwynn and his fellow-slaves, in the fury of the gale, stabbed the captain, overpowered and killed all the Spanish troops on board, and not only seized their own galley but captured another and sailed both vessels to Bayonne. From thence Gwynn travelled overland to Rochelle, had an interview with Henry of Navarre, and finally made his way to England to receive the Queen's commendations.

On occasions Elizabeth displayed all her wonted vigour and erudition. In 1597, when Paul Dialyn, the ambassador from King Sigismund of Poland, delivered an impertinent Latin harangue to her on the subject of her encouragement of the rebels in the Netherlands, she trounced him severely.

"God's death, my lords," said the Queen to her ministers, as she concluded, "I have been enforced this day to scour up my old Latin that hath lain long in rusting."

Now that Essex was gone, Sir Robert Cecil, Lord High Treasurer and First Secretary of State, was supreme in the Queen's counsels. It was said of him that "he was too proud, too rich, too powerful to be bribed". He was careful to keep himself in favour with the Queen, "not omitting in his absence daily to present Her Majesty with some jewel or toy that might be acceptable." He was also careful to look to the future. Elizabeth, although she had brought forward Arabella Stuart, when a child, as her possible successor in order to keep James I in subjection, for long had intended that the policy of Henry VII that England and Scotland should be one kingdom should be fulfilled after her death. She told Sully in 1601 that the King of Scotland would become one day King of Great Britain. As Miss Strickland observed, it should be remembered that it was Queen Elizabeth who gave the name of Great Britain to that prospective empire. The

Queen also mentioned the subject of James' succession to Nottingham, the Lord Admiral, and frequently wrote to the Scottish king instructing him in kingcraft. The usual response to these wise admonitions was a request for more money, although he might have made a better King of England by taking them to heart. It was therefore tacitly understood that the Protestant King of Scotland would succeed Elizabeth; and it was quite unnecessary for him to annoy her, as he often did, by pleas that she should recognize his claims openly.

In view of the Queen's age, the worldly wise at her Court were seeking to ingratiate themselves with King James, and Cecil himself maintained a secret correspondence with him through Lord Henry Howard. Queen Elizabeth had long allowed James a pension of £3,000 a year. In 1600, after much grumbling, Cecil persuaded her to increase it to £6,000. He also lent James £10,000. Raleigh, Cobham and the Earl of Northumberland were corresponding with King James, but Cecil counteracted their overtures by informing the King through Howard that he must not trust them, and saying of Raleigh and Cobham that "hell did never spew such a couple when it cast up Cerberus and Phlegethon."

On one occasion Cecil's correspondence with James was endangered, and only his presence of mind saved him from disgrace. A packet to him from James was brought in while he was having an audience of the Queen. She ordered him to open it and give her the news from Scotland. He obeyed, but observed as he was breaking the seals that the packet "had a strange and evil smell." The Queen fearing some infection or poisoning bade him take it away and have it purified. Thus the astute minister was able to remove any evidence of intriguing with King James before showing the letters to the Queen.

Spain continued to foment troubles in Ireland and to prevent further expeditions Admirals Levison and Monson took a fleet to the Spanish coast. They seized a large treasure-ship in the harbour of Sesimbria and returned home. Monson was immediately ordered out again and encountered six Spanish galleys stealing past the French coast. Before he could engage them they met a mixed squadron of English and Dutch ships. After some hard fighting, three of the galleys were sunk and the other three escaped into Sluys. This was the last clash with Spain in the Queen's reign.

In August, 1601, Queen Elizabeth hearing that King Henry IV was at Calais made a progress to Dover and invited him to cross the Channel to see her. She had a secret of great moment to divulge to him. It would have been an historic meeting, but Henry, with many compliments and expressions of delight at the request, regretted that it was impossible for him to leave French soil. He therefore courteously invited his good sister to visit him in France, which he knew was an empty compliment. It is said that Henry at first had some thoughts of acceptance or of arranging a meeting on a ship in mid-channel, but the fear of being captured by English or Spanish corsairs and being held to ransom deterred him. Consequently, he sent his chief minister, M. de Rosny, Duke of Sully, to Dover to hear the momentous communication.

The Queen's secret when it was revealed to him, says Sully in his *Memoirs*, astonished him, because it so closely resembled the project which Henry IV, independently, had in mind for preserving the balance of power in Europe. He marvelled at the grasp the Queen showed of foreign affairs and the clear and comprehensive view she took of almost every point in continental politics.

"She desired to see Germany restored to its ancient liberty in respect to the election of its emperors, and the nomination of a king of the Romans; to render the United Provinces an independent republic, and annexing to them some of the Germanic states; to do the same by Switzerland. To divide all Christendom into a certain number of powers as equal as might be; and last, to reduce all the various religions therein into three (Protestant, Roman Catholic and Islam), which should appear the most numerous and considerable."

Sully sums up his impressions in these words: "I cannot bestow praise upon the Queen of England equal to the merit which I discovered in her in this short time, both as to the qualities of her heart and her understanding." It was a notable tribute from a great statesman. Although this great conception for the pacification of Europe came to nothing, it is worth recording as evidence of Elizabeth's statecraft in the last years of her life.

The Queen summoned her last Parliament to meet at Westminster on October 27, 1601. Lord Henry Howard writing to the Earl of Mar (*Secret Correspondence of Sir Robert Cecil and James VI*) stated: "The Queen in all her robes had fallen the first day of the parliament, if some gentlemen had not suddenly cast themselves under that side that tottered and, supported her." This was only a passing weakness, due probably to the weight of the robes and the oppressive atmosphere, for she soon rallied and went through the ceremonial with her accustomed dignity and grace.

When the Commons' deputation waited upon her to return thanks for her concession about the monopolies, she made her last speech to them, in the course of which she said:

"For I know that the commonwealth is to be governed for the good and advantage of those that are committed to me, not of myself, to whom it is intrusted, and that an account is one day to be given before another judgment-seat. I think myself most happy that by God's assistance I have hitherto so prosperously governed the commonwealth in all respects, and that I have such subjects that for their good I would willingly lose both kingdoms and life."

It was true and her subjects honoured her for this life of dedication. There is little of substance in the report that after the execution of Essex she lost much of her former popularity.

Elizabeth had her moments of depression as when she

told M. de Beaumont, the French ambassador, "that she was aweary of life", and with sighs and tears bewailed the treason of Essex and the sad necessity for his execution. She was troubled with "a rheum in her arm. which vexeth her very much," and slept little by night or day. But she fought old age with courage. Her excellent physique, moderation in eating and drinking and regular mode of life and exercise, enabled her to outlive the usual span of royal lives. She strongly resented any mention of her advancing years. When the Bishop of St. David's preached a sermon on the text: "Lord teach us to number our days, that we may apply our hearts unto wisdom." Elizabeth, instead of giving him her customary thanks, told him that he might have kept his arithmetic for himself. "But I see," she added, "that the greatest clerks are not the wisest men."

She was equally indignant when a well-meaning courtier advised her at her years not to ride further on a stormy day. "Years, forsooth!" she exclaimed, and rode on in the wind and the rain. She was vain of her eyesight, showing a jewel to her courtiers with a minute inscription engraved on it, which none of them professed to be able to read and which she deciphered readily. She continued her wonted activities, riding, hunting and dancing, with a vigour which astonished her contemporaries.

It was not until February, 1602, that she showed signs that the years were taking their toll of her. She was then 68 years old. She took less exercise than formerly, and after an hour on horseback was sometimes compelled to rest for two days. Hearing that rumours of her bad health had reached the Scottish capital, she allowed the Scots ambassador to wait in a passage where he could see her dancing, as a hint to his master that his succession was not at all imminent. In April, she gave a feast to the Duke of Nevers and opened the ball with him; and on May Day she felt young enough to go a-maying in the woods of Lewisham. Lord Howard wrote to the Earl of Mar: "The Queen our sovereign was never so gallant many years, nor so set upon jollity." Another letter stated: "The queen walks often on Richmond Green with greater show of ability than can well stand with her years."

She frolicked and revelled in high spirits, ran off with a portrait of Cecil, which his niece, Lady Derby, wore round her neck, and rallied him on being in love with her. Cecil wrote a poem on this incident, had it set to music and sung to the Queen. In August, Northumberland wrote to Cobham:

"Wednesday night the Queen was not well, but would not be known of it, for the next day she walked abroad in the park, lest any should take notice of it. . . . The day of the remove, Her Majesty rode on horseback all the way, which was ten miles and also hunted, and whether she was weary or not I leave to your censure."

In September the Earl of Worcester described the Queen's revels:

"We are frolic here in Court; much dancing in the Privy Chamber of country dances before the Queen's Majesty, who is exceedingly pleased therewith. Irish tunes are at this time most pleasing; but in winter, "Lullaby", an old song of Mr. Bird's will be in most request, as I think."

These last flickers of recollected youth in the lamp of age are always pathetic. By December the Queen was visibly failing in health, for Sir John Harrington wrote to his wife, as follows:

"Our dear Queen, my royal godmother, and this State's natural mother, doth now bear show of human infirmity, too fast for that evil which we shall get by her death, and too slow for that good which we shall get by her releasement from pain and misery. It was not many days since I was bidden to her presence. I blessed the happy moment and found her in a most pitiable state."
There was some talk of Tyrone, and Harrington replied

that he had seen him with my Lord Deputy (Essex). At this reference to her former favourite, the Queen looked angry and grieved, "dropped a tear and smote her bosom." Harrington continues: "She held in her hand a golden cup which she often put to her lips; but in sooth her heart seemeth too full to lack more filling. She bade me come to the chamber at seven o'clock, when she inquired of some matters which I had written; and as she was pleased to note my fanciful brain, I was not unheedful to feed her humour and read some verses, whereat she smiled once, and was pleased to say: 'When thou dost feel creeping time at thy gate, these fooleries will please thee less. I am past my relish for such matters. Thou seest my bodily meat doth not suit me well; I have eaten but one ill-tasted cake since yesternight.' She rated most grievously at noon at some who minded not to bring certain matters of account. Several men had been sent to, and when ready at hand, Her Highness hath dismissed them in anger. But who, dearest Moll, shall say that Her Highness hath forgotten?"

She still planned progresses and festivities for the coming year, though she knew herself that her pilgrimage was nearing its end.

The New Year of 1603 came. Elizabeth felt somewhat better and was present at two State dinners. On January 12, she suffered from a cold, and on the advice of her physician, went to Richmond, which she said "was the warm winter-box to shelter her old age." At first she benefited by the change of air, but, as Robert Carey, her kinsman, relates, she was still indisposed and "kept her inner lodging."

He found the Queen in one of her withdrawing rooms, sitting low upon her cushions. He kissed her hand, and gave her his good wishes for long continued safety and health. She wrung his hand hard and said, "No, Robin, I am not well." She told him of her illness and that her heart had been sad and weary for ten or twelve days, sighing grievously the while. He was grieved to see her so dejected; he had only seen her sighing and weeping after the execution of the Queen of Scots, manifesting, as he says, her innocence that she never gave consent to the death of that queen. He endeavoured to distract her from her melancholy humour, but in vain. This was on a Saturday; on Sunday she intended going to chapel, but instead had cushions laid for her in the Privy Chamber, hard by, and there she heard the service. Afterwards she steadily grew worse, complained of continual thirst, and "had fallen into a state of moping, sighing and weeping melancholy". Her physicians could do nothing with her, for she refused everything they prescribed and all sustenance. (For the medical aspect of her illness see Chapter XV). Cecil and her ladies implored her to go to bed in vain. At length Cecil said that "to content the people she must go to bed." The Queen looked at him and her Tudor spirit once more flared up as she said:

"The word *must* was not used to princes. Little man, little man, if your father had lived you durst not have said so much; but you know I must die, and that makes you presumptuous."

At length the Earl of Nottingham induced her to take to her bed. The Council were assembled at Richmond Palace and sorrowfully awaited her death. On their behalf, on March 22, Nottingham again asked her pleasure about the succession, and she said: "My meaning was a King should succeed me; and who should that be but our cousin of Scotland." On March 23 she was unable to speak, but when Cecil asked her to confirm what she had said to Nottingham, she was said to have made a sign of assent when King James's name was mentioned. There were no near kith and kin to be with Elizabeth in her last hours. She was dying, as she had lived, a lonely queen.

At six o'clock in the evening, Elizabeth made signs for Archbishop Whitgift and her chaplains to draw near to her bedside. By signs she intimated her assent to the prelate's questions regarding the steadfastness of her religious faith, and he told her she shortly would yield her account of her stewardship as an earthly queen to the King of kings. He then knelt in prayer for a long while, and when the good man's knees were weary he gave her his blessing and would have left her, but twice she made signs to him to continue praying for a full hour. The Queen then sank into a deep sleep from which she never awakened.

Underneath the window of the Queen's bed-chamber, Sir Robert Carey, booted and spurred, with a saddled horse beside him, stood waiting in the watches of the night. At three o'clock in the morning of March 24, his sister, Lady Scrope, bending over the bed perceived that the Queen was dead. In the midst of the lamentations that ensued, she stole to the window and silently dropped a sapphire ring into Carey's outstretched hand. This was the "blue ring" sent to Lady Scrope by King James for a sign which was to announce the Queen's death. Sir Robert Carey immediately rode off post-haste for Scotland to give the tidings to the expectant King of Scots. It should be mentioned that Carey himself gave a different account of his proceedings in his autobiography, and said he went into the palace in the early morning on learning in his lodging that the Queen was dead.

At the conclusion of this book it is needless to expatiate on the qualities of this most illustrious woman, who ascended the throne as Queen of a divided, threatened and impoverished country and left it united, powerful and wealthy with its enemies subdued.

The story of her struggles and triumphs and of her self-dedication to her people has now been told anew from a medical view-point to show also how she combated successfully her bodily and psychological ills, and the debt which England owes to her should be fully apparent. Yet one cannot forbear from quoting three appreciations of Queen Elizabeth, two contemporary, the other more modern.

King Henry IV of France said many times in the

presence of his Court, that "she only was a king—and knew how to govern—how to support the dignity of her crown; and that the repose and weal of her subjects required the course she had taken." He alluded to the execution of Essex for whom he had interceded, but his words can rightly be taken as commendation of her rule throughout her reign.

The next quotation is from Lord Macaulay's essay on *Burleigh and his Times*. He wrote of Queen Elizabeth: "Yet she surely was a great woman. Of all the sovereigns who exercised a power which was seemingly absolute, but which in fact depended for support on the love and confidence of their subjects, she was by far the most illustrious."

Lastly, Edmund Spenser dedicated *The Faerie Queene* "to the most High, Mightie and Magnificent Empresse, renowned for Pietie, Vertue and all Gratious Government, Elizabeth, to live with the eternitie of her fame." Time has justified the truth of this dedication both for Queen and poet.

APPENDIX I

Husbands proposed for Queen Elizabeth

Date	Proposed Husband	Age of Elizabeth
1534	Duke of Angoulème (third son of Francis I)	1 year
1542(?)	A Prince of Portugal	9 years
1543	Son of the Earl of Arran	10 years
1544	Prince Philip (afterwards King Philip II)	10 years
1547	Sir Thomas Seymour	14 years
1552	Prince of Denmark	18 years
1553	Courtenay, Earl of Devonshire	20 years
1554	Philibert Emanuel, Duke of Savoy	20 years
1554	Prince of Denmark	20 years
1556	Prince Eric of Sweden	22 years
1556	Don Carlos (son of Philip II)	23 years
1559	King Philip II	25 years
1559	Prince Eric of Sweden	25 years
1559	The son of John Frederic, Duke of Saxony	25 years
1559	The Archduke Charles (son of the Emperor Ferdinand)	25 years
1559	Sir William Pickering	25 years
1559	The Earl of Arran	25 years
1559	Henry Fitzalan, Earl of Arundel	25 years
1559	Lord Robert Dudley (afterwards Earl of Leicester)	25 years
1560	King Eric of Sweden	26 years
1560	Adolphus, Duke of Holstein	26 years
1560	King Charles IX	26 years
1560	Duke of Anjou (afterwards King Henry III)	26 years
1566	The Earl of Leicester	31 years
1568	The Archduke Charles	33 years
1570	Duke of Anjou	35 years
1572–1585	Duke of Alençon (afterwards Duke of Anjou)	36–51 years

This gives a total of twenty suitors (some appear more than once in the list) whose suits were seriously put forward and considered. The suits of Ivan the Terrible and of King Henry IV of France were never seriously entertained and are therefore not included.

APPENDIX II

Queen Elizabeth's Physicians

The following are recorded in *Munk's Roll* and in the *Annals of the Royal College of Physicians* as being physicians to Queen Elizabeth I:

Robert Huicke, M.D., Oxon. et Cantab, F.R.C.P., Physician to King Henry VIII, Queen Catherine Parr, King Edward VI and Queen Elizabeth I. Disputed in the Physic Act at Cambridge University in 1654, the Queen jesting with him when he desired her licence. He was M.A., Oxon., Fellow of Merton College, Principal of St. Alban's Hall from 1543-5, M.D., Cantab. in 1538. In 1566 disputed in the Physic Act before the Queen at Oxford University and next day was incorporated M.D., Oxon. He was Censor, Elect and Consilarius of the College of Physicians and President in 1541, 1556, 1557, 1558 and 1559. Unhappy in his domestic life.

John Caius* (1510-1573), M.D., Padua and Cantab., F.R.C.P. Physician to King Edward VI, Queen Mary and Queen Elizabeth. His appointment to Queen Elizabeth is said to have been terminated in 1568 owing to his being a Roman Catholic. Fellow of Gonville Hall, Cambridge. Master of Gonville and Caius College of which he was co-founder. President of the College of Physicians, 1555-1560, 1562-1564, 1571.

Thomas Wendy* (d. 1560), M.D., Cantab. (incorporated on a foreign degree of M.D.), 1527. F.R.C.P. Educated at Gonville Hall, Cambridge. Physician to King Henry VIII, King Edward VI, Queen Mary and Queen Elizabeth. (For his attendance on the Queen when Princess Elizabeth see Chapter XV.)

Richard Master (d. 1588), M.D., Oxon. et Cantab., F.R.C.P. Youngest son of Robert Master of Streetend, Willesborough, Kent. In 1553 graduated B.A. and became Fellow of All Souls', Oxford. M.A. 1537. Joined Church of England in 1539, accepted a benefice, but resigned it as ill qualified to be a good clergyman. Studied medicine at Oxford. M.B. with licence to practice, 1545. Migrated to Christ Church. M.D. 1555, incorporated M.D. at Cambridge, 1571. In 1549 ill with fever (? malaria) for eighteen months. By patent, 26, June, 1559 physician to Queen Elizabeth at a salary of £100 per annum; became her personal physician. From 1562–5 was Prebendary of York. In 1564–5 the Queen for £590 6s. 4d. granted to him the site and lands of the late monastery of Cirencester. Moderator of the Physic Act kept before the Queen at Oxford, 1566. Censor, Elect, Consilarius and President of the College of Physicians in 1561. Had a high reputation for professional skill. Married Elizabeth Fulnethy of a Lincolnshire family and had seven sons. Died in his house in Silver Street, St. Olave, London.

Thomas Francis, M.D., Oxon., F.R.C.P. A native of Chester, educated at Christ Church, Oxford. First a theologian, he entered on the physic line in 1550, M.B. 1553 and M.D. 1554. Censor, Elect, Consilarius and President of the College of Physicians, 1568. Provost of Queen's College, Oxford in 1561. Subsequently physician to Queen Elizabeth "and much respected by her" (Wood).

Roger Giffard, Oxon., M.D., F.R.C.P., son of Ralph Giffard of Steeple Claydon, Bucks. Fellow of Merton College and All Souls' College, Oxford. M.B. 1563 and M.D. 1566. Censor, Consilarius and President of the College of Physicians, 1581–1584. Physician to Queen Elizabeth. He died of haematemesis, 1596–7 and was buried in the parish of St. Bride's, Fleet Street, London.

*Roderigo Lopus or Lopez**, F.R.C.P. Probably had a Spanish medical degree. Physician to St. Bartholomew's Hospital and chief physician to Queen Elizabeth. Hanged in 1594 for plotting to poison the Queen.

*Roger Marbeck**, M.D., Oxon, F.R.C.P., son of John

262

Marbeck, organist of Windsor. Educated at Christ Church, Oxford, of which he became a canon. Provost of Oriel, 1564, M.D., Oxon., 1573. First Registrar of the College of Physicians; in 1581 elected for life. Censor, Elect and Consilarius of the College. In expedition to Cadiz, 1596. Physician to Queen Elizabeth. Died in 1605 and was buried in St. Giles, Cripplegate, London.

*William Gilbert**, M.D., Cantab., F.R.C.P., son of Jerom Gilbert, recorder of Colchester, Essex. Fellow of St. John's College, Cambridge, M.D. 1569. Censor, Treasurer, Consilarius and finally President in 1600 of the College of Physicians. Physician to Queen Elizabeth whom he attended in her last illness. Founded sciences of magnetism and electricity.

*Walter Baily** (or Bayley), M.D., Oxon, F.R.C.P. Son of Henry Baily of Warnewell, Dorset, Esquire, born at Portsham, Dorset, educated at Winchester, Fellow of New College, Oxford. M.B., 1557, M.D., 1563. Proctor of the University, admitted to practise medicine, and Prebendary of Wells, 1558. Resigned his prebend, 1579. Regius Professor of Physic, Oxford, 1561. Physician to Queen Elizabeth. Elect and Consilarius, College of Physicians. Died March 3, 1592, aged 63; buried in inner chapel of New College (see also Chapter VI). His son-in-law, *Dr. Anthony Aylworth* succeeded him as Regius Professor of Physic and physician-in-ordinary to Queen Elizabeth. There is a memorial brass to Dr. Aylworth in the Antechapel, New College.

Lancelot Browne, M.D., Cantab., F.R.C.P. Educated at St. John's College, Cambridge. Fellow of Pembroke Hall. Licensed to practise physic by the University in 1570. Proctor, 1573, M.D., 1576. Censor, Elect and Consilarius, College of Physicians. Appointed first physician to James I. Died 1605. His daughter, Elizabeth, married Dr. William Harvey at St. Sepulchre's Church, Newgate, on November 24, 1604.

John James, M.D., Cantab. and Leyden, F.R.C.P. A native of Hampshire. Fellow of Trinity College, Cambridge, M.D. 1578. In September 1578 went to Leyden to study medicine and graduated M.D., also at that University. Censor, College of Physicians. M.P. for St. Ives, Cornwall in parliament of 1585 and for Newcastle-under-Lyme in that of 1592–3. Physician to the Queen's household in November, 1595. Died in 1600.

Robert Jacob*, M.D., Basle and Cantab., F.R.C.P., Fellow of Trinity College, Cambridge. Physician to Queen Elizabeth, who sent him to Russia to attend the Czarina (see Chapter XV).

Edward Atslowe*, M.D., Oxon., F.R.C.P. Educated at Winchester, Fellow of New College, Oxford. Created M.D. in 1554. Disputed before Queen Elizabeth in the Physic Act when she visited the University. Censor, Elect and Consilarius, College of Physicians. Believed to have been appointed physician to Queen Elizabeth, because she sent him with another physician, Mr. Barlthorp, to attend Dr. John Dee in 1571. As a zealous Catholic his involvement in plots to liberate Mary Queen of Scots must have terminated his Court appointment. In 1573 he married Frances Wingfield at Stoke Newington and died in 1594.

* For further particulars of John Caius, Thomas Wendy, Roderigo Lopez, Roger Marbeck, William Gilbert, Walter Baily, Robert Jacob and Edward Atslowe dealing with medicine in Queen Elizabeth's time, published in *The British Medical Journal* of May 30, 1953.

A.S.M.

Bibliography

ABRAHAM, J. J.: (1944) *The Early History of Syphilis*, Vicary Lecture for 1943–44, *Brit. J. Surg.*, XXXII.

BACON, F.: (1605) *Advancement of Learning*. The First Book. To the King.

BEESLY, E. S.: (1892) *Queen Elizabeth*, London.

CAMDEN, C.: (1952) *The Elizabethan Woman*, London

CAMDEN, W.: (1637) *Britannia*, trans. by Philemon Holland; (1615) *Annals of the Reign of Queen Elizabeth to 1588*.

CHAMBERLIN, F.: (1921) *The Private Character of Queen Elizabeth*, London.

CREIGHTON, C.: (1891) *A History of Epidemics in Britain*, Cambridge, I, 271.

CREIGHTON, M.: (1898) *Queen Elizabeth*, London.

CREIGHTON, M.: (1903) *The Early Renaissance in Englznd. Historical Lectures and Addresses*. London, 188–212.

Dictionary of National Biography, London

DORAN, A. H. G.: (1916) *Medicine in Shakespeare's England*, chap. 14, 413–443.

DURUY, V.: (1918) *A Short History of France*, 2 vols., Everyman Edition, London.

EDGAR, I. I.: "Medical Practice and the Physician in Elizabethan England and in Shakespeare's Dramas." *Med. Life*, n.s., XLI, 331–76.

FALLS, C.: (1950) *Elizabeth's Irish Wars*, London.

FOSTER, M. G.: (1919) "Sweating Sickness in Modern Times". Contrib. to *Medical and Biological Research*, II, 52–8, New York. *Dedicated to Sir William Osler in Honour of his Seventieth Birthday*.

FROUDE, J. A.: (1856–70) *History of England from the Fall of Wolsey to the Death of Elizabeth*, 12 vols., London.

GREEN, J. R.: (1874) *A Short History of the English People*, London.

GREEN, J. R.: (1880) *History of the English People*, vol. II, London.

HARRISON, F.: (1897) *William the Silent*, London.

HARRISON, G. B.: (1937) *The Life and Death of Robert Devereux, Earl of Essex*, London.

HARRISON, W.: (1586–7) *Description of England*.

BIBLIOGRAPHY

HORTON-SMITH, L. G. H.: (1952) *Dr. Walter Baily (or Bayley) c.* 1529–1592. The Campfield Press, St. Albans, Herts.
HUME, M. A. S.: (1897) *Sir Walter Ralegh*, London.
HUME, M. A. S.: (1899) *Philip II of Spain*, London.
KEEVIL, J. J.: (1952) *Hamey the Stranger*, London.
LANGDON-BROWN, W.: (1946) *Some Chapters in Cambridge Medical History*, Cambridge.
LETT, H.: (1943) "Anatomy at the Barber-Surgeons' Hall." Vicary Lecture, *Brit. J. Surg.* XXXI, 101–111.
Letters of Queen Elizabeth and James VI of Scotland (ed. J. Bruce, Camden Society).
LINDSAY, JEAN: (1950) *Life under the Tudors, Science*, Falcon Educational Books, London, chap. 7, 92–103.
LUBIMENKO, I.: "*Trois lettres inedités d' Elizabeth d'Angleterre à la cour de Russie*" in *Melanges d' histoire offerts à M. Charles Bémont*, Paris, 1913, p. 554.
MACMICHAEL, W.: (1830) *Lives of British Physicians*, London.
MACNALTY, A. S.: *The Doctor in Politics and Diplomacy*, MacAlister Lecture, 1937, London.
MACNALTY, A. S.: (1946) *The Renaissance and its Influence on English Medicine, Surgery and Public Health*, Vicary Lecture, R.C.S., 1945, London.
MACNALTY, A. S.: (1947) "*Sir Thomas More as Public Health Reformer*", a Chadwick Lecture, 1946, *J. Roy. Inst. Pub. Health and Hyg.*, X, 7–23.
MACNALTY, A. S.: *Henry VIII: A Difficult Patient*, London.
MARTIN, H.: *Histoire de France*, vols. IX, X, Paris.
MICHELET, J.: (1879) *Histoire de France*, new edn., vol. III, IV, Paris.
MOTLEY, J. L.: (1855) *The Rise of the Dutch Republic*, 3 vols., London and New York.
MOTLEY, J. L.: (1875) *History of the United Netherlands*, new edn., London.
MUNK, W.: (1878) *The Roll of the Royal College of Physicians of London*, 2nd edn., R.C.P., London, vol. I (contains biographies of Elizabethan Physicians).
NEAL, D.: (1822) *History of the Puritans: or Protestant Noncomformists; from the Reformation in* 1517 *to the Revolution in* 1688. 5 vols., London.
NEALE, J. E.: (1934) *Queen Elizabeth*, London.
NEALE, J. E.: (1943) *The Age of Catherine de Medici*, London.
NEALE, J. E.: (1949) *The Elizabethan House of Commons*, London.
NEALE, J. E.: (1953) *Elizabeth I and Her Parliaments*, London.
POMERANZ, H.: "Medicine in the Shakespearean Plays and Era", *Med. Life*, n.s. XLI, 479.
POWER, D'ARCY: (1907) "Dr. Walter Bayley and His Works, 1529–1572", *Med. Chir. Trans.*, XC, 415–449; and in *The Library* (1907) pp. 370–392.

266

POYNTER, F. N. L.: (1948) *Selected Writings of William Clowes*, 1544–1604, London.

PRESCOTT, W. H.: (1887) *History of the Reign of Philip the Second, King of Spain*, London.

PUTNAM, RUTH: (1895) *William the Silent*, New York and London.

RAE, J.: (1913) *The Deaths of the Kings of England*, London.

ROWSE, A. L.: (1950) *The England of Elizabeth: The Structure of Society*, London.

ROWSE, A. L.: (1953) *An Elizabethan Garland*, London.

SCOTT, SIR WALTER: (1830) *History of Scotland*, vol. II, London.

SINGER, C.: (1953) "Medicine in the Reign of Elizabeth I (1558–1603)", *Med. Annual*, 9–18.

SMITH, G.: (1940) "The Practice of Medicine in Tudor England". *Sci. Monthly, Wash.*, L, 65.

SPENCE, H. D. M.: (1898) *The Church of England*, vol. III.

SPENCER, H. R.: (1929) *Medicine in the Days of Shakespeare*, London.

STOW, J.: (1565) *Survey of London and Westminster;* (1580) *Summary of English Chronicles;* (1598) *Annals or a General Chronicle of England*.

STRICKLAND, AGNES: (1882) *Life of Mary Queen of Scots*, 2nd edn., 2 vols., London.

STRICKLAND, AGNES: (1899) *Life of Queen Elizabeth. Lives of Queens of England*, IX, London.

STRYPE, J.: (1698) *Life of Sir Thomas Smith;* Lives of *Sir John Cheke* (1705); *Archbishop Grindal* (1710); *Archbishop Parker* (1711) and *Archbishop Whitgift* (1718); *Annals of the Reformation* (1709-31) *Ecclesiastical Memorials*, 1513–58 (1721).

THOMSON, ST. CLAIR: (1916) "Shakespeare and Medicine". *Trans. Med. Soc. Lond.*, XXXIX, 257.

TREVELYAN, G. M.: (1929) *History of England*, London.

TREVELYAN, G. M.: (1942) *English Social History*, London.

UNDERWOOD, J. A.: (1953) "Medicine and the Crown," *Brit. Med. J.*, I, 1185.

UNDERWOOD, J. A.: (1953) "Pharmacy and Therapeutics in the Age of Elizabeth I", *Pharm. J.*, CXVI, 406-7, 411–15.

VERGIL, POLYDORE: (1570) *Hist. Angl.*, p. 167.

WALL, C.: (1932) *The London Apothecaries, their Society and their Hall.* Apothecaries' Hall, London.

WALDMAN, M.: (1944) *Elizabeth and Leicester*, London.

Table Showing Principal Relations of Queen Elizabeth

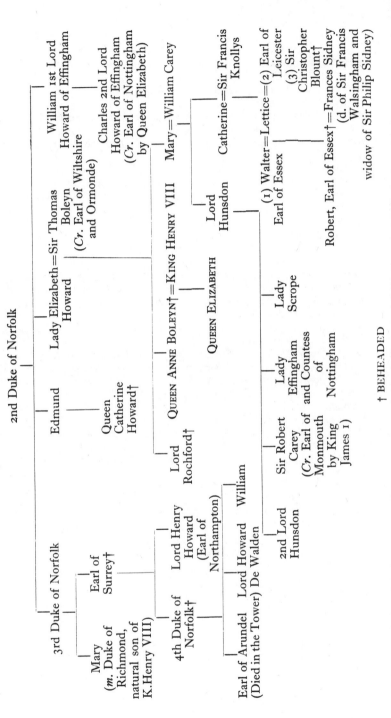

† BEHEADED

Index